Studies in Modern History

General Editor: **J. C. D. Clark**, Joyce and Elizabeth Hall Distinguished Professor of British History, University of Kansas

Titles include:

James B. Bell
THE IMPERIAL ORIGINS OF THE KING'S CHURCH IN EARLY AMERICA, 1607–1783

Jonathan Clark and Howard Erskine–Hill (editors)
SAMUEL JOHNSON IN HISTORICAL CONTEXT

Bernard Cottret (editor)
BOLINGBROKE'S POLITICAL WRITINGS
The Conservative Enlightenment

Richard R. Follet
EVANGELICALISM, PENAL THEORY AND THE POLITICS OF CRIMINAL LAW REFORM IN ENGLAND, 1808–30

Andrew Godley
JEWISH IMMIGRANT ENTREPRENEURSHIP IN NEW YORK AND LONDON, 1880–1914

William Anthony Hay
THE WHIG REVIVAL
1808–1830

Philip Hicks
NEOCLASSICAL HISTORY AND ENGLISH CULTURE
From Clarendon to Hume

Mark Keay
WILLIAM WORDSWORTH'S GOLDEN AGE THEORIES DURING THE INDUSTRIAL REVOLUTION IN ENGLAND, 1750–1850

William M. Kuhn
DEMOCRATIC ROYALISM
The Transformation of the British Monarchy, 1861–1914

Kim Lawes
PATERNALISM AND POLITICS
The Revival of Paternalism in Early Nineteenth-Century Britain

Marisa Linton
THE POLITICS OF VIRTUE IN ENLIGHTMENT FRANCE

Nancy D. LoPatin
POLITICAL UNIONS, POPULAR POLITICS AND THE GREAT REFORM ACT OF 1832

Karin J. MacHardy
WAR, RELIGION AND COURT PATRONAGE IN HABSBURG AUSTRIA
The Social and Cultural Dimensions of Political Interaction, 1521–1622

Robert J. Mayhew
LANDSCAPE, LITERATURE AND ENGLISH RELIGIOUS CULTURE, 1660–1800
Samuel Johnson and Languages of Natural Description

Marjorie Morgan
NATIONAL IDENTITIES AND TRAVEL IN VICTORIAN BRITAIN

James Muldoon
EMPIRE AND ORDER
The Concept of Empire, 800–1800

W. D. Rubinstein and Hilary Rubinstein
PHILOSEMITISM
Admiration and Support for Jews in the English-Speaking World, 1840–1939

Julia Rudolph
WHIG POLITICAL THOUGHT AND THE GLORIOUS REVOLUTION
James Tyrrell and the Theory of Resistance

Lisa Steffen
TREASON AND NATIONAL IDENTITY
Defining a British State, 1608–1820

Lynne Taylor
BETWEEN RESISTANCE AND COLLABORATION
Popular Protest in Northern France, 1940–45

Doron Zimmerman
THE JACOBITE MOVEMENT IN SCOTLAND AND IN EXILE, 1746–1759

Studies in Modern History
Series Standing Order ISBN 0–333–79328–5
(*outside North America only*)

You can receive future titles in this series as they are published by placing a standing order. Please contact your bookseller or, in case of difficulty, write to us at the address below with your name and address, the title of the series and the ISBN quoted above.

Customer Services Department, Macmillan Distribution Ltd, Houndmills, Basingstoke, Hampshire RG21 6XS, England

The Whig Revival, 1808–1830

William Anthony Hay

First published 2005 by
PALGRAVE MACMILLAN
Houndmills, Basingstoke, Hampshire RG21 6XS and
175 Fifth Avenue, New York, N. Y. 10010
Companies and representatives throughout the world

PALGRAVE MACMILLAN is the global academic imprint of the Palgrave
Macmillan division of St. Martin's Press, LLC and of Palgrave Macmillan Ltd.
Macmillan® is a registered trademark in the United States, United Kingdom
and other countries. Palgrave is a registered trademark in the European
Union and other countries.

ISBN 1–4039–1771–X

This book is printed on paper suitable for recycling and made from fully
managed and sustained forest sources.

A catalogue record for this book is available from the British Library.

Library of Congress Cataloging-in-Publication Data
Hay, William Anthony, 1968–
   The Whig revival, 1808–1830 / by William Anthony Hay.
      p. cm.
   Includes bibliographical references and index.
   ISBN 1-4039-1771-X
      1. Great Britain–Politics and government–1800–1837. 2. Whig Party
(Great Britain)–History–19th century. I. Title.
DA535.H39 2004
324.241'02–dc22   2004049122

10   9   8   7   6   5   4   3   2   1
14 13 12 11 10 09 08 07 06 05

Printed and bound in Great Britain by
Antony Rowe Ltd, Chippenham and Eastbourne

To Carolyn Jane

Contents

List of Illustrations		ix
Acknowledgements		xi
List of Abbreviations		xiv
Introduction		1
1	Party Structure and the Whigs in British Politics	10
2	Elections, the Press and Whig Tactics in Opposition: 1812–17	35
3	1818 and the Westmorland Election	66
4	Social Tension and Party Politics in 1819	91
5	Public Opinion and the Limits of Opposition: 1820–26	111
6	A Revolution in Parties: 1827–30	137
Conclusion		176
Notes		185
Bibliography		213
Index		225

List of Illustrations

1.1 'Sketch for a Prime Minister or how to purchase a Peace'
by [De Wilde]   26

1.2 'Which Drowns First Or Boney's Improved Bucket'   31

2.1 'The Death of the Property Tax' by G. Cruikshank   59

2.2 'A Patriot Luminary Extinguishing Noxious Gas!!!'   64

6.1 'The Three George's – The Patron – The Sovereign – and
the Patriot' by GW   142

6.2 'Diogenes in Search of an Honest Ministry' by H.H. [Heath]   148

6.3 'The Broom Sold'   150

6.4 'A Masked Battery' by HB   171

6.5 'Sampson and Dalilah' by HB   174

Acknowledgements

Although writing and historical research is a solitary occupation, its practitioners nonetheless work within a broader scholarly community that provides valuable support. I have incurred substantial debts to a variety of institutions and other scholars in the course of writing this book. The project began at the University of Virginia when a research paper for Enno Kraehe on opposition views of British foreign policy during the Napoleonic Wars led me into the byways of early nineteenth century domestic politics in Britain and the role of the Whig party. The late Martin Havran encouraged me to pursue a growing interest in party politics, and no adviser could have done more than Nicholas Edsall to encourage a student's intellectual independence. Both gentlemen provided invaluable advice on British archives and the personalities discussed in my book. Their comments on the dissertation from which this manuscript emerged strengthened it tremendously. Stephen Schuker trained me in diplomatic history at the University of Virginia and imbued me with standards of scholarship for which I will ever remain grateful. I am honoured to count him a friend, and his critical analysis and questioning helped me set developments in British politics during the second and third decades of the nineteenth century within the broader context of European and Atlantic history.

James Sack and John Severn offered welcome advice and companionship during my archival research in London. Professor Sack kindly gave the manuscript a line-by-line reading and encouraged me to read through the provincial press. Richard Davis and Harry Dickinson also provided invaluable guidance on sources and fielded questions as I began the project. William Banks Taylor put at my disposal his research on debates among the Whigs over foreign policy and the career of Francis Horner and Lord Thanet. Charles Perry, John Hutcheson, Samuel Williamson, and Jeremy Black directed me to sources, offered comment on my views and assisted me in overcoming barriers to research. Jonathan Steinberg, Matthew Davis, Paul Gottfried, and Jennifer Siegel each set aside their work in other fields to comment on my draft. Mary Katherine Barbier saved me from occasional infelicities of language as I prepared the final draft, and Pamela Edwards, Philip Harling, Arthur Herman, and Jonathan Clark each took the time to read the entire manuscript and offer comments based on their deep knowledge of the long eighteenth century in British history.

Much of the book was written during my time as a research fellow at the Foreign Policy Research Institute in Philadelphia. The trustees, fellows, and staff at FPRI provided a congenial and intellectually stimulating working environment for three years, and Charles B. Grace Jr, Alan and Jan Luxenberg, and Harry Richlin merit special thanks for their kindness. Dr Harvey Sicherman, FPRI's President, encouraged my efforts with advice and often applied his years of government experience to illuminating my questions on an earlier era. My colleagues Walter McDougall and James Kurth also took time from their busy schedules to discuss the Whig Revival from the perspectives of American history and political science. Their comments and criticisms made the final manuscript far better than it would have otherwise been.

I would like to thank Dr Godfrey Uziogwe, Head of the History Department at Mississippi State University, for providing a generous grant to cover the cost of illustrations. Besides assisting me with a grant for this project, Dr Uziogwe has combined with other faculties and Dr Phil Oldham, Dean of the College of Arts and Sciences, to foster a commitment to research and scholarship at Mississippi State that deserves special recognition.

I also wish to express my deep appreciation to the archivists and librarians who assisted my research, especially the staff at the University of Virginia's Alderman Library. Lew Purifoy, Holly Shifflet, and Peggy Holley in the Interlibrary Services Department at Alderman demonstrated great facility in locating obscure pamphlets and memoirs, along with cheerful patience with my requests. The British Museum's Department of Prints and Drawings handled my inquiries with the utmost courtesy and professionalism, and I appreciate their kind permission to reproduce images from their collection of print satires. I wish to thank the owners and custodians of manuscripts for permission to cite from their collections: Christopher Wright, Keeper of Manuscripts at the British Library; the British Library's Newspaper Archive at Colindale; University College, London; the Earl of Lonsdale and the Cumbria Record Office branches at Kendall and Carlisle; the Hampshire Record Office; Durham University Library at Palace Green; the Liverpool Record Office; Arlene Shy, Librarian at the William L. Clements Library at the University of Michigan, Ann Arbor; and the Earl of Harewood and the West Yorkshire Archive Service in Leeds. The assistance I received from the staff at these archives made my research a real pleasure.

Compelling personal debts remain for last. Dandridge Woodworth provided much appreciated hospitality while in Durham, and Daniel McCardle entertained me in Washington on several research trips to the Library of Congress. The camaraderie that Mike Kelly and Edward Rix shared in Philadelphia eased the burden of revisions. My wife Carolyn Jane Hay has been a constant friend and inspiration, and she patiently read through several drafts of the manuscript. It is to her that I dedicate this book. Margaret Hampton, Sarah Jane, and Wills have also made a contribution of sorts to this project, and they can now reclaim their father's attention from political conflict in early nineteenth century Britain.

West Point, Mississippi   WILLIAM ANTHONY HAY

List of Abbreviations

Manuscript collections

Add. MSS	British Library Additional Manuscripts Collection
Althorp MSS	Manuscripts: Lansdowne Papers Althorp (Spencer) Papers
Brougham MSS	Brougham Papers, University College, London
Croker MSS	John Wilson Croker Papers William L. Clements Library, University of Michigan, Ann Arbor
Grey MSS	Grey Papers Durham University Library
Lansdowne MSS	British Library Uncatalogued
Lowther MSS	Lowther Papers Cumbria Record Office, Carlisle
Roscoe MSS	William Roscoe Papers Liverpool Record Office
Tierney MSS	George Tierney Papers Hampshire Record Office

Published books

Brougham's Life and Times	Henry Brougham, *The Life and Times of Henry, Lord Brougham*, 3 vols (London: William Blackwood & Sons, 1871).
Creevey Papers	Sir Herbert Maxwell, ed., *The Creevey Papers: A Selection of the Correspondence and Diaries of Sir Thomas Creevey, MP* 2 vols (London: John Murray, 1903).

Creevey's Life and Times	John Gore, ed., *Creevey's Life and Times: A Further Selection from the Correspondence of Thomas Creevey* (London: John Murray, 1937).
Croker Papers	Louis J. Jennings, ed., *The Croker Papers: The Correspondence and Diaries of John Wilson Croker*, 3 vols (London: John Murray, 1885).
Dropmore Papers	*Report on the Manuscripts of J.B. Fortescue Esq. Preserved at Dropmore.*, 10 vols (London: HMSO, 1894).
Formation of Canning's Ministry	Arthur Aspinall, ed., *The Formation of Canning's Ministry, February to August 1827* (London: Royal Historical Society, 1927).
Greville Memoirs	Roger Fulford and Lytton Strachey, eds, *The Greville Memoirs*, 7 vols (London: Macmillan & Co., 1938).
Holland, Memoirs	Henry Richard Vassall Fox, 3rd Baron Holland, *Memoirs of the Whig Party.*, 2 vols (London: Longmans, Brown, Green & Longmans, 1852–4).
Holland, Further Memoirs	Henry Richard Vassall Fox, 3rd Baron Holland, *Further Memoirs of the Whig Party, 1807–12 with Miscellaneous Recollections* (New York: Dutton & Co., 1905).
Horner Papers	Kenneth Bourne and William Banks Taylor, eds, *The Horner Papers: Selections from the Letters and Miscellaneous Papers of Francis Horner, MP, 1795–1817* (Edinburgh: Edinburgh University Press, 1994).
Letters of George IV	Arthur Aspinall, ed., *Letters of King George IV*, 3 vols (Cambridge: Cambridge University Press, 1938).

Pope of Holland House

Seymour, Lady, *The 'Pope' of Holland House: Selections from the Correspondence of John Wishaw and His Friends, 1813–14* (London: T.F. Unwin, 1906).

Smart

William Smart, *Economic Annals of the Nineteenth Century*, 2 vols (London: Macmillan & Co., 1910 and 1917).

Thorne

R.G. Thorne, ed., *The House of Commons, 1790–1820*, 5 vols (London: Secker & Warburg, 1986).

Wilson, Narrative

Sir Robert Wilson, *Narrative of the Formation of Canning's Administration, 1827*, Herbert Randolph, ed. (London: Rivingtons, 1872).

Wordsworth Letters

Mary Moorman and Alan G. Hill, eds, *Letters of William and Dorothy Wordsworth*, 3 vols (Oxford: Clarendon Press, 1970).

Introduction

In Britain, the early decades of the nineteenth century saw the qualified development of a two-party representative system different in key respects from earlier periods of party rivalry. Few observers in 1800 would have predicted the revival of the Foxite Whigs or the post-1832 political structure in which organized parties with popular support beyond Westminster alternated in office. Those changes fostered a broader political nation in which provincial opinion carried greater weight in national political discussion at Westminster. Together they laid the foundation for nineteenth century parliamentary liberalism and the Whig–Liberal ascendancy that lasted until William Gladstone split the party over Irish Home Rule in 1886. The political scene in which the Foxite Whigs reestablished themselves as an effective opposition between 1808 and 1830 thus provides valuable insights into the development of modern British politics.

With the end of a formal Whig–Tory rivalry in the 1750s, the concept of party had only a tenuous legitimacy until Edmund Burke crafted a systematic defence for concerted opposition to George III's ministers by the Rockingham Whigs. Cautious references to outside agitation and public opinion were only outdoor gestures by the Rockingham Whigs in support of an essentially indoor struggle, and Burke's own insistence that Parliament maintain its independence from external pressure set limits on how a ministry's critics appealed beyond Westminster.[1] Splits within the opposition provided another problem that set the government against competing factions rather than a solid opposition. Despite ministerial reshuffles in the 1760s, Lord North, William Pitt the Younger, and Lord Liverpool successfully piloted what was effectively a one-party state into the 1820s.[2]

The Foxite Whigs in the first decades of the nineteenth century stood between their undistinguished recent past and uncertain prospects for the future. Excluded from office, save for Charles James Fox's short-lived Whig-dominated Talents Ministry in 1806–7, the party saw its ranks thinning and prospects for office slim. Byron's *Don Juan* quipped that 'Nought's permanent among the human race/Except the Whigs *not* getting into place', and a later historian argued persuasively that 'the Whigs had established a powerful claim to be considered the least effective party of modern times, doomed to permanent opposition'.[3] The political scene changed dramatically with the turmoil that followed Lord Liverpool's crippling stroke in 1827 and the Tory split over Catholic Emancipation. The Whigs had established their claims as a credible governing party by 1830, and they formed the core of Earl Grey's reform ministry later that autumn. The Reform government and its Whig successor under Lord Melbourne initiated a decade of reform through such measures as the Reform Act of 1832, the New Poor Law of 1834, and the Municipal Corporations Act of 1835 and thereby solidified the coalition that came to define parliamentary liberalism. By the 1840s, the very success with which the coalition of Whigs and liberal reformers had recast political discourse obscured the scale of their achievement.

Henry Brougham, a leading Whig MP, barrister, and publicist, played a key role in his party's revival by building an alliance with provincial interests. Where Edmund Burke had earlier crafted an intellectual justification of party activity, Brougham applied the concept and extended it beyond the House of Commons to the nation as a whole. His appeal to provincial merchants and manufacturers frustrated at their exclusion from influence helped transform a faction of aristocratic, metropolitan-oriented Foxites into a national party. Although his career peaked in 1830, he transformed British politics through an achievement whose significance was clouded only by the later eccentricities that ended Brougham's chances to hold office or remain a serious political figure.

Several facets of Brougham's approach fit together in his effort to bring the Whigs from opposition to office. Brougham pioneered a new style of parliamentary opposition through 'petition and debate' tactics that combined local petitioning meetings with press reports and debates in the House of Commons to create a cycle linking provincial opinion with the political contest at Westminster. The tactic helped Brougham defeat the regulatory Orders in Council in 1812 and the income tax in 1816, and Richard Cobden used Brougham's campaign against the Orders as a model for the Anti-Corn Law League in the 1840s. Opening county and borough politics through contested parliamentary elections served as another way to extend the party contest from Westminster to constituencies. Brougham's efforts to capture a seat in Westmorland controlled by the Earl of Lonsdale's interest attracted national attention as a symbolic confrontation between the Whigs and Lord Liverpool's Tory government, and his 1818 canvass in Westmorland prefigured William Gladstone's Midlothian crusade in 1879–80. Observers viewed Brougham's election in July 1830 as MP for Yorkshire, England's largest county, as a declaration of popular support for reform. Parliamentary opposition and election campaigns both involved extensive work with the press, and Brougham used periodicals along with both London and provincial newspapers to make the Whigs' case. His strategy eventually harnessed in support of the Whigs many middle class activists who drove the period's liberal reform movements. More than any other figure of the time, he educated public opinion and brought it to bear on national affairs.[4]

As Donald Read has shown, the nineteenth century was the great age of provincial consciousness with cities like Manchester and Birmingham shaping national politics more than before or since.[5] Expansion of the political nation between 1808 and 1830 to include new interests throughout the country made possible the provincial role that Read describes. During the early and mid-eighteenth century, the city of London and borough of Westminster led extra-parliamentary opinion in spirit and organization. This reinforced the importance of the metropolitan world focused on London that included established commercial interests along with high politics in Parliament, government administration, and the court. Popular activism in the borough of Westminster, with what amounted to manhood suffrage and a well organized plebeian radical interest, provided another facet to the political context.

The need to describe interests developing beyond London gave the term provinces a new application in the 1780s. Groups like Christopher Wyvill's Yorkshire Association established in 1779 and the General Chamber of Manufacturers that followed in 1785 marked the beginning of organized provincial interests, especially in Northern England and the Midlands, with perspectives distinct from those of metropolitan London. The growing reach of provincial newspapers after 1790 encouraged their growth, but Brougham's campaigns accelerated it and made it a political force at Westminster. He described public opinion and the press in 1812 as the main check on Lord Liverpool's government, and public opinion by the 1820s was associated with the provincial middle classes.[6] Such respectable groups had a standing within the community that their radical counterparts lacked, and Whigs uneasy with popular agitation found them more agreeable partners in finding new issues on which to challenge the government. Agitation by London radicals had less of an impact than slow and profound shifts of allegiance in the country at large and the ways in which politicians learned to turn those changing attitudes to their advantage.[7]

Opposition to monopolies in commerce, religion, and politics gave Whigs and the provincial interests Brougham cultivated an ideological bond that became the foundation for a more effective challenge to the Pittite Tory ascendancy than Foxite efforts before 1812. During those years Whigs had stressed divisive issues like retrenchment, scandal, and peace that lacked coherence as a programme and looked back to eighteenth century country party rhetoric. Besides creating differences among Whigs by drawing Foxites into uncomfortable relations with metropolitan radicals, opposition along those lines painted Whigs as factious and self-interested. Brougham's developing strategy in the 1810s and 1820s fitted better with Whig principles that emphasized liberty and resistance to arbitrary power. It also helped move the party from its eighteenth-century obsession with secret influences and the power of the Crown toward a wider concern with the liberties of other groups within the realm that was more likely to draw support beyond their own aristocratic circle. Campaigns highlighted Whig ideological differences with the government as well as questions of policy, painting ministers as part of an incorrigible Tory establishment.[8] Brougham's critique drew provincial reformers towards the Whigs and informed the changes in public attitudes that laid the foundations for Victorian liberalism. Jonathan Parry has defined nineteenth century liberal government as a system in which potentially incompatible interests accepted an overall code that guaranteed a variety of liberties. The open politics that liberals practised reflected their desire to respond to popular grievances, and liberals defined themselves as opponents to government by class, sect, or interest.[9] Attention to public opinion and the importance of debate seen in what the Victorian journalist Walter Bagehot described as Parliament's role in articulating grievances felt in the country followed from this approach which contrasted with the Pittite regime's administrative mentality and exclusive ethos.[10]

Despite the metropolitan orientation of most Foxites, a number of Whigs shared Brougham's awareness of politics beyond metropolitan London and the opportunities it provided for cooperation with middle class interest groups. The fact that the middle classes were defined by a coherent set of 'respectable' cultural and moral values that gentry and aristocrats could appropriate rather than strictly economic criteria removed barriers to exploring common ground.[11] Lords Milton and

Althorp, whose views had been shaped by their families' parliamentary interests and social role in Yorkshire and Northamptonshire, appreciated the dynamics of local politics and sought to establish the Whigs as leaders of 'popular' elements in the country that their party's leaders had neglected. Accordingly, they lent support during the 1820s to movements favouring parliamentary reform and removal of disabilities on religious nonconformists.[12] Others appreciated the growing desire among the middle classes for a voice in government policy and understood that the Whigs must provide leadership or risk 'falling into contempt...as an incapable and useless body'.[13] Even during the bleak days following Fox's death in 1806, the Edinburgh-raised economist and politician Francis Horner saw in the respectable middling orders a broad foundation for a popular party.[14]

Nonetheless, Brougham brought a unique perspective and energy to the Whig opposition that merits close attention. A provincial man raised in Edinburgh and steeped in the Scottish Enlightenment, his awareness of commercial society and communities in Britain whose concerns differed from metropolitan preoccupations shaped an outlook different from other Foxites. Brougham's family originated across the border in Westmorland where his father had been a Whig squire, but his formidable mother Eleanor Syme was the niece of William Robertson, a distinguished historian and principal of Edinburgh University. The Virginia orator and patriot Patrick Henry was Brougham's cousin on his mother's side, and both families acknowledged the relationship. Robertson had traced Europe's transition from rudeness to refinement through the development of commercial society and was a moderate Whig who opposed slavery and sympathized with the American colonies.[15]

Raised in a culture that stressed self-improvement by study and practice, Brougham displayed an early penchant for classics and mathematics at the Edinburgh High School before entering the University at fourteen where he studied with Dugald Stewart and John Playfair. Two papers on scientific topics that he wrote in his teens were read before the Royal Society and later published in its *Transactions*. A firmly empirical intellectual environment marked Brougham's adult writings and set him apart from radicals and utilitarians like Jeremy Bentham. From an early age, Brougham strove to pose as a prodigy and displayed an impressive range of interests throughout his career.[16] Friends within his circle founded the *Edinburgh Review* in 1802, and within five years he had taken the lead in what became the most influential periodical of the age. Youthful exuberance combined with Edinburgh's vibrant intellectual milieu set the journal's early tone. Brougham's essays not only covered a remarkable range of topics, but also showed a gift for invective that often went beyond prudence.

Exclusion from preferment as a young Whig in Scotland under Henry Dundas's Tory hegemony sharpened Brougham's stridency along with his political views. Admitted to the Scottish bar in 1800, he found few briefs and filled his time with writing. Brougham moved to London in 1804 and built his career in England as a barrister on the Northern Circuit. Francis Horner, who had preceded Brougham and developed ties with the Holland House circle, introduced him to Whig society. Brougham's *Inquiry into the Colonial Policy of the European Powers* drew national attention when it appeared in 1806 and established him as an authority on political economy. Lord Holland persuaded him to write a pamphlet defending the Talents ministry in 1806, and Brougham received his first political appointment that year as secretary to a failed diplomatic mission to Portugal. He managed the press campaign for the Whigs during the 1807 general election and, with some assistance from Holland and John Allen, wrote most of the party's material. According to Holland, he 'filled every bookseller's shop with pamphlets, most London newspapers and country ones without exception with paragraphs'.[17] Brougham's awareness of the most effective ways to influence public opinion through the press made him peculiarly well fitted for the task, but he disliked compromising his independence by remaining long in a subordinate capacity as a hired pamphleteer.[18] Ambition spurred Brougham to gain a seat in Parliament and claim a leading public role.

Brougham's wit drew an audience from an early age, and his achievements as a barrister and parliamentarian reflected a passion to be seen. As a young man he attended a theatre performance in which every attempt at humour over four acts had misfired. When the curtain rose for the next act with the stage set for a dinner scene, an actor called for a toast. Brougham replied from the audience, 'I humbly propose "good afternoon"', the customary toast for ending a party, and waved his hat for others to follow as the theatre emptied behind him. Pranks and wild boisterousness among Brougham's Edinburgh circle showed a different side of his personality than treatises on colonial policy. He boasted that a closet in his father's house contained brass knockers torn from doors in Edinburgh's new town. Brougham and a group of friends pulled the bronze sign from Manderson's druggist shop after a banquet, and on another occasion he called out the city watch as a prank on his companions after instigating a similar expedition for the sign from another apothecary.[19] Conviviality drew forth the same energy as work and scholarship, while all revealed an erratic streak.

Temperament defined the course of Brougham's career as much as anything else. A man with tremendous presence, Brougham had a depressive personality in which periods of frenetic activity and gaiety alternated with periods of blackest gloom. Periodic retreats to his Westmorland estate punctuated his busy social and professional life. Impatience and querulousness spoiled Brougham's charm over time. Whig aristocrats and intellectuals alike became suspicious of their awkward, headstrong colleague.[20] Grey once likened Brougham to Edmund Burke as the most eminent man of his day, and, like the Irish-born Burke, Brougham served as the intellectual mentor and strategist for the Whig party of his generation.[21] The two men shared other attributes that merit attention: both were perceptive outsiders with a shrewd grasp of the political scene and both proved difficult colleagues who pushed their fellow Whigs to raise questions that they otherwise hesitated to press in such strident tones.

Brougham entered the House of Commons in 1810 for Camelford and quickly became the Pittite government's most formidable parliamentary critic. Connections from legal work, particularly representing Liverpool merchants petitioning against the Orders in Council prior to entering the Commons, and the campaign against slavery and other reform movements, such as the Society for the Diffusion of Useful Knowledge, helped build formidable support in the country. Although his interest in these issues was sincere, political ambition drove Brougham's multifarious activities.[22] Involvement with reform efforts and educational initiatives enhanced his image and provided contacts with networks of respectable supporters across the country. Consequently, few other Whigs and no radicals could match Brougham's influence over liberal opinion in the provinces that played so important a role in the Whig revival.

This study of the Whigs' move from opposition to office contributes to a substantial recent literature on early nineteenth century British political culture. Richard Brent, Jonathan Parry, and Peter Mandler have explored the development of liberal politics with an emphasis on events after 1830, and Mandler's work captures the aristocratic Whig style whose influence persisted into the 1840s. His analysis of the Foxite connection explains much of their cohesion and survival through decades of opposition. Broader studies by Frank O'Gorman and H.T. Dickinson of the Hanoverian electoral system and popular politics over the long eighteenth century indicate a more vibrant and participatory scene than earlier accounts credit. Public opinion and political activity existed largely within the framework of local and constituency politics that formed a political culture of its own, and elites devoted considerable attention to maintain their influence. Only in the early nineteenth century did national parties at Westminster systematically engage constituency networks as part of their struggle for advantage.[23]

Each of these works, however, largely examines developments between the collapse of the Talents ministry and Grey's accession to office in 1830 as part of another story rather than closely engaging the period on its own terms. Older narratives of the Whig years in opposition by Michael Roberts and Austin Mitchell focus on the manoeuvres of high politics among party leaders and thereby neglect the impact of questions related to civil and religious liberty, commercial interests, and opinion beyond Westminster during these years in opposition. Far from being the defeated and fragmented force that Roberts presents, the Whigs showed the capacity to expand by seeking new issues and appealing to new constituencies. While the factionalism he and Mitchell describe impeded attempts to revive the party, Whigs nonetheless sustained a bond in opposition that provided the basis for their subsequent revival. Close study of manuscript sources, newspapers, and other print media of the period indicates the importance of building provincial support during the halting process of Whig revival that profoundly changed British politics. Analysis of the shift in the two decades before 1830 thus requires close attention to trends beyond the parliamentary struggle at Westminster that past accounts or scholarship focused on other periods do not provide.

This book presents the Whig revival as a key episode in the political history and party development between 1808 and 1830. Chapter 1 opens with a discussion of parliamentary politics and the factors behind the Whigs' exclusion from office before addressing the specific issues on which Brougham and his party drew support and the limits they faced in exploiting their tactical success. Chapter 2 sets high politics into the broader context of social and economic forces beyond Westminster and considers the role of the press and local politics. Subsequent chapters examine Whig efforts to seize advantage over the government between 1818 and 1830. Election campaigns in Westmorland and Yorkshire gave Brougham a prominent platform outside Parliament and served a similar objective of building support, as did issue-oriented campaigns in the Commons. Each of those elections provides insight into Brougham's developing strategy, its effectiveness, and political tensions of the period. Political conflict and the struggle for power itself became the catalyst for change, and Whig efforts at responding to its exigencies played a vital part in developing the liberal approach that emerged in the 1820s. The Whigs' halting progress underlines their difficulty in gaining traction against the government. Brougham nevertheless combined electioneering with pressure tactics that gradually shifted opinion in the country to establish the Whigs as a viable governing party and allowed them to seize the opportunity presented by the final Tory split in 1830.

1
Party Structure and the Whigs in British Politics

After the Foxite-dominated Ministry of All the Talents collapsed in 1807, the main body of the Whigs spent over two decades out of office, and the brief tenure of the Talents itself marked only a short caesura in the party's exclusion from power since the early 1780s. William Pitt the Younger and his political heirs had held together a remarkably resilient set of administrations, which continued through the last years of the war against France and the peace that followed. Lord Liverpool, who governed longest of Pitt's protégés from 1812 until his stroke in 1827, faced severe pressure without irretrievably losing the confidence of the Crown or the House of Commons. His Whig opponents led by Lord Grey consistently failed to establish their standing as an alternative source of leadership in spite of their ability to inflict occasional defeats on issues such as the Orders in Council and income tax. Repeated failures to translate those victories into a change of administration left the Whigs increasingly on the political margins.

Although it appeared likely that the Whigs would come to power in 1810–11 under the Prince Regent, any trust in the future George IV was misplaced. Their exclusion involved more than royal disfavour, since recent experience had demonstrated that a sovereign could no longer enforce his will against the wishes of a wider bloc in or outside Parliament. Popular sentiment also distrusted Whigs. They had faced charges of 'a more than tacit connivance given to all irreligion and immorality' as early as the 1740s, and attacks on Whig amorality elaborated in lurid detail became a staple of the Tory press from the 1790s. Public perceptions of the Whigs' openly profligate behaviour became associated with latitudinarian and sceptical religious views and radical politics.[1]

The public style that Whigs cultivated also set them further apart from elite and popular attitudes in the 1790s and beyond. After 1765 the high Whig aristocracy became the primary conduit for bringing continental fashions to London and they consciously set their cosmopolitan outlook against the narrower view of their counterparts focused on local concerns. Travel on the continent enhanced Whig claims for a special objectivity, for it was through the Grand Tour that tastes were refined and political horizons broadened.[2] Foxite support for the French Revolution and opposition to the war against France raised further doubts about the Whigs' trustworthiness. J.W. Ward wrote that 'a suspicion of being too much attached to foreign notions or foreign manners' could irretrievably ruin a public man, and, if not actually clothed in foreign ways, many Whigs appeared at least to wear accepted English ones very lightly.[3]

The arithmetic of parliamentary seats underlined more nebulous questions of public image. Dividing members between the two categories of government and opposition gives a deceptively clear picture of a complicated political scene, but, despite a degree of oversimplification, it illustrates the problem behind the Whigs' plight. The Talents, like all other governments, held a majority in the House of Commons based upon their own supporters, sympathetic independents, and borough owners who sought the potential rewards of cooperating with the ministry in office regardless of its complexion.[4] Once they left office in 1807, however, the coalition split, and support from uncommitted members evaporated. A motion on the new administration saw the Whigs defeated with 226 votes against 258 for the Duke of Portland's government. Some members opportunistically changed sides, and others who in 1806 and 1807 had preferred Pitt's friends, but found active opposition in wartime unpalatable, returned to give Portland their support.[5] Pitt's friends, who gradually assumed the name Tory, relied on support beyond the usual backing given the King's ministers. John Wilson Croker calculated in 1827 that Tory peers and commoners returned 203 English members to the House of Commons against roughly 73 seats controlled by Whigs.[6] Henry Dundas, 1st Viscount Melville, created a reliable phalanx of Pittite support among Scottish members by exploiting an electoral system open to manipulation. Public opinion carried scant weight outside ruling circles, and the eligibility for official appointments among most voters gave the ambitious an incentive for cooperation. Melville's influence declined after his fall from office in 1805, but as late as 1818 his machine ensured Liverpool's government support from 66 per cent of active Scottish members. Only 55 per cent of members overall voted as favourably, and the Scots were only half as likely to cast mixed votes as members generally.[7]

Voting patterns illustrate the Whigs' problem. The 1807 election called to bolster the Duke of Portland's government returned 388 government supporters, 224 opposition members, 29 independents, 17 doubtfuls, and 12 designated neutral. A Treasury analysis from March 1808 listed 378 members supporting the government, 256 against, 10 hopeful, and 14 doubtful. It then divided hopefuls and doubtfuls to project 389 pro and 267 con.[8] Portland thus had a majority of between 122 and 146 depending upon attendance and the subject at hand. Animosity between George Canning and Lord Castlereagh broke up Portland's government, and after his resignation George III turned to Spencer Perceval. Although Perceval, and, following his assassination in 1812, Liverpool, sought several times to broaden their government with opposition support, talks with Whig and Grenvillite leaders failed. Instead, Perceval and Liverpool attracted other parliamentary factions, including those of both former Pittites, like Canning, and others like the friends of Lords Sidmouth and Wellesley who had been courted by both sides. More divided these groups from the Whigs than from one another, however, and their support contributed to the government's strength in the 1810s and early 1820s.[9]

As his government's fortunes rose in late 1812, Liverpool called an election which returned 419 supporters against 239 in opposition, and, factoring in members who voted with less consistency, created a majority of 180, some 60 more than in the previous session.[10] The Whigs lost some of their leading men in the Commons, including Brougham, and others had to be hastily returned for pocket boroughs after defeat elsewhere. Consistent voting, at rates of 70 per cent or more, and low attendance made the government secure on all but the most controversial questions between 1818 and 1827. Divisions among the Whigs, including the secession of the Grenvillites, widened the gap by 1818, giving Liverpool 411 votes and a majority of roughly 212.[11] Hence, the government's revival after 1812 left the Whigs little hope of driving Liverpool from office without renewed quarrels among ministers or an extraordinary, and unlikely, degree of royal dissatisfaction.

Liverpool maintained his position with considerably less direct patronage than earlier Prime Ministers. He had only ten seats under his control in 1826, and the drop of placemen and pensioners from 200 in 1760 to fewer than 50 in 1821 suggests patronage was a waning asset. Liverpool also broke with the earlier practice of spending secret service money on elections, since Curwen's Act of 1809 had prohibited the

open purchase of seats.[12] The government viewed accusations of illegitimate influence very seriously, and Liverpool reduced its use of offices
and state funds for political purposes in order to avoid scandal. Along
with efforts to economize after 1815, the policy forced Liverpool regularly to refuse patronage requests, thereby lessening his potential
control over the Commons.[13] Support came more from loyalty to the
King's ministers and fear of radical tendencies among the Whigs, than
from the emoluments that had lubricated Sir Robert Walpole's and
Lord North's system in the previous century. Individuals concerned
with protecting their offices and pensions from a change of government no longer defected from ministers under fire as they had done
earlier, and opposition pressure tended to strengthen governments
rather than speed their decline. Conflicts over principles revived ministerial support among members who distrusted the Whigs and doubted
their ability to govern effectively.[14]

The political balance in the House of Commons was more complicated
than the terms government and opposition suggest. The Commons held
two main parties, several factions of varying significance, and independents who rejected the concept of party altogether. Most observers at the
time took the language of party for granted as a means of defining the
political landscape. The labels 'Whig' and 'Tory' represented divisions
dating largely from the 1780s and 1790s, even though the words themselves came from earlier conflicts.[15] Some historians have questioned
whether party labels accurately describe late Hanoverian politics, and
one writer has made the valid point that dividing members into groups
on the basis of their votes superimposes a mechanical grid on fine shades
of personal opinion and political connection.[16] Moreover, at times contemporaries showed unease with the Jacobite and Stuart implications of
Toryism. Nevertheless, what James Boswell called in the 1760s 'these
ludicrous terms' stuck because:

> They give us instantly the ideas of these different parties and give it
> with a particular force which explanation does not give...We have
> been accustomed to hear these words from our earliest youth in a
> particular sense. Consequently they make a more lively impression
> than a long argument.[17]

Sir Thomas Lethbridge in 1827 offered a similar view of two different
parties professing opposite principles. He thought the terms, and the
choice they implied, useful and believed people 'knew where to find
[Whigs and Tories] when they were wanted'.[18]

The term Tory gradually came into general use once more as an epithet aimed at Pittites accused of following reactionary policies on law and order, radicalism, limiting religious toleration, and defence of the monarchy and constitution.[19] Beyond specific issues, Croker believed that temperament played a role as the parties represented 'two great antagonistic principles at the root of all government – *stability* and *experiment*'.[20] Toryism thus reflected the desire for stability. Although some ministers baulked at the label on the grounds that all Englishmen who accepted the settlement of 1688 were Whigs of one kind or other, Canning described Pittites as Tories. Liverpool, then as Lord Hawkesbury, described Tories as 'firm, steady, and persevering support-ers of the monarchy and Established Church', and appealed for Tory support against Catholic Emancipation as early as 1805. Croker defined Toryism as 'morality, legality, [and] respect for constituted authority', and promoted acceptance of the word in the press. Whig became the sole possession of the Rockinghams who supported Fox through the 1780s and, momentarily divided by the French Revolution, largely reassembled themselves by 1803–6. The terms gained currency in the 1807 election, and by 1815 largely had replaced the earlier labels Pittite and Foxite.[21]

The parties themselves at this period differed greatly both from their earlier incarnations and their late nineteenth and twentieth century successors. A political party in Britain is an organized group possessing or aspiring to political power, and thus political office, which cultivates popular support for its beliefs and focuses its attention on Parliament. Parties also act at different times as vehicles of ideology, dispensers of patronage, and instruments of government.[22] Whigs and, to a lesser extent in this period, Tories met the criteria of party even though the absence of a mass electorate focused attention on the Commons itself. Since few members owed election to a party label or machine, unity relied on personal loyalty, shared ideological commitments, and, above all, the desire for office and its perquisites. Parties can be understood best as coalitions reflecting a spectrum of political opinion within agreed bounds rather than a more disciplined and homogeneous body. If differences at times weakened party cohesion, breadth of opinion also became a strength in drawing support from outsiders who might gradually merge into the group.[23] Debates over ideologically charged issues that emphasized identity strengthened the role of parties, while party sentiment receded when such matters of principle became muted and the unity they brought faded. Centrifugal forces often blurred dis-tinctions and made parties appear as two centres of gravity rather than the organized and disciplined bodies acting in sharp opposition usually associated with the concept.[24]

The system's flexibility encouraged small, cohesive groups, acting both within parties and as separate forces. Factions depended upon their leader's fortunes and differed from parties in the scope of their ambitions, their size and popular support, and in having a distinctive ideology.[25] Contemporaries often used the terms party and faction interchangeably, a practice that may derive as much from the ill-repute associated with factions as from confusion over the standing of particular groups. When not used as a synonym for party, faction described a smaller unit of narrower interests whose actions, though similar to those of a party, 'were condemned as illegitimate since directed to the benefit of individuals'.[26] Self-interest, more than the public interest, appeared the driving force behind faction. Factions like the Canningites and Grenvillites received so much attention because many governments exercised only limited control over their supporters and thus in many cases relied upon a shifting majority drawn from such groups.[27] Factions were most effective either as part of a larger party or in negotiating for an alliance with one. Otherwise, they withered as their supporters sought opportunity elsewhere.

A substantial cohort within the Commons completely rejected the concept of party. The number of men recognized as independents fell from 29 in 1790 and 1797 to 9 in 1806 and 12 in 1807, before rising once more to 24 in 1812 and 32 in 1818.[28] Historians often group together the seemingly irreconcilable independents and radicals on the basis of their shared repudiation of party and commitment to local freedom of election.[29] Independents generally represented counties or rural boroughs and entered Parliament to promote local interests or maintain their family's status. Many of them espoused conservative or even reactionary positions, and they resembled radicals only in their close scrutiny of ministerial conduct and their opposition to taxation. Independents, however, declined in significance through the nineteenth century, especially in the 1830s. Radicals drew their strength from educated artisans and Dissenters in boroughs like Westminster, with its large electorate and almost open suffrage. Where birth, preferment, or political adoption made a man a Whig or Tory, radicalism arose from doubts of the justice in conferring power on such grounds. It sought to replace the rival and equally corrupt aristocratic factions with a more pure system that left no place for parties. Radicalism as it emerged in the 1810s also involved a theoretical critique of revealed religion and an institutional critique of the Established Church and the overall social and political order.[30] The line between Whig and radical appeared blurred at times, but the Whigs' deep commitment to party as a facet of their corporate identity and their insistence on property as the qualification for political participation limited cooperation. Another key difference lay in the view among Whigs that radicals could not be trusted because their social and economic situation left them devoid of honour, a qualification required of governors. Francis Place echoed his fellow radicals in accusing Whigs and Tories of neglecting the public good and only considering measures 'as may conduce to the views of the faction'.[31] Independents steeped in country party rhetoric of the eighteenth century would likely have endorsed Place's description.

Most active politicians in the Commons, however, valued party ties. Castlereagh claimed public business could not be better managed or so well managed, if it were not for the system of parties. The success of Britain's government indeed derived from 'that conflict of parties, chastened by the principles of the constitution, and subdued by the principle of decorum'. Even when differing from his fellow Whigs, Charles Western acknowledged 'the necessity of acting generally, though by no means invariably, in a party with those who concur in opinion upon great fundamental principles'.[32] Creevey was equally certain that 'without [party] nothing can be done'.[33] Croker accepted the existence of a party system and contrasted party with faction, insisting that where factionalism had brought confusion early in George III's reign, the party system of the 1810s and 1820s brought stability by balancing interest with principle.[34] Public figures spoke and acted as though they operated within a party system, albeit a flexible one, and deviations from it provoked sufficient comment to suggest party was the normal condition of political life.

The political scene after 1800 took shape from realignments during the 1780s and reactions to the French Revolution in the 1790s. George III replaced the Fox–North coalition in December 1783 with the 24-year-old William Pitt. Despite Pitt's description of himself as an Independent Whig and his refusal to accept party, the 'King's friends' who brought Pitt into office and sustained him there had adopted party techniques, including attendance letters, pairing arrangements, organized propaganda, and election planning.[35] The Rockingham Whigs led by Fox already had an intellectual justification of party crafted by Edmund Burke that drove their opposition. The French Revolution split the Whig opposition and isolated Foxites from growing conservative sentiment in the country, producing an exaggerated group loyalty centred on Fox's person and principles with a corresponding hatred of Pitt and his system.[36]

An alliance between Fox and Lord Grenville in 1804 revived the opposition by drawing many Whigs who had broken with Fox over the French Revolution back to the party. Grenville's disagreements with Pitt and Addington over conducting the war and the Catholic question had separated him from the Pittites, while his differences with Fox no longer involved current concerns. Fox himself believed strongly in systematic opposition to what he long had considered renascent Toryism lurking behind the throne, and his emphasis on the need for a group of loyal and honest men in Parliament who could stand against both men and measures became part of the Foxite creed that guided Grey and others after their leader's death.[37] Fox had already urged his friends to cooperate with Grenville and the conservative Whigs, and personal ties that had never completely faded encouraged the reunion. Grenville, along with the Burkean Whigs led by William Windham, and Lords Spencer and Fitzwilliam, proposed joining Fox's systematic opposition intended to defeat the current government and construct a broadly based replacement. The opposition would focus on the war with France and a more liberal policy toward Ireland, and it became the largest single group in the Commons.[38] After Pitt's death in 1806, this opposition joined with Addington's supporters to form the short-lived Talents ministry. Its dismissal over a minor measure of Catholic relief in 1807 brought Whig members of the government together again in opposition.

Along with its Foxite core, the Grenvillites and Samuel Whitbread's 'Mountain' of radical Whigs comprised the opposition, but the two factions gradually declined in importance. Lord Grenville led the opposition until his retirement in 1817 from active politics, but the Grenvillites lacked the commitment to Fox's memory that characterized most Whigs. As early as 1809, Leigh Hunt's *Examiner* observed that Whig was little more than a name for the Foxite party.[39] Nevertheless, Grey cooperated closely with Grenville and refused to supercede him as party leader or hear of a break. True to Fox's precepts on opposition, Grey insisted on the value of the Foxite-Grenville connection and worked hard to preserve it.[40] Grenville provided qualities of character and experience other Whigs lacked, but his declining ambition and lessening interest in politics led Grenvillites and Burkean Whigs in both Houses to drift gradually into the Foxite camp. The group's core by 1812 'was soft and its outer layers rapidly decomposing', with the result that the Grenvillites who seceded from the Whigs in 1817 amounted to a less formidable force than they once had been.[41]

Other divisions, mainly involving cooperation with radicals, created tensions on the party's other wing. Whitbread and his Mountain, named in ironic reference to Robespierre's allies in the National Convention, urged cooperation with independent radicals in attacking the war and denouncing abuses. Voting patterns marked the Mountain, which became known for its members' 'moral earnestness and extreme anti-ministerial fervour', as a recognizable faction by 1809. A cartoon even depicted Creevey, the group's whip in the Commons, as a badger for his incessant criticism of ministers.[42] The Mountain invited comparisons with the Foxites of the late 1790s both in style and substance, and Whitbread deliberately used Fox's legacy as a rallying point for Whigs uneasy with their party's tentative approach to opposition. A number of Mountaineers cited qualities they admired in Fox as reasons for their support, but the faction also attracted professional men like Brougham and Sir Samuel Romilly who acted for different reasons.[43] Whitbread's desire to work with radicals and groups outside Parliament anticipated Brougham's later efforts, but personal quarrels with Grey and other Whigs drove Whitbread from the party in 1812 and the Mountain dissolved as a separate faction after his suicide in 1815.

In spite of the Whigs' divisions, Lord Holland's lament that the party agreed on little besides Catholic Emancipation missed the fact that the issue involved broader concerns over civil liberties lying at the heart of the party's identity.[44] Agreement on the Catholic question not only overshadowed other differences among Whig factions, it also contrasted sharply with the divisions seen within the government that tended to amplify the views of exclusionist Toryism. Commitment to religious liberty expressed Whig opposition to any proscription of the liberty of British subjects by arbitrary power. Sydney Smith and others may have viewed Catholicism as error, but they saw anti-Catholicism as a form of bigotry with dangerous political consequences.[45] Political disabilities against Roman Catholics raised questions about other forms of political exclusion in a way that made Catholic Emancipation a symbolic issue for Whigs. Indeed, it was important enough to be a *sine qua non* for the Duke of Bedford to give Brougham a seat for one of his pocket boroughs. The defence of religious freedom more broadly created an influential political alliance between evangelical nonconformists, heterodox Unitarians, and Whigs that provided important support outside Parliament and grew over successive decades.[46]

The party joined aristocratic landowners and professional men whose liberalism derived from different sources. Brougham, like his friend and rival Francis Horner, epitomized a type of Whig more at home among statistics and economic theories than the social whirl of London and the great country houses, and whose hagiology drew on Adam Smith rather than Algernon Sidney.[47] Efforts to forge a firm consensus between what Brougham called the high and low Whigs, not to mention factions, threatened to divide the party at times. Grenvillites and the Mountain operated as pressure groups, with Grenville restraining the Whigs from flirting with radicalism and Whitbread demanding more aggressive opposition. Even so, Grenville consistently took more liberal positions on economic policy than Grey or Holland, and he cannot be seen simply as a misplaced conservative. Indeed, Grenville and many of his followers shared with Brougham and others among Whitbread's friends a commercial orientation and appreciation of financial issues that most Foxites lacked. Divisions, including those that crossed factional lines, inhibited efforts to set an accepted agenda beyond driving the government from office and hence made the party difficult to lead.[48]

Finding effective leadership that the majority of Whigs would accept posed major problems. Neither Grenville nor Grey found favour among the country gentlemen, and both of them spent considerable time away from the political arena. The real challenge involved replacing Grey's leadership in the Commons after he acceded to his father's peerage in 1807. Various disqualifications weakened the claims of Lord Henry Petty, Whitbread, Richard Brinsley Sheridan, and Thomas Grenville, and no clear choice emerged.[49] Grey had anticipated the situation by promoting his wife's uncle, George Ponsonby, for the job, but that solution raised other difficulties. Grenville originally wanted the post for his brother Thomas Grenville, who disliked taking an active role himself and backed Ponsonby instead. Whitbread reluctantly accepted Ponsonby as a compromise, and Tierney also set aside his ambitions in deference to Grey, while noting the situation's disadvantages. Ponsonby accepted on 23 November 1807, agreeing that declining the proposal would cause more harm than his acceptance. Whether he could lead a group of gentlemen 'with scarcely twenty of whom he was personally acquainted' seemed in doubt, but Whigs in the Commons agreed to acquiesce in Ponsonby's leadership.[50]

Ponsonby's appointment as nominal leader simply shifted attention to the competition between Tierney and Whitbread for the effective leadership. Grenville, and many Foxites, disliked Whitbread's aggressive style, and even Brougham noted his friend's limitations. Rejection grated on Whitbread's sensibilities and encouraged his drift from regular opposition to an erratic radicalism. Tierney, dubbed 'Mrs. Cole' after a brothel keeper in one of Samuel Foote's farces who shared Tierney's habit of referring flatteringly to his own character, faced distrust from others critical of his tentative approach. Brougham complained that Tierney tended to 'pour cold water on all that is proposed' and accused him of a 'generally discouraging habit' that diminished the man's acknowledged merits along with his support in the party. But Brougham also criticized Ponsonby for committing the party to positions on the war with Napoleonic France, reform, and humanitarian issues that countered what many others considered Fox's view, thereby 'reducing us all to the dilemma of either being supposed to agree with him or (what is hurtful both personally and to the party) getting up and disclaiming'.[51] Such open disagreements hurt the party's standing in Parliament.

The possibility of replacing Ponsonby arose in 1810, when rumours circulated that he wished to lay down the burden. He quickly repelled the attack on his leadership, but failed to assert his authority in doing so.[52] Holland complained that the party could not prosper without a leader in the Commons 'who does not only inspire full confidence but who really has some degree of ascendancy over our minds'. Creevey phrased the point differently by claiming that a man 'must make himself our leader by his talents, his courage, and above all by the excellence and consistency of his public principles'.[53] Under Ponsonby's leadership, or lack thereof, the party seemed unable to manage itself, let alone the government, and the absence of a clear voice diminished the Commons' willingness to hear the Whigs' case.

Discussions over possibly forming a government proved as divisive as settling on a leader in the Commons. The weakness of Pittite governments until mid-1812 prompted several offers to the Whigs. Hesitating to strengthen the government and accept responsibility for its measures, Grey and Grenville rejected coalition proposals in 1809 and 1812. They realized that such a step would merely provide cover for an essentially Tory government while undercutting Whig principles by compromising their own and the party's reputation. The most significant opportunity arose in 1811 when creation of a Regency raised the possibility that the Prince of Wales might replace Perceval's government with a Whig ministry, but the prospect of office only heightened factional quarrels. The Whigs and the Prince had drifted apart since Fox's death, and the Regent's eventual decision to support Liverpool's government forced a split. Abandoning the Regent's favour then forced the Whigs to consider an alternative path out of the political wilderness.

The Whigs' approach to specific issues demonstrated the party's problems in the Commons. The Talents Ministry's poor record gave their successors a fatally easy means of replying by reproaching their predecessors 'with some similar error or job'.[54] Foreign and military policy left the Whigs most vulnerable to such *tu quoque* arguments. Whigs differed among themselves as well, with some joining Whitbread's zealous demand for peace and others, like Grenville and Grey, unable to see how it could be secured honourably at present. Uncertainty made them hesitate to move beyond criticizing the present government, and that position made them seem motivated by opportunism rather than national interest.[55] Whigs faced steady criticism for asserting 'the interests of every country in preference to those of England', and for raising questions solely from party spirit and personal animosity.[56] While Grey, for practical as well as patriotic reasons, sought to 'avoid giving any fair occasion to the charge of carrying on a vexatious & harrying opposition', Whitbread and the Mountain took a different view, and the cautious approach of Tierney and Ponsonby only split the party further.[57] Disputes over policy, like the leadership quarrels, made the Whigs appear disorganized, while at the same time raising doubts about their patriotism.

Whig attacks on the expedition mounted in 1807 to seize the Danish fleet at Copenhagen and prevent Napoleon from using it against Britain united the party to a degree during 1808's parliamentary session. A vote of thanks passed the Commons on 29 January 1808 by 100 to 19, with mostly Mountaineers in the minority. Tierney criticized the government's motion as an attempt to give what he called a relatively minor action 'the utmost possible importance'.[58] Ponsonby requested correspondence related to Denmark in a motion on 3 February 1808 intended to challenge the attack's justification. He accused the government of bullying the Danes and making an unprovoked act of aggression. Ponsonby's motion failed by 145 votes, and the Commons rejected by 155 votes a similar motion by Richard Sharp, who presented Britain as a more active aggressor than France.[59] Whitbread's attempt to press the matter further by requesting diplomatic correspondence relating to Russia only sparked Sir Thomas Turton's sharp accusation of partisanship.[60] The opposition's case failed to convince despite the vehemence of its presentation.

The Spanish rising in response to Napoleon's decision to install his brother Joseph on the Spanish throne after forcing the legitimate sovereign's abdication brought strong Whig support for intervention in Spain, and the party united around the policy with varying degrees of enthusiasm. Whitbread, who saw negotiation with Napoleon as the surer path to securing Spain's independence, and Grenville, who privately urged that Britain husband its resources in order to act decisively against France when an opportunity arose, were the only exceptions. Grey described aiding Spain as 'morally and politically one of the highest duties a nation ever had to perform', while the chief Whig newspaper, the *Morning Chronicle*, insisted upon the public's willingness to sacrifice for the Spanish cause, 'so truly and intimately do they sympathize with the struggle of a people for liberty'. Brougham believed the Whigs could gain popularity by supporting the Spaniards and avoiding attacks on the government's Spanish policy.[61]

The Whigs backed aid to Spain when they had opposed other wartime measures because the Spanish rising was a popular movement distinct from other British and allied concerns, and their reason for action raised as many doubts about their commitment to the existing order as the Whigs' general opposition to the war. Brougham expressed many of his friends' sentiments in claiming that the Spaniards' success would bring 'the downfall of our own govt...[and] an end to the high aristocratic tone of the upper orders & the whole discredit brought on democracy by the Reign of Terror'.[62] In an *Edinburgh Review* article written with Francis Jeffrey, the journal's editor, Brougham, insisted that whoever wished Spain well understood that

> he has been espousing the popular side of the greatest question of the present day; that he has been praying most fervently for the success of the people against their rulers; that he has, in plain terms, been, as far as in him lay, a party to revolutionary measures.[63]

Spain's king and nobility had deserted the country leaving the people to save themselves, and their achievement was bound to have an effect in Britain as well. In the article, Jeffrey and Brougham asked:

> What man will now dare to brand his political adversary with the name of a revolutionist, or try to hunt those down, as enemies of order, who expose the follies and corruptions of an unprincipled and unthinking administration?

They argued that:

> [the Spanish revolt would save] our declining country, by the only remedy for its malady – a recurrence to those wholesome popular feelings in which its greatness has been planted and nursed up.[64]

Brougham's article provoked a storm of controversy, and, regardless of their views, few Whigs would state their position as baldly as he had done. Sydney Smith warned Jeffrey the article was imprudent in its language and wrong in its doctrines, but Smith and other Whigs still viewed Spain's opposition to Napoleon as profoundly different from that of Britain and other states. Lady Bessborough noted as late as 1813 the contradiction in Whig attitudes toward Spain and other theatres of war that was explicable only by a preference for Napoleon over the despotisms of Austria, Prussia, and Russia.[65] The war in Spain caught the Whigs in support of radical democracy; their demands for intervention created a conflict with their previous demands either for peace or a defensive strategy.

Another problem arose for the Whigs from their pessimistic response to setbacks in the Peninsular War. By allowing the French free passage home with their baggage and equipment, the Convention of Cintra cast an embarrassing pall over the victory Sir Arthur Wellesley, later Duke of Wellington won over General Junot at Vimero on 21 August 1808. Sir John Moore replaced Wellesley, and his two superiors responsible for the agreement, Sir Hew Dalrymple and Sir Harry Burrard, in command of British forces in the peninsula. Moore's Spanish campaign ended in a retreat from Salamanaca to Corunna and the general's death. The early euphoria and the national unity over intervention in Spain faded with news of Cintra, and the political storm over Moore's campaign worsened the damage.[66] Events appeared to have borne out Grenville's pessimism, but the opposition remained split over how to criticize the government. Foxites and conservative Whigs aligned with Grenville on other issues opposed his wish to raise the broad question of continental expeditions, and pressed instead for a censure of the war's management. Grenville himself hesitated to press ministers for fear of fueling domestic tensions raised by a scandal over bribes for army appointments involving the Duke of York.[67]

Disagreements among the Whigs on wartime strategy and how to act as an opposition blunted effective criticism of the government's overall policy, but the 1809 parliamentary session set a pattern for opposition attacks based upon the details of campaigns rather than the policy behind them. Doubtful of the prospects for future campaigns, Whig leaders received copious, if often inaccurate, information from officers with the army that confirmed their suspicions. Grey closely followed the guidance of Sir Robert Wilson, who consistently deprecated Wellington's plans and ability, and Wilson's advice shaped Grey's criticism of the war from the 1810 defence of Lisbon to an abortive Spanish campaign in

1811 and contributed to the Whigs' surprise at Wellington's successes after January 1812.[68] The Talents' record in office, moreover, gave ministers ammunition that made their Whig critics seem wilfully pessimistic:

Should men who France invincible believ'd
Conduct a warfare they so misconceiv'd
Should prophets, who to Spain foreboded ill,
Get pow'r, and thus their prophecies fulfil
For they, without reserve, would mischief do
To make the mischief they predicted true.[69]

Grenville realized the problems that the Whigs faced from giving the impression of a factious opposition, but the party failed to find a way around them in spite of its early sympathy for the Spanish people.

Even in the Walcheren Expedition of 1809, where the government appeared genuinely at fault, the Whigs failed to make a case that convinced independents in the Commons. The campaign had been an attempt to help Austria by distracting Napoleon, but poor planning and delays produced a disaster when the expedition failed to advance on Antwerp after capturing the island of Walcheren in the Scheldt estuary, where disease took a heavy toll. Once Napoleon defeated Austria, the government abandoned the attempt and withdrew the expedition. Although responsibility lay with ministers, the two commanders, Sir Richard Strachan and the Earl of Chatham, drew blame for allowing the French time to defend Antwerp. As a doggerel mockingly claimed, 'The Earl of Chatham, with sword drawn/Stood waiting for Sir Richard Strachan/Sir Richard, longing to be at 'em/Stood waiting for the Earl of Chatham'.[70] Canning and Castlereagh, whose duel arose from disputes related in part to Walcheren, showed more aggression toward each other than toward the French, and the whole fiasco placed the government in awkward straits.

With the aid of Castlereagh, now out of office and seeking vindication, the Whigs won the vote for a committee of enquiry on 26 January 1810, and Whitbread passed a motion a month later in a thinly attended sitting that censured Chatham for conducting a private correspondence with the King about the affair. Romilly warned the Commons in January 1810 that 'by giving impunity to former ministers in cases of former failures they had given them confidence to bring fresh disasters on the country'. The House took a different view, expressed in majorities of 51 to 23 against the Whigs in a series of votes taken on 30 March 1810.[71]

Why was the Commons willing to approve investigating the Walcheren Expedition, yet equally unwilling to censure it? Independent members disliked the idea of placing affairs 'into the hands of a party that had neither policy, nor prospect of uniting upon one, nor ability to carry it out'.[72] Francis Horner, a Whig MP and colleague of Brougham at the *Edinburgh Review*, thought that the Commons backed the government despite its desire to censure the expedition to avoid forcing it from office and bringing in the Whigs.[73] A pamphleteer insisted that 'it will be a matter of eternal reproach to the opposition that, in this crucial conjecture [1810], they seize every occasion of introducing, night after night, idle and unnecessary discussion, evidently for no object but to tease, to harm, to wear out ministers'. The author likened the motives of politicians who 'agitated the public mind' with 'banditti exhibiting false lights that they may derive plunder from the wreck' that resulted from the confusion.[74] Grey knew such opposition carried all the negative connotations of faction discussed earlier, and Foxite criticism of the war implied pro-French sympathies that pamphleteers attacked in scurrilous tracts like 'The Patriots and the Whigs: the Most Dangerous Enemies of the State' and 'The French Spy'. A cartoon from 1811 showed Lord and Lady Holland – she wearing the breeches and he a skirt – attempting to storm the Treasury with Napoleon in tow muttering *'et moi aussi'*.[75] Whigs reduced their coordinated criticism of the government's military policy, and one backbench Whig claimed the next year that 'all attempts at regular opposition in the House of Commons seem to have been abandoned'.[76]

The Orders in Council, however, provided an issue in which the Whigs effectively challenged the government and forced a change in policy. Although the Orders involved aspects of foreign and military policy, the Whigs primarily addressed their economic impact. The campaign to repeal the Orders brought Brougham to prominence and it illustrated both the problems and opportunities facing the Whigs. Castlereagh recognized the triumph of provincial merchants and manufacturers whose views conflicted with established commercial interests as a portent for the future. A Birmingham leader echoed the point with his insistence that the issue taught Parliament 'it is not the colonial interest nor the shipping interest, two rocks on which England has well-nigh split, but the manufacturing interest on which the prosperity of England depends'.[77] Later groups such as the Manchester-based anti-Corn Law League saw the campaign as an explicit model for their efforts. Defeat over the Orders marked the government's lowest point from the formation of Portland's cabinet in 1807 to Liverpool's stroke

Illustration 1.1   Cartoon from the 1811 showing Lord and Lady Holland approaching the treasury with Napoleon in tow. Reproduced with kind permission of the British Museum.

twenty years later, and the repeal campaign's challenge to political conventions shaped Brougham's strategy over the next two decades.[78]

The Orders in Council were a series of regulations governing trade with French-occupied Europe adopted in response to French attempts at economic warfare. Napoleon's Berlin Decree of November 1806 forbade trade with Britain and made British and colonial goods fair prizes of war.[79] Retaliatory measures instigated by the Talents brought subsequent French decrees that in 1807 declared any vessel following British regulations a lawful prize and again in 1810 ordered the confiscation of British manufactures and of colonial and American goods shipped through Britain. The first Orders in Council issued by the Talents prohibited trade between French-controlled ports, and Perceval expanded them to create a licensing system requiring all trade with Europe to pass through British ports. He insisted on Britain's right to retaliate while realizing a strict blockade would alienate neutrals, especially America. Managing French trade with the wider world would provide sufficient retaliation and benefit Britain without interfering excessively with neutral trade.[80]

The policy set out in the Orders drew sharp criticism in Parliament and the press, but the Whigs did not unite in opposition because many, including Grey and Holland, failed to grasp its implications. Leadership on the issue fell to those better versed in the technicalities of economic policy. Lord Auckland warned the Lords on 28 January 1808 that any policy restricting trade could only bring mutual destruction. He compared the Orders with the efforts of men who, in seeking to starve one another, grasped at 'the inevitable means of starving themselves'.[81] Brougham challenged the Orders' legal justification in the *Edinburgh Review* on the grounds that Napoleon's blockade could not be enforced, and therefore was a legal nullity that gave no grounds for reprisal.[82] Lord Henry Petty made a similar point in the Commons and asked why the government had not waited to see whether Napoleon enforced his decrees against America before taking reprisals, but Perceval rejected implications that the Orders were aimed against the Unites States.[83] Richard Ryder, the Advocate General, further claimed that British trade would face exclusion from Europe without the Orders, since France would use neutral shipping to secure 'all the advantages of peace by having an ample supply of all sorts of goods'.[84] The Whig motion for a committee of inquiry failed by 55 to 118, and the government secured the Orders in Council Bill's passage with a majority of 100.[85]

Events belied Perceval's belief that Britain could dictate the terms of trade between Europe and the wider world without objections from America and other neutral countries. Smuggling limited the Continental System's effectiveness and reduced pressures on Britain, but attempts to mitigate the blockade's impact worked only in part. Periods of strict enforcement by the French between July 1807 and July

1808 and from 1810 to 1811 closed markets as Napoleon strengthened his hold on the Continent.[86] President James Madison's decision in November 1810 to renew non-intercourse the next year if Britain continued the Orders and the implementation of non-intercourse by the Macon Act of 1811 closed America as an alternative to the closed European market. Stockpiles of unshippable goods collected, and many smaller merchants dependent upon American business faced bankruptcy.[87] Declining trade and inflation contributed to a general depression, and, while the country had suffered unemployment earlier in the war, the situation was worse than in recent memory.[88]

Here, the reality of the Orders' economic impact became less important than the public's belief that the policy lay at the root of their problems. Ministers had taken their early cue from established commercial interests that benefited from government intervention, but groups dependant on other markets felt increasingly aggrieved by the policy. Merchants and manufacturers with little previous involvement in repeal took a new interest in the matter that Brougham turned to his advantage in the winter of 1811–12 through tactics he described as 'petition and debate'. Petitioning meetings and newspaper notices prior to the parliamentary session captured attention usually devoted to debates. Each presentation of a petition during the session prompted discussion of the petition's subject, and the resulting publicity spurred more meetings and petitions. Members committed themselves in debate or by presenting a petition or endorsing its sentiments, which further influenced parliamentary sentiment.[89] The tactic brought together popular and parliamentary politics as delegations supported the petition drives by coming to London and meeting directly with Perceval and George Rose, Vice-President of the Board of Trade.

Although an earlier petitioning effort in 1807 had failed, members of the repeal movement learned from their experience and the trade depression gave them a stronger position. Brougham took charge of the campaign in late 1811, and support across the country confirmed his plans for another petition drive to be followed with agitation in the House of Commons. William Roscoe and Thomas Thornley renewed the Liverpool merchants' contact with Brougham, who provided his friends with detailed advice on the form and content of petitions that they shared with other groups.[90] Roscoe later withheld one of Brougham's letters from publication to avoid the impression he had been behind the petitions. As he told Brougham, the idea that petitioners had not spoken of their own accord 'might in some degree prevent the good effects of [Brougham's] exertions to be told in the House'.[91]

Efforts had to be seen as local initiatives for their weight to be felt. A Liverpool petitioning attempt in December 1811 faced opposition from the Mayor backed by the established West India interest, and its organizers abandoned a proposed meeting to call instead upon supporters to sign a prepared address to the Prince Regent.[92]

Richard Spooner and Thomas Attwood, both Tories, organized Birmingham manufacturers, and in other areas Dissenters such as the Staffordshire Wedgwoods led local repeal efforts. Anti-war radicals whose activity dated from the 1790s brought Leeds and Sheffield into the campaign.[93] A January letter to the *Leeds Mercury* commented ironically on local distress by claiming it was impossible 'to devise an expedient so well calculated for keeping clean mills as those famous instruments called the "Orders in Council"'. By late February, Yorkshire woollen manufacturers had recognized the real cause of the depression and mounted a petitioning drive that ended with a public meeting at the Cloth Hall in Leeds.[94] Brougham informed Holland of petitioning efforts in Liverpool, Staffordshire, and Birmingham as well as Leeds, which had been less affected than other areas, and noted firm opposition in Yorkshire to an American war.[95] Coverage in both London and provincial papers stimulated discussion and, although Brougham started the campaign, local groups drove its early stages and provided the petitions that kept the Orders alive as an issue before the Commons.

Parliamentary discussion of the Orders began with Whitbread's request on 13 February 1812 for diplomatic correspondence between Britain and America. The tactic had become a common method of forcing the discussion of issues, and Whitbread stressed the need for information in light of reports that President Monroe had declared that British policy made war with America inevitable.[96] While the motion failed, Brougham began a debate specifically on the Orders on 3 March by moving for an inquiry on the state of trade. His speech reviewed the now familiar arguments against the policy while insisting on the need for an inquiry to determine the Orders' effects. Rose replied that Britain had a right to demand that neutral powers willing to tolerate regulations inimical to Britain also accept measures to defend British interests. While he accepted that distress existed, Rose complained that 'great art had been used to make the suffering individuals believe that their evils originated in the Orders in Council'.[97] Alexander Baring, who had business interests in America and an American wife, dismissed Rose's defence as irrelevant to whether something radically wrong in the economy called for an inquiry. Perceval objected to an inquiry that he doubted would bring any benefit, and the government defeated Brougham by 216 to 144.[98]

Repeal petitions arrived through March and April. A petition from the framework knitters of Leicester had 1100 signatures, and another from Sunderland shipowners complained specifically about losing trade to foreign ships that had received licences exempting them from the Orders.[99] One Liverpool petition on peace sparked a dispute over alleged comments by George Rose to a Birmingham delegation. Rose vehemently denied any words likening Britain and France to two men each with their head in a bucket of water struggling to see who would drown first. A cartoon of Rose holding a man's head underwater in a contest with a caricatured Yankee and Napoleon captured an incident that already had attracted public notice as a symbol of government indifference.[100] On 28 April Castlereagh conceded an inquiry after Lord Stanley offered a formal motion, but denied that the change involved any admission on the merits of the policy. The inquiry, Castlereagh said, was 'merely a concession to the wishes of the country', but his sentiment was as disingenuous as Stephen's view that if yellow fever were felt to be caused by the Orders, an inquiry would be justified merely to remove the false impression.[101] Advocates of repeal took the contrary view that the public discontent had led ministers to judge it 'inexpedient any longer to oppose an inquiry into the effects of their favourite measure', and insisted their demands 'must sooner or later prevail over every opposition'.[102]

The Commons conducted the inquiry as a committee of the whole house before which strangers presented evidence. Brougham managed the presentation of evidence for repeal, but Perceval's murder by a lunatic outside the Commons on 11 May interrupted the hearings. His death deprived the Orders of their strongest supporter and threw the government into disarray, and Lord Holland credited Brougham for braving his enemies' censure and shocking 'the more timid and gentle of his friends' by demanding that the inquiry proceed so as not to inconvenience witnesses.[103] Manufacturers testified on the policy's local impact, and emphasized the need to export since the home market could not absorb all their goods. Joseph Stanley, a Wolverhampton screwmaker, stated that half his production was for America and until that market opened no relief from distress could be found. Josiah Wedgwood of the potteries spoke two days later, claiming over-reliance on domestic sales had forced prices down by 20 to 25 per cent and wages by almost half. While his business mainly exported to Europe, he also attributed problems in Staffordshire to the closed American market.

Illustration 1.2   Print from 1812 that satirizes the orders in council showing George Rose, Vice-President of the Board of Trade, with a caricatured Yankee and Napoleon. Reproduced with the kind permission of the British Museum.

Thomas Millwood, a Birmingham spoonmaker, declared 'he had orders to ship as soon as they [the Orders] are done away with'.[104]

Brougham opened his offensive when debate on the inquiry's results began on 16 June. He blamed the Orders for the hardship described in petitions and testimony, suggesting merchants would prefer Parliament 'abandon them to the hostility of their enemies and spare them the merciless hostility of the protection under which they are groaning'.[105] Evidence had shown Britain's dependence on American markets as well as the fact that the Orders hindered the war effort by bringing distress and provoking quarrels with America. Brougham then closed by moving an address to the Prince Regent favouring repeal.

Rose accepted the inquiry's account while insisting that Napoleon bore sole responsibility for the hardship the Orders brought. Repeal would be a concession to France, not America. Baring countered that the Orders were linked with distress, and repeal would remove the only barrier to reviving American trade.[106] Castlereagh realized that the temper of the Commons had turned against the government, and the debate offers a remarkable instance of a government forced to concede its critics' point and then abandon its position entirely. Like Rose, he sought to defend the Orders while accepting unmistakable evidence of their impact. His professed willingness to conciliate America gave Whitbread an opening to press for the government's specific intentions. Castlereagh offered at first to abandon the Orders once America repealed its restrictions, but Whitbread denounced the inadequacy of half-measures. Castlereagh then agreed to suspend the Orders that June, and it was done.[107]

The startling victory over the Orders in Council contrasted sharply with the Whigs' overall performance in opposition. Brougham demonstrated the policy's detrimental effects by mobilizing provincial opinion, but he failed to place responsibility for the Orders' impact squarely on the government. Perceval's death may have eased Brougham's efforts to secure repeal, but it also helped the government to evade blame for the policy. Grey criticized Brougham for giving the government 'unqualified credit' for repeal rather than press the case by denouncing the minister for persisting in a disastrous policy, but party divisions offer a better reason why the issue died so quickly.[108] Whigs failed to engage the issue together in a systematic way from an early stage. Grey had expressed early doubts about the repeal campaign, and Lord Thanet, a leading Foxite peer, thought Whitbread had been drunk when he suggested the Whigs unite around opposition to the Orders. Thomas Grenville refused to join the campaign for repeal, an issue originally raised by Grenvillites, on the grounds that Brougham had gone over to 'Burdett and the Jacobins'. The parliamentary aspect of the 1812 repeal campaign fell largely to the Mountain, and other Whigs took an ambivalent view of the petition and debate tactics Brougham exploited so effectively.[109] Appealing for public support involved cooperation with radicals most Whigs distrusted, and problems created by earlier flirtations with popular movements left most Foxites, let alone more conservative Whigs, with a lingering distaste for agitation outside Parliament. Repeal essentially had been Brougham's own achievement, but even the popularity he gained failed to sustain his election campaign in Liverpool during the autumn of 1812.

Nevertheless, the controversy over the Orders illustrated the possibilities open to the Whigs. The role of organized provincial interests was, as Castlereagh noted, a portent of future trends. Significantly, the repeal campaign stressed the theme of major interests excluded unjustly from a voice on matters that touched them directly. Coordinating local efforts with press reports balanced the Whigs' weak position in Parliament, and Brougham's campaign showed how pressure tactics that drew on provincial support could defeat the government on a major issue. Similar petition efforts against Lord Sidmouth's proposal in 1811 to regulate nonconformist ministers and in favour of amending the East India Company charter in 1813 to permit missionary work in India underlined the value of Brougham's tactics. Dissenters had produced nearly 700 petitions against Sidmouth's bill at short notice, and 250 Methodist petitions contained nearly 30,000 signatures. The 1813 campaign to permit missionary activity in India brought some 908 petitions in 1913 with nearly half a million signatures.[110] Along with Brougham's success against the Orders, these efforts highlighted the effectiveness of appealing beyond Westminster for support and provided a model for activists that cast a shadow well into the 1840s.

The Whigs found themselves during the first decades of the nineteenth century continually at a disadvantage in the House of Commons, where both numbers and sentiment stood against them. While majorities could be built by ministers with support from the Crown and opinion out of doors, the Whigs lacked those advantages, and suffered instead from internal divisions and accusations of factious opposition that limited their effectiveness. Perceval once noted that 'nothing can fling Ministers on their backs in this country unless others are forward on their legs showing themselves willing and able and ready in an apparent sufficiency to supply their places'.[111] Many Whigs were unwilling to accept the responsibility of governing, and the party as a whole failed to offer itself as a plausible alternative to the ruling government.

The comment by Brougham's friend, John William Ward, that the country 'preferred anything to the Grenvilles' applied with equal force to the Whigs generally.[112] The war's turn in Britain's favour after 1812 bolstered the government, while the Regent's break with the Whigs further reduced their hopes of office. Brougham realized that support among those provincial merchants and manufacturers who had shown their strength in the repeal campaign offered the Whigs their best opportunity to gain power. Gaining their support became central to his activities over the next twenty years.

2
Elections, the Press and Whig Tactics in Opposition: 1812–17

The Whigs' fortunes stood at a low tide in 1812 as the party's leaders responded with uncertainty to their extended political isolation. Francis Jeffrey, editor of the *Edinburgh Review*, had urged them in 1810 to conciliate and lead what he called the 'popular party', insisting that 'like faithful generals whose troops have mutinied', Whigs join them to guide an unsettled public opinion.[1] But how could this be done? The metropolitan focus of Holland House set Whigs apart from popular movements except for radicals in London and Westminster who were tainted by association with extremism or sedition. Although they had long spoken of being a terror to Tories and democrats alike, Whig aristocrats deeply distrusted public opinion. Cautious early efforts at agitation by the Rockingham Whigs in Burke's day were primarily outdoor gestures in support of an essentially indoor struggle.[2] Subsequent Whig appeals to the country in the 1790s had exposed differences with liberal advocacy groups while also tainting Whigs with radicalism. That failure led Fox back to a conventional parliamentary opposition based on tactical manoeuvering and coalition with other parliamentary groups. The need to maintain party unity after 1805 encouraged a hesitant approach, especially on issues like reform that touched on the social order and risked dividing the party anew.[3] Given the limits of their own base, however, Whigs also needed a strategy to draw wider support beyond Parliament. Whig leaders thus faced the challenge of mounting an effective opposition to Liverpool's government while avoiding trouble from radicals whose agenda remained inconsistent with the party's fundamental interests.

The alliance between Whigs, local commercial interests, and the press that Brougham had forged in his campaign against the Orders in Council offered an alternative strategy that kept the party apart from plebeian radicals. Like Jeffrey, Brougham saw public appeals as a way to guide opinion while bolstering his party's position, and he emphasized looking to the 'well informed and weighty parts of the community' whose interests lay with the Whigs in order to move the party beyond a factionalism built on a few families or individuals.[4] Doing so would also undercut radicals who attacked Whigs as well as Tories. Brougham repeatedly claimed that Francis Burdett and other radicals 'would have been nobody' save for the Whigs' failure to 'show as well as feel popular sentiments'.[5] The balance of seats within the House of Commons gave further reasons to avoid the 'terrible error of despising the people & neglecting popular courses'.[6] Brougham meant by popular courses an appeal beyond Westminster to local interests and elites whose support would strengthen the party's effectiveness in opposition. His strategy combined electoral efforts with cultivation of the press and a search for issues to use effectively against the government.

Brougham's approach recognized that most people in Britain experienced politics at the local level and within the framework of parliamentary constituencies.[7] Elections periodically connected the web of local interests and relationships with national politics at Westminster. Controversial issues might dominate parliamentary elections, but they also provided an arena for conflict between factions and interests within constituencies. The circumstances of each case dictated which pressures would exert the greatest impact. The challenge for the Whigs lay in opening constituency politics to engage wider questions related to party conflict at Westminster. Despite their trouble and expense, Brougham believed popular contests served an important purpose in bringing men together to hear 'free and sound language'.[8] The prestige conferred by representing important constituencies was particularly important to the Whig claim to represent popular interests, and in 1811 Brougham had entertained a proposal to stand for Worcester at the next election.[9] A year later, he capitalized on his popularity by standing for Liverpool along with Thomas Creevey.

As a sequel to Brougham's campaign against the Orders, the Liverpool election of 1812 reflected both the strengths and weaknesses of his position. The Duke of Bedford's plan to sell Brougham's Camelford seat threatened to leave him out of Parliament after the next election, and that possibility cannot have been far from his mind in 1812. Although Brougham's relations with Bedford, Grey, and Holland remained warm, many Whigs viewed his aggressive tactics with unease and considered him as difficult a colleague as Whitbread. Brougham and Creevey entered the election campaign without their party's firm support and were left to rely on Roscoe's local reforming Whig interest.

Brougham's use of petitions and contacts with local groups during the repeal campaign had led Whigs, including Grey and Allen, to question whether he had joined Whitbread on the radical periphery.[10] Strident rhetoric, including a speech at a Liverpool dinner in September, heightened those worries. Brougham claimed that the Mountaineers were the 'real and best' Whigs because they stood up for 'Fox *against* Pitt – at the moment when the others are saying "Never mention the word Foxite – be quiet as to Pitt".'[11] Politics framed in terms of Fox against Pitt reminded many Whigs of their isolation in the 1790s and alarmed others who had broken with Fox until 1804. As Fox then had appeared too much a firebrand for conservative Whigs, so Brougham seemed in 1812. His insistence on attacking Pitt and his legacy followed from his view that Whigs stood against a system of policy as much as a set of ministers, but it was more aggressive than many Whigs liked.[12] Brougham's friend John William Ward believed that such attacks on Pitt hurt Brougham more than the Tories.[13]

Brougham's most fervent support came from beyond Whig ranks in Parliament. News of repeal had prompted the *Leeds Mercury* to speak of public opinion's victory over the ministry and the country's indebtedness to Brougham.[14] Merchants in Leeds voted their thanks, and Thomas Attwood told a Birmingham meeting in late July that justice and public gratitude tied Brougham to the popular interest and ranked him as a statesman with Burke, Pitt, and Fox.[15] A Liverpool meeting that praised Brougham's consistent support for the sound principles of a liberal and enlightened policy ignored the city's sitting members, Banastre Tarleton and Issac Gascoigne.[16] Enthusiasm that had followed Brougham's victory over the Orders in Council encouraged William Roscoe's belief that the Whigs could win both of Liverpool's seats at the next election. He conferred with Lord Sefton, a local Whig peer who urged Brougham's candidacy, and organized a public dinner to raise support.[17]

As an extension of the earlier struggle against the Orders in Council, the Liverpool election also brought out the local conflict between proreform Whigs associated with Dissent and the American trade and the Anglican establishment backed by West India merchants and represented by the city corporation.[18] Freemen eligible to vote in Liverpool formed a socially mixed body that included a variety of craftsmen as well as merchants, brokers, and gentlemen, but a substantial number of respectable and prosperous men found themselves excluded and economic dependence placed many plebeian freemen under pressure from their employers. While the franchise in Liverpool came largely by birth or service as an apprentice in the borough, the Corporation controlled the admission of new freemen which was the only other means of gaining the vote. Local Whigs bitterly resented the Corporation's influence in this matter.[19] As Brougham later told Leigh Hunt, 'think of such men as Roscoe having no vote, while every slave captain who served seven years apprenticeship to that traffic of blood was enabled to vote against the person who made it a felony'.[20] Although Brougham and Creevey benefited from association with campaigns against unpopular commercial policies, they suffered from becoming embroiled in a test of strength between Roscoe's friends and the Corporation.

Observers rightly thought an attempt to carry both seats provocative, while Brougham's having written the Felony Act that enforced the ban on slave trading guaranteed opposition in the city that had dominated the trade. Bitterness over the issue added to local divisions as Roscoe had been driven from the poll in 1807 for his part in abolishing the slave trade. Rumours circulated that Liverpool Tories led by John Gladstone, a local merchant and stalwart of the West India interest, would back George Canning's candidacy. Canning, who was first approached in March 1812, originally resisted the idea, and only accepted on condition supporters paid all expenses and accepted his non-alignment with the government. Gladstone and his friends subscribed £10,000 and pledged to raise double or more if necessary, but Canning delayed until after Parliament's dissolution on September 29.[21] Concerns grew among Whigs about the chances of electing two candidates, and Sefton accordingly warned against promoting the hesitant Creevey at Brougham's expense.[22]

Preparations for the 1812 election accelerated in anticipation of Parliament's dissolution. Unlike the previous election in 1807 dominated by the Talents' resignation over Catholic Emancipation, the 1812 election involved little controversy over specific national issues. Local interests and concerns dominated the campaign. In many cases neither government nor opposition found candidates for available places, and Tierney complained that voters were 'left entirely to themselves to manage their concerns in their own way'.[23] Liverpool's election illustrated Tierney's point, while the presence of Brougham and Canning made it the most closely watched and controversial contest.

The election began in the first week of October with official announcements and the public arrival of candidates in Liverpool. Brougham cited his record to show his 'attachment to those principles of liberty which have been long the bulwark of the Country'. Creevey stressed his ties with Liverpool and pledged to promote its trade and general prosperity.[24] Both letters circulated as handbills, along with songs and election material written by both sides. Brougham entered Liverpool with Roscoe and other Whig leaders on 5 October in a large procession that met Canning's supporters, resulting in a brief scuffle. Creevey, to Brougham's irritation, did not arrive for several days.[25] Although a few violent encounters occurred between rival groups, observers remarked that the election was Liverpool's most peaceful in recent years; Creevey called the people as 'tractable as lambs'.[26] Candidates restrained supporters, and part of a letter to Grey suppressed in Brougham's memoirs describes Canning's embarrassment over an anonymous pamphlet accusing Brougham of 'unnatural acts'. While Brougham admitted that most election squibs came from the Whigs, he forbade retaliation after Canning pledged help finding those responsible for the attack.[27] Canvassing involved candidates in a series of public speeches during each day, followed by evenings with electors at local political clubs that included speeches and toasts at each stop.[28]

Brougham campaigned on a platform of 'peace and reform', blaming war with America on ministerial intransigence. He insisted that Whig and radical grievances boiled down to the 'Pitt system', a set of false principles backed by corruption, that all true patriots must oppose. On the evening of the fourth day of polling, Brougham denounced Pitt as

Immortal in the miseries of his devoted country! Immortal in the miseries of her bleeding liberties! Immortal in the cruel wars which sprang from his cold miscalculating ambition! Immortal in the intolerable taxes, the countless loads of debt which these wars have flung upon us – which the youngest man amongst us will not live to see the end of![29]

Creevey described the speech, made on the last day of polling, as having 'shook the very square and all the houses in it from the applause it met with'.[30]

On a lighter note, a song cleverly turned Pitt's reputation as 'the pilot who weathered the storm' into a tag urging voters who hoped that England would 'weather the storm' to 'vote for the champions of peace and reform'. Another verse contrasted Canning, whose 'mother and sisters are pensioned by you', with the independent Creevey and Brougham.[31] The *Liverpool Mercury* echoed these sentiments in setting Brougham and Creevey apart from Canning and Gascoyne, whom it dismissed as the Corporation's puppet.[32] Canning's presence encouraged

Whigs to connect questions of local and national corruption, and Sefton said that Gladstone's party was the backside rather than the backbone of Liverpool. A poem, entitled 'Backbone of Liverpool', concluded 'down, down with the Rump'. Opponents taunted in reply to the tune of 'Yankee Doodle' that 'the mighty Brougham's come to town/ to sweep away corruption/and other filth, but ten to one/he'll meet with interruption'.[33]

Canning led at the end of the first day's poll on Thursday, 8 October, with Brougham close behind and Creevey trailing Gascoyne. By Tuesday, Canning had 926 votes to Brougham's 892, Creevey's 866, and Gascoyne's 864. Tarleton was quickly squeezed out of the field and finished at the bottom of the poll with only 11 votes. He declined to withdraw officially so his friends would not give Canning their votes.[34] Brougham rejected subsequent proposals for a joint return with either Gascoyne or Canning, partly for fear of ruining his reputation.[35] Although such compromises were common, abandoning Creevey would bring accusations of duplicity, while partnership with Canning would open both men to charges of inconsistency. Canning then turned to Gascoyne.[36] By the poll's close on Wednesday, Canning had a solid lead of 1361 with Gascoyne ahead of Brougham by 1276 to 1105, and Creevey at the rear with 1055. Brougham kept the poll open another day at his supporters' request, but denied any effort to put his opponents to added expense and inconvenience by delay. Privately he noted that he could have kept the poll open a week longer and forced the enemy to spend £10,000.[37] Brougham and Creevey abandoned the contest the next day, and the sheriff declared Canning and Gascoyne duly elected.

The Tory press cited Brougham's defeat as evidence of the Whigs' failure to win popular support. The *Courier* described Brougham and Romilly as

'picked men' expressly dispatched by the Whig commanders to take the two great rivals in commerce [Liverpool and Bristol] by a sort of coup de main...[and] the unexpected defeat of these immaculate candidates – the very flower of the party and pink of patriotism – shows their ignorance of their fellow countrymen is almost equal to what they have so repeatedly displayed in regard to those of foreign nations.[38]

The criticism vastly overestimated the Whigs' organization, and ignored local factors. As Creevey told his wife, 'we had to do with artists who did not know their trade...Poor Roscoe made too sanguine an estimate of our strength'.[39] Other Whigs concurred that Roscoe's attempt to carry both seats reached too far. Likening him to a man who would 'drive a wedge the broad end foremost', Horner lamented that neither Roscoe's own experience nor that of others would ever make him practical.[40] The *Morning Chronicle* described Liverpool's election as a caricature of an election in a populous borough and denied its result reflected the inhabitants choice.[41] Brougham denounced Liverpool as a rotten borough with a coerced electorate. Complaining of the Corporation's influence, he thus described voters who declared that their hearts were with the Whigs despite being forced to give Canning and Gascoyne their votes.[42]

His criticism emphasized the disparity in size between Liverpool's electorate and population, with only 3 per cent voting in 1812, as well as the nature of the franchise.[43] Even so, Liverpool was considered a large borough, and Lord Lansdowne rejected Brougham's claim since the 'proportion of voters to inhabitants signifies nothing when the positive number is so great'.[44] Popular enthusiasm failed to outweigh the Corporation's backing for Canning and Gascoyne, or Brougham and Creevey's failure to win support beyond the Whig reformers. Brougham revealingly stated that the election closed with an immediate and cordial reunion of factions he described as high and low, or radical, Whigs. The internal division suggests that Roscoe's miscalculations and Corporation influence were not Brougham's only impediments.[45] 'A Liverpool Cry' in the *Courier* best summarized the situation: '"New Brooms to sell", cries Roscoe, "Won't you buy?/"No",says the Town of Liverpool, "Not I"/ And so Poor Roscoe at the Hustings stands/With his new Brooms returned upon his hands!'[46]

Comments on the Liverpool results appeared in the general election's broader context. Lord Liverpool expressed satisfaction with early results, claiming success in every popular election where the government had a proper candidate. Croker, an astute observer and government press manager, later complained the results were not as favourable as government supporters originally calculated.[47] The *Courier* predictably seized upon Whig losses as a demonstration of the public's contempt and claimed their 'desperate experiment' only revealed the government's popularity and the Whigs' inability to read events.[48] The attack roused the *Morning Chronicle*, which had been notably silent during the election itself. Foxites had declined invitations to stand from numerous constituencies, the paper weakly retorted, and, far from reflecting ministerial popularity, the result in popular boroughs like Liverpool and Bristol 'displayed the degrading effects of mercenary influence on the mind'.[49]

Broadly speaking, the Whigs maintained their strength in spite of painful and well-publicized defeats. Before the election, Tierney had predicted the loss of active men with little change in numbers. Although he lamented the defeat of able and stalwart Whigs such as Brougham, Horner spoke optimistically about the party's strength and opportunities for an alliance with Canning or Lord Wellesley.[50] John Goodwin, a freelance Whig agent, claimed Whig victories in several smaller Tory boroughs: 15 Whigs had taken Tory seats against nine Whig seats lost to Tories.[51] An accurate tally of party strength would only come in the next session with divisions on important issues, though the Treasury expected a majority of 180, with an increase of 60 over their previous 120 supporters.[52] Beyond the numbers, however, the absence of national controversy limited the election's value as a test of party support. No issue comparable with the Catholic question in 1807 arose to outweigh local alignments and make the election a national contest. Public apathy benefited the Whigs at a point when the war and economic conditions stood in the government's favour, and 1812 saw substantially fewer contested English borough elections than in subsequent elections of the period: 50 contested in 1812 rose to 86 in 1818, 69 in 1820, 84 in 1826, and 78 in 1830.[53]

The defeat of leading Whig spokesmen in the Commons made the results appear worse than they were, even though the losses impaired their efforts for several years. Finding seats at short notice forced Whig reformers to 'have recourse to those very Boroughs which they have represented as the disgrace and scandal of the constitution'.[54] Individual patrons disposed of 42 seats in Whig-controlled nomination boroughs, and those seats ensured a core of Whig support in the Commons while strengthening the influence of peers who controlled them. But Whig leaders could not coordinate their use for party interests because patrons themselves set the terms. Family members filled many seats, while other boroughs required a substantial financial commitment just short of outright purchase.[55] Each situation differed according to circumstance and the parties involved.

Several cases highlighted the financial, personal, and political factors that shaped the marriage between patron and candidate, and tensions over political views made finding seats for leading men difficult. Mutual forbearance only partly alleviated Horner's acute dilemma as a Foxite holding a Grenvillite seat.[56] Tierney specifically named the peers from whom he would take a seat and wrote further that he would consider himself beholden to Grey rather than the real patron since Grey in substance would be the recipient.[57] William Lamb, who failed to find a seat in 1812, bitterly asked Grey 'whether those who afford so little mutual assistance can in any reasonable sense of the word be said to act together'. Describing the letter from Lamb as 'wrong-headed', Grey warned Holland that it indicated dangerous tensions within the party and urged steps to ease resentment by preventing 'our most efficient friends from being' out of Parliament.[58] Nothing was done, however, and the failure to provide for those unexpectedly defeated caused greater trouble than the whims of borough owners.

Brougham's exclusion from Parliament until Grey secured a seat for him at Winchelsea in July 1815 from William Harry Vane, 2nd Earl of Darlington, illustrated the problem. Brougham doubted Whig borough owners would 'return a reformer & one who has shown himself an indifferent party man', while 'Westminster & other *really* popular places' were already filled.[59] Defeat in Liverpool thus left him no other recourse. Brougham also feared that another immediate defeat would imply a repudiation by party members, many of whom already had criticized his conduct in the last session. He had asserted his Foxite credentials pointedly in Liverpool, and believed the appearance of being out by choice would dampen talk that he was a firebrand desperate to stay in Parliament but unwilling to heed party leaders.[60] Ward, who remained Brougham's friend after shifting his allegiance from the Whigs to Canning, thought being out of Parliament would leave Brougham bitterly angry and, despite claims to the contrary, lead him to 'turn downright Jacobin'.[61]

Brougham never equated being out of Parliament with retirement from active politics. He had entered politics as a Whig publicist and appreciated the vital role of the press in mobilizing public support. Before the Liverpool election, Brougham had assured Roscoe that, if defeated, he would pursue his plans through the press. And although he promised supporters to use his legal work to 'share in the protection of our sacred rights against the wiles of corruption or the violence of power', Brougham's journalism was equally important.[62] An article in the November *Edinburgh Review*, entitled 'Rights and Duties of the People', stressed the need for public discussion of major issues in a way that pointed toward Brougham's agenda. It also gave credence to the *Courier*'s acid remark that he and other Whigs remained 'ready to seize the goose quills of reform, and lay their opponents on the rack of a review'.[63]

The press, as Brougham repeatedly argued, played a vital part in shaping public opinion, and it was to a change in opinion that Whigs must turn for their future revival. By appealing to 'the sense of the people' Brougham believed Whig efforts to mobilize opposition outside Parliament had prevented the government from persisting with bad measures.[64] Dissemination of criticism through the press and the subsequent response enhanced the effectiveness of Whig appeals to public opinion. The party's exclusion from office also encouraged its leaders to look beyond their immediate audience in the Commons when discussing an issue. Brougham told Leigh Hunt that the press and its reports of discussions in Parliament alone could save the country from the current ministry.[65] Better than his contemporaries, Brougham saw both the Whigs' need to look beyond Westminster and opportunities such efforts afforded.

The growth in newspaper circulation and readership, two very different, though related, things, shows why Brougham and other politicians devoted so much time and consideration to newspapers. Commercial expansion in the eighteenth century had encouraged a demand for news and advertising, and the publication of parliamentary debates had become a popular feature that editors neglected at their peril.[66] After 1800, newspapers came into their own. Successful papers like *The Times* and the *Morning Chronicle* saw sales rise steadily, and numerous attempts to start new papers in London suggested the perception of an expanding, if highly competitive, market. Printing technology limited the press run until the development of high-speed rotary presses that later heralded mass-circulation papers, while newspaper duties, criticized as 'taxes on knowledge', imposed another barrier as they reached their highest levels between 1815 and 1830.

Readership still far exceeded the copies sold. Coffee houses, barber shops, and taverns attracted customers by providing papers, and 'penny newsrooms' made a variety of London and provincial papers available at a nominal charge to readers otherwise unable to afford them.[67] More people read each copy than in later years, and the costs, kept artificially high by taxation, ironically boosted readership by making newspapers articles of value exchanged among friends and neighbours. Richard Cobden's comment that newsrooms provided the main attraction of mechanics' institutes reflected the popularity of newspapers among all social classes, and readership magnified a paper's influence beyond a relatively narrow circulation.

Newspapers, as Brougham noted, disseminated political discussion to a growing audience in the early nineteenth century as they became more sophisticated and provided better coverage. Magistrates complained that newspapers read aloud in public houses fostered discontent, but William Cobbett saw that cheap papers brought home where wives and children could read them provided families a potent means of influencing husbands and fathers.[68] His comment on the role newspapers could play in linking the domestic sphere with public discussion showed how newspapers expanded the range of public participation under the unreformed political system despite strenuous efforts to limit their impact. A Tory pamphleteer concluded public opinion exerted an influence over Parliament that made it impossible for ministers to impose a truly unpopular policy against concerted opposition.[69]

The Whigs faced problems in turning the influence of the press to serve their party's interest. With a few significant exceptions like the *Morning Chronicle's* proprietor, James Perry, respectable people saw journalists, as 'blackguard news-writers' beyond the social pale. A strange dichotomy existed between admiration for a free press as 'the palladium of the British Constitution' and contempt for the men who conducted it. Disparaging newspaper editors, Sir Walter Scott wrote in 1829 that he would 'rather sell gin to the poor people and poison them that way'.[70] Abhorrence of close ties with journalists cut across the political spectrum, and many politicians boasted of never having communications with them. Fear of journalists' mercurial willingness to change their politics for pecuniary advantage or violate confidences heightened the wariness of those politicians who did cooperate.[71] The press's licentious tone partly explained the distaste, and critics noted the corrosive social effects of character attacks on men of exalted rank and illustrious station.[72]

The tradition of unsigned articles both in newspapers and the more respected periodical press encouraged vituperative attacks, even though defenders of the practice insisted the public gained 'a full and free discussion without any mixture of that egotism and self intrusion which are almost inseparable from compositions of any individual writer in his own personal character'.[73] The custom also allowed politicians to provide sympathetic papers with squibs and paragraphs, but Brougham and Holland lamented that few of those they called upon for material chose to help. Brougham wrote in intervals between parliamentary and legal activity, and referring to articles on the Orders in Council, he complained that writing in a 'desperate hurry' ensured they were 'very ill-executed'. Yet he remained convinced that 'it is more important to have many and speedy publications on these points than to have good ones'.[74]

Circulating what propaganda the Whigs produced was difficult since the party lacked the government's ability to manipulate the press through subsidies, advertising from government departments, and the purchase of papers, though the efficacy of such practices had declined rapidly since 1800. Proprietors chose to forgo government support as they became conscious of the growth in opinion outside Parliament, and they often saw such independence as a virtue in itself. Advertising income based on circulation, however, made their shift from subservience to independence possible.[75]

As a result, cooperation with even the most sympathetic papers was far from guaranteed. Friends and foes alike saw James Perry's *Morning Chronicle* as a Whig paper, but, while acknowledging the fact, it sharply denied being 'a tool of party'. Instead, the paper insisted that 'a man should take counsel of his friends...make known his sentiments on every topic of a public nature, and if he differs from his party on any question avow his difference with an independent spirit'.[76] Perry considered his newspaper a guardian of Fox's memory, but he did not believe that task required constant cooperation with the Whig party. Grey, Brougham, and other Whigs remarked especially on the *Morning Chronicle*'s neglect of party concerns during the 1812 election. Although Perry expanded the paper by 25 per cent in 1810, advertisements continued to fill half of each edition, and Whigs deplored what they saw as a conflict between news and advertising.[77]

The need for an effective Whig newspaper brought several attempts by Brougham to find an alternative to the *Morning Chronicle*. A proposal in 1812 to establish 'a good and independent paper set up...for us of the Mountain' that involved an effort by 10 men to raise £6,000 capital never passed beyond the planning stage.[78] In 1817, Brougham brought the *Guardian* briefly into operation as a Whig evening paper. Grey appreciated the need for 'a good paper' and saw Brougham's scheme as the best chance of establishing one, but the enterprise soon foundered.[79] While Perry took no offence, he expected the paper to fail and a lack of enthusiasm among the Whigs who pledged financial support crippled it from the start. Brougham worked hard to make the paper a success and floated other proposals in later years with encouragement from fellow Whigs. In the end, however, the party continued its reliance on Perry, and Brougham grudgingly admitted the proprietor's merits on his death in 1821.[80]

Although the party lacked a reliable organ in the *Morning Chronicle*, individual Whigs cultivated support elsewhere and Brougham took the lead in providing paragraphs and information to sympathetic papers. Successfully defending the Hunt brothers in a controversial libel case guaranteed positive coverage in the *Examiner*, a radical weekly, and Brougham regularly corresponded with Leigh Hunt from 1811 to 1818.

His relationship with Thomas Barnes of *The Times* gave Brougham a significant influence over its coverage and editorial policy as it became Britain's most widely circulated paper, growing from between 2,500 and 3,000 copies in 1801 to 7,000 by 1821. In November 1814, *The Times* installed steam presses that increased the number of copies produced and gained a decisive advantage among morning dailies that increased in successive years, though the *Courier*, a Tory evening paper, sold 8,000 copies a day at the climax of the Napoleonic wars.[81]

Brougham wrote several leading articles for *The Times* and contributed material for others, and *The Times* gave his legal work and parliamentary activities extensive, sympathetic coverage. The relationship with Barnes began when Brougham met the future editor at the Inner Temple and persuaded him to choose journalism over law. It continued after Brougham became Lord Chancellor in 1830, despite Barnes's differences with the Whig government, and became the basis for Brougham's influence with *The Times*.[82] An overview of *The Times'* pages from 1812 to 1830 shows a striking concurrence of opinion with Brougham that attracted notice at the time. The paper's position during several periods of agitation, including the campaign against the income tax and Queen Caroline's trial, encouraged Tory attempts to create an alternative publication that never matched its parent's success.[83] *The Times* served Brougham rather than the party as a whole, but the distinction seemed moot.

The provincial press provided other important Whig outlets. Arthur Aspinall stated that the government ignored English provincial papers, which were the only ones read by a large part of the public, because most had a small circulation and lacked their own national news or commentary.[84] While true in many cases, provincial papers varied greatly in form and content. Some were little more than advertising broadsheets whose owners feared alienating any large sector of the public, and political comment in many papers serving rural areas remained muted well into the nineteenth century.[85] But many others provided sophisticated coverage tailored to local interests and some made their name as party or ideological organs. The *Liverpool Mercury*'s index and tabloid pages designed to facilitate the paper's preservation in bound volumes made it resemble a periodical. It was an unabashedly liberal paper created as a voice for Roscoe and other Liverpool reformers that serialized pamphlets on major issues. Although the *Morning Chronicle* claimed that provincial newspapers supported the government – a logical assumption given the interest of their editors in cultivating support among the local establishment – between 1817 and 1820, a sizeable number of them came to the attention of local magistrates and the Home Office for allegedly printing seditious articles, and these included papers in Birmingham, Leeds, and Manchester.[86] Papers serving industrial and commercial areas had pushed campaigns against the Orders in Council and renewal of the East India Company monopoly, and their combination of parliamentary coverage and awareness of local concerns suited them well to the task.

Brougham's success against the Orders in Council raised his standing among provincial editors. Announcing Wilberforce's retirement from Parliament in 1812, the *Leeds Mercury* insisted that a popular statesman, like Brougham or Whitbread, could win his seat for Yorkshire by pledging 'if you will elect me freely, I will serve you faithfully'.[87] The paper's encouragement for Brougham foreshadowed its enthusiastic support for his 1830 candidacy for Yorkshire. Edward Baines deserves attention both for his connection with Brougham and his paper's influence as the most important English provincial weekly. His initiative in exposing an agent provocateur in 1817 known as Oliver the Spy won a national reputation. An estimate in 1839 claimed each issue of the *Leeds Mercury* had an average of fifteen to twenty readers and it circulated throughout the woollen district from the 1810s.[88]

Baines's paper took a consistently liberal Whig line urging peaceful, comprehensive reform to meet the needs of industrial society, and generally sympathized with the Whigs, whom he believed most likely to follow that course. Baines saw government paternalism and mob violence as two sides of the same coin, with anarchy being the worst kind of tyranny. Speaking for the commercial and industrial middle class, the *Leeds Mercury* distinguished its commitment to popular rights from calls for anarchy by citing Horne Tooke's statement that 'I had rather be governed by St James than St Giles'. Christopher Wyvill, another Yorkshireman and leader of provincial opinion, had spoken along similar lines, warning in 1792 against the extremes of 'a powerful aristocracy' and 'the violence of a furious populace'. Baines's ardent support for Lord Milton in the 1807 Yorkshire election marked his debut as a political combatant and built ties with Milton's father, Lord Fitzwilliam.[89] Once established as a Whig paper, the *Leeds Mercury* played an important part in electoral politics and reform agitation that carried an influence beyond Yorkshire.

The strident middle-class press epitomized by Baines's *Leeds Mercury* demonstrated a growing provincial involvement in national debate and the decline of instinctive deference to established institutions among new local interests.[90] Journalists and many politicians gave the concept of public opinion greater attention from the mid-1810s than before. Dissenters figured prominently among the commercial and industrial middle class Brougham sought to cultivate, and their political exclusion automatically set them against 'Church and King' Tories. Despite other differences, Whigs agreed on what Grey called 'a principle of moderation & liberality...[in religion] complete toleration, or to speak more properly the rejection of all intolerance whether in the severer form of penal or the milder form of disqualifying statutes' that united them against the government.[91] The principle formed a bond between Whig and middle-class interests with broader implications for nineteenth century politics. Access not only to parliamentary representation, but also to local corporations, which were far less responsive than Parliament in many cases, gradually drew middle-class groups into politics where they provided electoral support for the Whigs. As the connection grew during these years, genuinely shared sympathy in outlook also developed that held Whigs and provincial liberals together in the nineteenth century despite a social gulf between them.[92] Charges of apostasy against Whigs and radicals in the Tory press during the 1810s and 1820s showed an appreciation of Dissenters' political activity and its potential advantage to the Whigs. While keenly aware of the damage such attacks brought, Brougham saw the value of middle-class support and cultivated the provincial press to get it.

The *Edinburgh Review*, to which Brougham devoted a majority of his attention as a writer after 1807, became the prime Whig vehicle for shaping opinion. While newspapers could justly be likened to a shrub that lost its leaves daily and bore little fruit, periodicals excited great interest and sparked debates from their pages. A group of Scots intellectuals that included Brougham, Horner, Jeffrey, and Sydney Smith founded the *Edinburgh Review* in 1802, and the quarterly journal soon achieved a dominant position. Like its later rivals, the *Quarterly* and the *Westminster*, the *Edinburgh Review* attracted readers mainly from educated and serious-minded members of the middle class. 'Information' and 'point of fact' became key words in these quarterly journals, which deliberately eschewed sensationalism in favour of providing measured judgements and informed opinions.[93] The *Edinburgh Review* popularized the economic and philosophical doctrines of the Scottish school, including its critique of mercantilism. As a mark of its influence, Lord Holland cited Robert Southey's complaint that its editor, Francis Jeffrey, should have power to hurt sales of the poet's work, though 'in physical stature [Jeffrey] did not reach his shoulder, nor in intellectual dimension his ankle'.[94] Another Tory lamented that men who accepted unquestioningly the literary judgements of reviewers would not be very scrupulous in heeding the same oracle on more serious matters.[95] William Hazlett reinforced the point by remarking that readers found political discussion palatable only when inserted into a sandwich of literature, and the linkage between politics and literature testified to the quarterlies' status.[96] As general interest periodicals with a wide readership among those with intellectual aspirations, they had influence beyond the politically engaged.

Although the *Edinburgh Review's* founders held Whig sympathies, it remained for a time outside party politics and attracted some Tory contributors including Sir Walter Scott. Brougham gradually drew the magazine toward the Whigs, and the decisive break came in October 1808 with the 'Don Cevallos' article on Spain co-authored by Brougham and Jeffrey. The piece celebrated the Spanish uprising as a blow against reactionary governments across Europe as well as Napoleonic aggression, and, although it was unsigned, Brougham's involvement became an open secret. Sydney Smith noted the consternation provoked by Brougham's 'attack on the titled orders', with subscriptions cancelled, back issues returned to the bookseller, and library shelves ostentatiously cleansed. The Earl of Buchan famously set the offending issue on his doorstep and publicly kicked it into the street to be trodden underfoot by man and beast.[97] More constructively, Scott accelerated plans for a rival journal that began in 1809 as the *Quarterly Review*. The *Edinburgh's* drift already had alienated Scott, but the 'Don Cevallos' article, which shocked many Whigs as well as Tories, brought the dispute into the open.[98]

The article marked the *Edinburgh Review's* emergence as a radicalizing force on the progressive wing of the Whig party and changed perceptions of the magazine.[99] An avalanche of criticism denounced it in terms that recalled attacks on Foxites in the 1790s. A satire that interestingly numbered Scott and Cobbett among the journal's 'cabinet council' complained that 'Not friends to Kirk or Synagogue,/they play the role of demagogue,/and keep the popular tune in time/By ridicule and pantomime'.[100] Another piece claimed that, while the *Edinburgh Review's* editor was 'really rather a rational man', its writers insisted that he insert their 'Jacobinical effusions' in order to keep their services. While 'one can only forgive Englishmen who write like Scotch Reviewers', the poet concluded, 'there is no pardon for Scotch Reviewers who write like Frenchmen'.[101]

Comparing Whigs and reform-minded intellectuals with Jacobins and *philosophes* was a common rhetorical trope in the Tory press. Some critics expanded on it to offer more serious warnings of the *Edinburgh Review*'s sympathetic presentation of seditious ideas, describing its authors as conspirators actively promoting the 'delusive, execrable doctrines of the Rights of Man, to justify rebellion', and ready to provoke 'the most malignant passions of the lower classes...[and] incite them to discontent, disaffection and outrage'. Only in their article on Spain did the reviewers 'abandon the reptile form of concealment, in which they whispered seductive casuistry to our disordered fancy, and in the terrific magnitude of their natural form, like the first apostate they disclos[ed] their whole design and treachery'.[102] The *Courier* remarked of the 'Don Cevallos' article that 'Thomas Paine never published anything more seditious than the last No. of the *Edinburgh Review*'. Continual references to the 'diabolical features of jacobinism' and the author's prior reluctance to put 'the cloven foot beyond the hem of his didactic toga' further evoked the fear and hatred with which many Tories viewed the *Edinburgh Review* in its new guise.[103]

Such cries reached their highest pitch when most ineffectual, and establishment of the Tory *Quarterly* implicitly paid tribute to the *Edinburgh Review*'s success. In stark contrast with newspaper journalists, writers associated with the periodicals spawned from the *Edinburgh*'s success gained prestige, and respected literary figures coveted the post of editor, which provided access to the highest social circles along with a munificent salary.[104] Regular contributors to the *Edinburgh Review* took full advantage of a respected platform to further their interests. Brougham opened his two campaigns against the Orders in Council in its pages, and, even before the 'Don Cevallos' article, Brougham had used a review of Whitbread's pamphlet on Spain to advance the intervention policy he and the Holland House circle supported. Jeffrey pressed the Whigs on reform from his editorial perch, and Horner used articles to promote the financial policies developed by the bullion committee he chaired. Anonymity allowed the reviewer to benefit from what a commentator described as 'the obscurity in which his real shape is enveloped'.[105] Brougham seized the opportunity to review favourably his own pamphlet on the Polish question, and he consistently took advantage of journalistic anonymity to coordinate speeches with reviews and newspaper reports.[106] The *Edinburgh Review* therefore played an important role in generating effective publicity for the Whigs. Brougham's ability to raise issues simultaneously in different forums that combined to draw sustained attention showed his sophistication in the understanding of public relations that multiplied the effectiveness of his campaigns.

Public discussion in parliament and the press offered valuable opportunities for shaping public opinion, but Whigs had to pick their issues carefully to mobilize support. Economic distress provided the most favourable grounds for opposition other than major scandals along with the weakest position for ministers to defend, though religious issues mobilized Dissenting congregations and consistently brought the largest numbers of petitions. Effective political agitation during the early nineteenth century usually coincided with economic distress. Distress could make the public more receptive to the Whigs' message, as it did for Brougham's 1812 campaign against the Orders in Council. Prosperity, however, reduced public interest in politics and strengthened the government's position. The economist W.W. Rostow calculated social tension for the period by plotting the business cycle and high wheat prices, which assumes that unemployment and high food prices played a roughly equal part in unrest. Social tension peaked in 1812, 1819, 1826, and 1829, with other high points in 1813, 1816–17, and 1827–8. Rostow's calculations describe influences on the industrial working class, but they can lead to other conclusions.[107] Low wheat prices cut incomes of both landowners who dominated England's political class and agricultural labourers whose distress brought pauperism, crime, and the swing riots of the early 1830s. The scissors effect produced by the combination of low earnings and high fixed costs, including taxation, fuelled political agitation from 1816 to 1830.

Trade cycles often vary from agricultural ones, but the situation in 1810, when low wheat prices coincided with a severe trade depression, reflected the unusual pressures of economic war and cannot provide a benchmark for comparison. The years 1811, 1816, 1819, 1826, and 1829 marked low points in the cycle, and major political agitation occurred in each of these years or the one immediately following.[108] By contrast, the prosperous years 1824–5 were relatively quiescent.

The economic transition from war to peace and its social impact presented Liverpool's government with its greatest challenge. Grey and Holland, like Fox before them, had little interest in political economy, but they saw the opportunities public disaffection offered. The need for support from the financial market placed ministers on the side of fundholders against landowning and business interests squeezed by high taxes and low incomes from 1814 to 1817. Brougham updated old country Whig rhetoric from the eighteenth century that attacked extravagant court government by presenting himself as a defender of the industrious middle classes who defined themselves against clergy, courtiers, and members of the new administrative classes. Pamphlets and satirical prints developed this critique of a parasitic administrative and rentier class at length over the next decade.[109] Taxpayers bearing the burden of government were contrasted with those who profited from government expenditure. From a different perspective, the rentier element within Pitt and Liverpool's administration found little favour among county gentlemen and backbenchers whose constituents felt sorely pressed by war debts and taxes.[110] These factors came increasingly to the fore as the loyalist sentiments fuelled by the threat of Napoleonic France receded.

Whig views on foreign policy, particularly the war with France, created a more immediate problem as they set the party at odds with public opinion after 1812. The country generally rejoiced over a change in the war's course that vindicated ministers, and a petitioning drive in 1813 that Whitbread and Holland organized in favour of negotiations stalled when local groups changed their mind and requested their petitions not be presented before Parliament. Grey resisted the effort partly because he thought it interfered with ministerial discretion, but also to avoid a break with the Grenvillites and other Whigs who had differed with Fox's view of France in the 1790s.[111]

The prospect of peace raised uncomfortable questions about the origins of the war, and Grenville bluntly told Grey in 1813 that every succeeding event had confirmed his original view of the need to act against Revolutionary France in 1792.[112] Thomas Grenville complained that Holland House had become unapproachable by mid-March of 1814 as the only place in London 'where our success is disparaged and our allies abused'.[113] Deliberate amnesia about disagreements over France in 1792–3 had secured cooperation between Grenvillites and Foxites that since 1804 had been based on a combination of shared views and practical interests. Cooperation would now require more forbearance on both sides than before. Grey considered Grenville 'a little unfair', or at least unwilling to make the same concessions he demanded of others.[114] But he and Holland retained their respect for Grenville and wished to avoid a break.

Peace in April 1814 prevented further tensions until Napoleon's return from Elba cast ministers in the role of bemused spectators to disputes that isolated Grenville from Foxites, conservative Whigs and even younger members of his own family. A series of divisions in May 1815 that saw Grenvillites in both houses voting with Foxites marked the faction's final decline.[115] By November, Tierney thought the Grenvillites' diminished standing made them favour a reconciliation and that even a slight disposition to compromise among Foxites would keep the party together. Grey saw no impediment to cooperation so long as Grenville continued his opposition to standing armies and a costly peacetime military.[116] Brougham thought the party would pull together as it put aside the crippling issues of war and peace to focus on other matters, and he now anticipated a more favourable political climate.[117]

Long before returning to the Commons in June 1815, Brougham envisioned using the tactics that defeated the Orders in Council in a campaign against the income tax. In late 1812, Brougham suggested capitalizing on their victory with a vigorous assault on the tax and told Grey he had received numerous letters on the subject.[118] Brougham placed an investigation into the income tax on his agenda for the next parliamentary session, and a song during the Liverpool election framed assessed taxes, particularly the income tax, as a barrier to prosperity.[119]

Pitt had introduced an income tax in 1799 in response to pressure on public credit and expenditures related to the war. Addington had bowed later to public pressure by ending the tax after the Peace of Amiens in 1802, but revived it at a higher rate and with a more efficient enforcement mechanism with the war's renewal in 1803. Ministers and the public alike understood the measure as a wartime expedient.[120] Called the Land and Property or Rent and Funds tax, it levied a shilling in the pound on rents received by English landowners and 9d on the pound paid by tenants (Scottish tenants paid only 6d). The impost also covered net profits of all trades and professions along with dividends from the public funds, with the exception of dividends due to foreigners residing outside the country. While sometimes described as a property tax, the measure taxed income earned by property or enterprise and was generally called an income tax.[121]

Opposition to the income tax derived from its novelty as a direct tax and the intrusive nature of its assessment as much as from its burden on taxpayers. The banker Alexander Baring told the Commons in 1816 that 'nothing could be more odious than that a man should be catechized by persons who possessed more than inquisitorial powers'. Indeed, Baring would prefer being summoned before bishops to be tested on his religious doctrine than to answer questions as to the exact amount of his worldly goods.[122] Members of the political nation resented the intrusion of the state into their private affairs through the income tax, and it was attacked on grounds of liberty as well as economy. Brougham specifically linked the income tax with a large military establishment as two examples of arbitrary power.[123]

Napoleon's final defeat at Waterloo on 18 June, 1815 removed any pretext for continuing the income tax as a war measure. Arguing that the public found nothing so intolerable as the tax, Grey urged Brougham in November to stir discussion on it before Parliament met again.[124] On 12 January, 1816, the *Morning Chronicle* reported government plans to retain an income tax, charging ministers with violating their solemn pledge that it should wholly cease on 5 April. Within less than a fortnight, the paper reported meetings in Yorkshire against the tax and expressed satisfaction on the public impact of its earlier notice.[125] The *Leeds Mercury* attributed the tax's possible continuation to wasteful administration and plans for an excessive peacetime military establishment.[126] Other newspapers picked up the issue, though ignorance of the government's exact intentions held back politicians and press alike.

On 1 February, 1816, Vansittart confirmed plans to continue the income tax on the modified scale of five per cent.[127] Brougham condemned the tax as 'still more oppressive in detail than in the bulk', and asked whether it would become a source of permanent revenue. Baring later forced Vansittart to admit that the government sought to continue the tax in a modified form for another two or three years, after which Parliament could act as it thought proper.[128] The news catalyzed opposition, prompting *The Times* to denounce the policy. While accepting that taxation may become more rigorous in periods of great public danger, *The Times* insisted that the increased burden should end with the threat that had justified its imposition. Vansittart's desire to retain the tax implied that it was seen by ministers as an ordinary financial measure rather than an emergency levy, and the editors warned the public to act quickly lest it be permanently saddled with an income tax.[129]

Petitions against the tax came before the Commons on 7 February in a steadily increasing volume. As before in 1812, the presentation of petitions created an opportunity for debate. John Lambton used a Durham petition to call for others to convince ministers that Englishmen would not 'endure the pressure of taxation for the express purpose of supporting unprincipled tyrants' in France and Spain.[130] Sir William Curtis's speech presenting a London petition from the Lord Mayor and liverymen attacked the tax's peacetime retention as 'a violation of the most solemn engagement, highly irritating to a loyal and generous people'.[131] On 22 February, Sir Charles Burrell submitted a Sussex petition against the tax that also complained of agricultural distress, and Althorp introduced another that blamed the tax on the costs of an excessive peacetime establishment.[132]

Coverage of petitioning meetings and debates when petitions were brought before the Commons gave newspapers the opportunity to comment on the issue. The *Leeds Mercury* rejected Vansittart's modification of the tax with the assertion that 'the merest driveller in politics must perceive that the proposed limit of two or three years may be extended to an indefinite period and pretexts for such an extension will very easily be found'. Any delay in expressing opposition would mean defeat.[133] The *Morning Chronicle* urged that no time be lost in assembling meetings as delay played into the government's hands. A firm stand now would force upon ministers the retrenchment 'that can alone save us from ruin'.[134]

Forceful imagery fuelled public opposition. One letter to the *Times* against the tax denounced it as 'a lay inquisition' that undermines the whole fabric of English freedom.[135] Brougham illustrated the point with the tale of a man who purchased cheese wrapped in a neighbour's tax return. On confronting the cheesemonger, he found that the merchant had purchased a quantity of old paper that contained tax records for the jurisdiction allowing customers to devour reports of their neighbours' finances along with their cheese.[136] Reports of a Hull meeting described a physician who paid more money in income tax than he left to his wife and children; the tax had taken up his savings and forced the family on to the parish after his death. The meeting ended with a unanimous resolution to petition against the tax.[137]

The *Liverpool Mercury* pointedly distinguished between taxing property and incomes that varied according to fortune. A man dependent upon a salary subject to taxation 'may literally be worth nothing' compared to another with property to bequeath, 'and to impose an equal burden upon each is to violate every principle of common sense and common honesty'. The paper later described 'the tradesman, the farmer, the gentleman of small means, or the man whose industry and economy have enabled him to invest a modest competency in the public funds...who form the great middle portion of society' as the income tax's main victims. It not only tore profit or even a portion of capital diminished by an insecure speculation from a man of industry and enterprise, but impeded commerce by intruding into private business.[138] By explicitly denouncing it as a tax on the middle classes, critics cast ministers as opponents of commercial and manufacturing interests as well as landowners. Ministers became the agents of a parasitical regime of courtiers and fundholders that fed on Britain's productive classes. Debate over taxation raised broader questions about the burden of public expenditure on administration and the rentier class that held government debt. George Cruikshank's 'The British Atlas, or John Bull Supporting the Peace Establishment' presented the conflicts between established interests and the country at large by depicting a long suffering Englishman bearing the burden of the court and an excessively large army.[139] Newspaper coverage and public meetings drew on this image to focus sentiment against ministers, thereby adopting the role Brougham had envisioned for the press and public opinion in the November 1812 *Edinburgh Review*.

Pressure to organize meetings grew quickly since the Commons could only hear petitions before a measure's first reading. Brougham complained on 26 February, 1816 that petitioners across the country feared that they would not be heard.[140] The debate itself became a topic of discussion when Tierney, gently mocking Castlereagh's ill-chosen reference to the public's 'ignorant impatience of taxation', called for each petition to be read fully so 'petitioners might be heard for themselves'. When William Cartwright, an old Perceval supporter, questioned the exercise, Tierney responded that hearing complaints was the least the House could do, but he could not help it if gentlemen chose not to listen.[141] Tierney later requested a delay until Parliament could receive petitions being prepared against the tax. Brougham believed that waiting a few more days would defeat the tax, and Sir James Mackintosh warned that proceeding to a vote would virtually deprive the people of their right to petition.[142] Cartwright's view opened the government to charges of indifference to public concerns about the burden of the tax. By conceding a delay, Vansittart effectively acknowledged public opinion's role and gave his opponents the upper hand.

The government's weakness lay in more than Vansittart's inadequacy as a debater. Although a solid case existed for retaining the income tax to liquidate debt, maintain public credit, and avoid recourse to a loan from the sinking fund, public discontent simply overwhelmed Vansittart's efforts to respond. Critics both in Parliament and the country simply refused to hear his arguments. Brougham accused Vansittart of issuing a threat when the Chancellor observed that without the income tax other measures would be needed to meet the shortfall.[143] Horner parried Castlereagh's resort to the *tu quoque* argument that the Talents government had endorsed the income tax and even raised its rate by noting the very different circumstances in the two cases and reminding the Commons that the strongest opposition to the tax then had come from Castlereagh's own party.[144] With finance, unlike foreign affairs, ministers failed to embarrass the Whigs with reference to their past. The government privately drew back from the tax, but Liverpool declined to abandon it willingly, insisting that critics in the Commons bear the final responsibility for repeal.[145]

Opposition reached a critical mass by March, when only the government's firmest supporters remained loyal. The economic slump that accompanied the transition from war to peace in 1815–16 fed discontent, partly because deflation hurt merchants, manufacturers, and landholders alike, producing an alliance of town and county taxpayers against creditors, fundholders, and officials with incomes fixed at a time of high prices.[146] Aristocratic landowners suffered from the policy along with the commercial and industrial middle class, and the number of petitions from rural areas in 1816 marked a contrast with the campaign against the Orders in Council. Independent country gentlemen, as well as some government supporters, joined Whig magnates in organizing petitions. Whigs united against the tax, and Fitzwilliam placed his interest behind the campaign, supporting meetings in Yorkshire and Northamptonshire.[147] A verse addressed to 'John Bull' in the *Morning Chronicle* captured public sentiment; 'Good God, says the Leach, why treat me so rough/Let Friend Van have his way, he will bleed you enough'.[148]

Both sides expected a close vote, but the government only anticipated a dangerously slim majority. The final debate on 18 March consisted of set speeches where critics of the tax rehearsed earlier arguments, while ministers insisted on the need for the tax and urged Parliament not to abandon its deliberations before the weight of petitions. Brougham concluded by reading the clause of the Property Tax Act stipulating its continuance until 'the 6th of April next after the definitive signature of a treaty of peace, and no longer'. Wilberforce abandoned trying to speak amid loud shouting before the Commons divided 201 to 238 against continuing the tax.[149]

Brougham received public credit for the majority of 37 against the government, and a print playing on a popular brand of snuff called Hardmans 37 showed him offering the Prince Regent a sniff of 'Brougham's 37'. Another caricature by George Cruikshank depicted Brougham leading John Bull and a lion against a hydra representing the tax. Holding a roll of papers incised 'petitions from every town in the United Kingdom [against] the Property Tax', John Bull urged Brougham to strike the finishing blow with his 'glorious majority of 37'. Ministers and the Prince Regent fled in the background along a path marked 'economy', and a scroll proclaimed 'a nation's gratitude to Mr. Brougham and other patriots that delivered England from the property tax'.[150]

Illustration 2.1 'The Death of the Property Tax' by George Cruikshank depicts Brougham and John Bull slaying the hydra-headed property tax with the aid of petitions as Lord Liverpool, George IV and Castlereagh flee in the background. Reproduced with kind permission of the British Museum.

The majority against the property tax marked a victory for Brougham's tactics of mobilizing public opinion, though it failed to inflict on Liverpool's government the 37 mortal wounds Cruikshank supposed. The *Morning Chronicle* used the vote to insist that no government could 'safely treat the judgement of Englishmen with indifference', and the *Leeds Mercury* attributed the 'glorious triumph' over 'fiscal oppression' to the voice of the people, the right of petitioning, and an independent press. *The Times*, doubtless at Brougham's cue, called the opposition's victory as important as any ever obtained over Napoleon.[151] Tierney had deprecated the Whigs' earlier effort in 1815 by claiming agitation had 'resulted entirely from the impatience of the country at large and cannot be attributed in any way to the exertions of the opposition'.[152] While non-party men and even Tories backed petitions in 1816, Tierney's view reflected more of what Brougham called his 'discouraging manner' than political reality.[153] Whig activity in the press and Brougham's tactics focused opposition into an effective force. Criticism from ministers and backbenchers like George Holme Sumner, a treasury supporter who protested against those who made every petition a vehicle for 'calumnious misrepresentations', implicitly recognized the effect. As a Tory pamphleteer complained:

The moment Br–m pronounces, 'something wrong'
'Here' shouts each Ex, the lobbies 'Here' prolong.
Chophouses clamour, newspapers indict,
And 'something wrong' soon turns to 'nothing right'.
Pil'd Babels of petitions heaven ascend,
And call Reform from Hebrid to Lands End.[154]

The main question now was whether the Whigs could exploit their success. Brougham told Francis Place, the radical organizer in Westminster, that he sought to obtain a letter Castlereagh purportedly had written that defined the issue as one of whether Brougham held power over the government, and then read it before the Commons to announce his willingness to form a reform ministry.[155] Exultation betrayed Brougham into a reckless attack on the Prince Regent during debate over salaries for the Secretaries of the Admiralty in which he accused the Prince of lavishing public money on favourites and surrounding himself with an 'establishment of mercenaries'.[156] The rash speech and his actions preceding it exemplified how Brougham's intemperate behaviour could so quickly alienate his party and other sympathizers who respected his talents. Besides frustrating his friends, the incident foreshadowed the outbursts and quarrels that destroyed his career in the 1830s.

Holland, who attributed the income tax victory to Brougham, believed the speech estranged men who had voted with the Whigs against the income tax and squandered the earlier achievement. Thomas Wishaw thought it simply gave those eager to break with the Whigs a pretext, but Brougham's speech aroused enough consternation among Whigs for Brougham to tell Grey he would leave Parliament if doing so would help the party.[157] Place and Leigh Hunt, however, responded positively to language that Brougham's friend Romilly thought better fitted to describe the Emperor Tiberius.[158] The incident marred Brougham's success by alienating his fellow Whigs, and the contrast between their reaction and that of leading radicals pointed to the tensions that led Brougham to break with Place in 1817. As with Whitbread before him, Brougham's frustration with the formidable problems of working with radicals threw him back upon the Whigs.

The government won the vote of 20 March, 1816 by too narrow a margin in a thinly attended House to be perceived as having recovered the initiative. Ministers only secured the clear vote of confidence they needed when Croker defeated Tierney's attack on the Navy estimates a few days later in a debate that exposed Whig opportunism.[159] The income tax vote had cost Liverpool's government a key part of its economic programme while denting its prestige and placing ministers on the defensive. They recognized the need to justify policies before the Commons because 'silence on their side, broken only by the tromp of marching feet into the lobby', encouraged suspicions that the government's power derived from something besides the confidence of the House. After 1815, Liverpool adopted parliamentary tactics to conciliate the disaffected, catch opponents off guard, and at times hide his government's true intentions.[160] Defeat on a measure as important as the income tax forced the government's opponents and friends alike to confront the possibility of its collapse. The Commons faced a choice between persisting in votes that would bring in the Whigs by expressing a lack of confidence in the government or ceasing to reject its legislation.

In spite of their success against the income tax, the Whigs failed to build the general support at this stage that would show them to be a viable governing party. Grey privately admitted at the beginning of the 1816 session that turning power over to the Whigs would be Liverpool's most effective way to embarrass them.[161] The Tory press continued attacking the Whigs record on the war and branding them with the Talents' lacklustre record. Grey complained to Lady Holland about the party being caught between the Tory *Courier* and William Cobbett's radicalism, and her husband saw the Whigs' failure to take a clear position on important issues as their fundamental problem.[162] Factional differences resurfaced after the 1816 session closed on 27 June. Grenville's views on foreign policy, which led him to oppose reductions in the army, and his opposition to reform made agreement impossible, while the lack of an authoritative leader in the House of Commons further impeded concerted action.

Moreover, the 1816 campaign had emboldened popular critics of the government to begin agitation on other questions. Petitions and public meetings to discuss parliamentary reform dominated the early part of the 1817 session. The Spa Fields riot in December 1816 and an attack on the Regent following his return from opening Parliament sparked fears that distress had revived the instability of the 1790s. Robert Southey struck a particularly alarming note in the January 1817 *Quarterly Review* where he complained that 'pure obstinacy of party feeling' kept the Whigs from seeing what their conduct tended to promote. Divisions among the Whigs held them back from channelling public discontent in another direction, and radical groups led popular campaigns.[163] The government appointed secret committees of both Houses on 5 February to inquire into a possible conspiracy against the Crown. With that move, Brougham and Lord Thanet realized that all hopes of challenging the government had ended.[164]

The situation brought disagreements among Whigs over the proper scope of civil liberties. Grenville's concerns about threats to public order led him to favour a repressive approach at odds with the traditionally libertarian Foxite view. Holland and Grey criticized what they saw as alarmism among Grenvillites and conservative Whigs. Reports from the secret committees provided the justification for legislation to suspend habeas corpus and reimpose a 1795 restriction on public meetings.[165] Debate in the Lords made tensions among the Whigs clear after Grey strongly opposed suspension while Grenville stated that a clear case for it existed. The conflict led Grenville to announce his withdrawal from active politics.[166]

Although the Grenvillite secession from the Whigs failed to cause significant reduction in the party's strength, concerns over social stability placed it in a defensive position that crippled attempts to rally opposition. Brougham and Grey, both of whom had supported parliamentary reform, refused to endorse radical efforts in 1817. Grey blamed John Cartwright, Hunt, and other radicals for blocking the possibility of prudent reform.[167] Along with their distrust of plebeian radicals, Whigs feared being characterized as working with them to undermine the social order. Canning's charge during a debate on reform that the Whigs would 'pull down the building to obtain possession of the ruins' showed their vulnerability to such criticism from the right.[168]

Radicals themselves accused Whigs of wavering in their support for reform. Place had given Lord Cochrane Brougham's 1814 statement on parliamentary reform to Westminster radicals that had endorsed their agenda including annual parliaments to present before the Commons as evidence of his inconsistency on the subject.[169] Brougham retorted that he would not turn from his public duty in order to maintain a childish appearance of consistency, but the impression of opportunism it left did him little credit. Brougham aligned himself firmly against the radicals during the session's debates; a Cruikshank cartoon from February 1817 entitled 'A Patriot Luminary Extinguishing Noxious Gas!!!' depicted him using a fire extinguisher manned by Castlereagh to put out a boiler emitting steam from the heads of Cobbett, Hunt, and Cochrane.[170] Brougham joined others in walking out of a Westminster meeting when Henry Hunt attacked the Whigs as placehunters and opponents of reform. The *Times'* report warned that publishing the speech would violate public decorum, and Brougham privately complained that Hunt's 'blackguard conduct' offended respectable men present.[171] He clearly saw the limited prospects for cooperation with radicals like Hunt and Place.

In spite of their ability to challenge ministers in the Commons and rally support outside Parliament, the Whigs remained caught between Tories and radicals. Brougham demonstrated the possibilities that petition and debate offered, but he laboured under the distrust of a significant number of his own party. He had sought to establish himself as the Whig leader in the Commons after returning to Parliament in 1815, while at the same time building a following in the country. Other Whigs resisted his claims for leadership even though he stood out as the party's most active member. Brougham's assertiveness in debate antagonized fellow Whigs, particularly after his attack on the Prince Regent in 1816. Holland noted that Brougham,

> by his unwearied exertions and wonderful powers, made himself very formidable to his enemies; he was frequently very serviceable to his cause, and occasionally very popular out of doors. The House did not like him, but they always feared him and sometimes admired him.[172]

Such qualities did little to persuade other Whigs to accept Brougham's leadership.

Illustration 2.2   A Cruickshank cartoon from February 1817 showing Brougham using a fire extinguisher manned by Castlereagh against a boiler emitting steam from the heads of Cobbett, Hunt, and Cochrane. Reproduced with kind permission of the British Museum.

Ponsonby's death in July 1817 left Whigs in the Commons without an acknowledged leader, and Grey's detachment from the political scene left the party adrift. Disillusionment prevailed, and Brougham complained to Lambton that slender hopes of place had created 'a disposition in all the shabby ones to leave us...[and] some others less shabby are tired of opposition'.[173] The transition from war to peace had done less for the Whigs than expected, and the situation forced the party's attention toward electoral prospects and strengthening its parliamentary organization.

3
1818 and the Westmorland Election

Brougham had confidently predicted in 1814 that 'the gag is gone which used to stop our mouths as often as any reform was mentioned – revolution first, and then invasion', and he believed that with peace 'the game is in the hands of the Opposition'.[1] Although he correctly foresaw the discontent that the transition from war to peace would produce, Brougham misjudged his party's ability to turn it to their advantage. Whigs who accepted public opinion as a useful tool against the government still distrusted what they saw as a fickle and turbulent populace. Parliamentary elections offered a better chance to restore Whig ties to the public by appealing to respectable freeholders in boroughs and shires. Opening constituency politics to national debates during the 1820s marked a key point in the growth of a broader political nation. Brougham saw that parliamentary elections could serve the same objectives as petition and debate tactics while shifting the party contest from the House of Commons to constituencies.

As only one Parliament since 1768 had lasted more than six years, anticipation of a general election grew in late 1817. Ministers found the Commons increasingly difficult to manage as its members sought to gratify their constituents' wishes at the last possible moment before the poll.[2] False rumours of a general election had circulated in the autumn of 1816, and interested parties in the various constituencies undertook arrangements for the next contest. Lord Liverpool began warning supporters about the coming election in May 1818, several weeks before the 10 June dissolution, and observers predicted a greater number of seats to be under contention than usual.[3] Lord Darlington, who controlled Brougham's seat at Winchelsea, believed he would raise his influence and help the party by moving from a pocket borough to a popular constituency. Darlington told Brougham of a confidential letter inquiring whether he would be willing to be returned along with Canning and encouraged him to contest Liverpool once more.[4]

Brougham had different intentions. Since entering Parliament in 1810, Brougham and his brother James had increased their family's land holdings in Westmorland and Cumberland. By late 1817, their interest in local politics drew the Broughams into considering a challenge to the Tory Earl of Lonsdale's control over Westmorland's two parliamentary seats, an ascendancy that had stood undisputed since the county's last contested election in 1774. The *Kendal Chronicle* carried an announcement on 6 December, urging freeholders to withhold their votes for 'a gentleman of independent principles' who would stand at the next election.[5] Unable to find a willing candidate in the county itself, organizers made little progress until James Brougham pressed his brother into service on 26 January. Brougham's involvement transformed the situation from a local insurgency against a county's dominant interest into perhaps the most spectacular case in which party rivalry shaped an election before 1832. A contest that pitted the Lowther brothers against the star of the Whig front bench drew national attention as a symbolic confrontation between government and opposition.[6]

Lord Lonsdale had returned his younger son, Colonel Henry Lowther, for Westmorland in 1812, and the next year filled the county's other seat with his heir, William Viscount Lowther, when the sitting member died unexpectedly. Lonsdale later claimed that he had done so only after several Westmorland gentlemen declined to stand.[7] Rarely did a single interest control both seats in a county as opposed to a borough, and it was unheard of for two brothers to represent the same county. When the Whig John Lambton entered Parliament for the neighbouring county of Durham in 1813, his uncle, Ralph Lambton, gave up a seat for the city because he felt it neither just nor expedient for one family to hold two of the four seats for the city and county.[8] That example suggests the unease raised by the Lowther monopoly in Westmorland.

The Lowthers had faced ineffective opposition from local Whigs earlier and the Broughams had a history in the county. Before moving to Edinburgh, Brougham's father had set his modest interest as a Westmorland squire against the Lowthers. Despite his own Whig ties, Henry Brougham had proposed an arrangement to Lonsdale through William Wilberforce in 1806 that would have returned Brougham for Westmorland as a candidate of the Talents government. With support from Fox and Lord Henry Petty, later Lord Lansdowne, Brougham had hoped to negotiate a compromise between Westmorland's Whig and Tory interests that would return him to the Commons. Lonsdale's contemptuous dismissal of this unusual proposal earned Brougham's deep resentment. Sydney Smith later credited the incident with having provoked Brougham's challenge in 1818 since 'his hatreds are not the least durable of his feelings'.[9]

Party differences compounded the local and personal rivalries behind the contest since the Lowthers held the largest bloc of seats controlled by a single Tory patron. Sir James Lowther, who had established the family's political interest in the later eighteenth century and became 1st Earl of Lonsdale in 1784, had returned Pitt and Robert Banks Jenkinson, the future Lord Liverpool, for a Lowther seat at Appleby. His nephew, Sir William Lowther, became Viscount Lowther upon his uncle's death in 1802, and Earl of Lonsdale by a second creation of the title in 1809. Lonsdale's strong government ties dated from his early friendship with Pitt. As Sir William Lowther, he seconded the reply to the King's speech in 1796 at Pitt's request.[10] Lonsdale joined Pittite opposition to the Talents, but, although the Marquess of Buckingham saw him in 1807 as among the best feathers of the Tory wing, Lonsdale pointedly declined to lead an opposition party.[11] The Lowther interest, whose representatives were called the Lowther ninepins, staunchly backed Perceval and Liverpool, and Lord Lowther held minor posts at the Treasury and India Board. Income from land and coal mining gave the Lowthers sufficient wealth to dissuade most challengers.

The Lowther's control over Westmorland, however, had weakened enough to make Brougham's candidacy more than a forlorn hope. Though born and reared in Edinburgh, Brougham's family ties and local property enabled supporters to claim him as a native. Sackville Tufton, 9th Earl of Thanet and leader of Westmorland's Whig interest, stood firmly behind him. A Whig peer more Foxite than his idol Charles James Fox, Thanet had close ties with the Hollands and James Brougham, and Lord Holland described him as having joined Grey in promoting Brougham's return to the Commons in 1815.[12] Only an agreement in 1807 to divide control over Appleby had suspended his family's rivalry with the Lowthers, and Brougham noted Thanet's resentment of their pretensions.[13] Thanet's property and standing as hereditary sheriff of Westmorland bolstered his local political strength. Appleby Castle, Thanet's Westmorland residence, stood by the town where polling for county elections took place and he controlled one of the borough's seats. The peer showed scant interest when James Atkinson, Secretary to the

London Committee of Westmorland Freeholders, approached him in late November 1817, and warned that his family would not supply a candidate. Thanet's attitude changed by mid-January when he wrote to James Brougham about the relative merits of potential candidates and the need for a committee to manage affairs and collect funds.[14] Thanet backed Brougham enthusiastically in 1818, and contributed to subsequent efforts until his death in January 1825.

Rivalry between the Thanets and Lowthers no longer defined Westmorland politics, as William Wordsworth admitted in dismissing the idea that Thanet's purse or interest alone could sustain Brougham.[15] Dissenters and businessmen, mainly from the county's leading town of Kendal, joined other interests excluded by the Lowthers in supporting Brougham. The first stirring of this opposition had come in 1816, when the *Kendal Chronicle*'s proprietors voted to set the paper against Liverpool's government. A minority of shareholders aligned with the Lowthers strongly opposed the shift. Local elites, which included Quaker manufacturers as well as Tory Anglicans, had remained united during the Napoleonic Wars, and only split under the pressures of postwar economic distress.[16] Such economic issues joined with matters of religion and local politics to heighten the resentments fuelling opposition to the Lowthers.

Kendal's society reflected the duality of its two roles, both as a county town providing a focus for the surrounding countryside and as a coherent community in its own right. Institutions like the Kendal Book Club, founded in 1761, primarily served gentlemen living in the county and was part of the social hierarchy Lord Lonsdale headed.[17] Other groups focused on inhabitants of Kendal itself, particularly the Dissenters excluded from county society. Nonconformity tended to be restricted to towns and Kendal was its strongest base. Religious differences reinforced political divisions, and, since almost every congregation in Kendal included one of the town's leading families, Dissenting churches provided a base for the growing anti-Lowther interest. John Harrison, a Unitarian minister in Kendal from 1796 to 1833, carried his congregation into Brougham's camp. William Jennings, a prosperous merchant active in radical politics, supported the New Union Building Society that helped build houses that later gave Lowther opponents votes in the 1820 and 1826 elections.[18] The Kendal Fell Trust, established in 1767 to aid the local poor through proceeds from enclosed wastelands near town, offered Dissenters an important opportunity for civic leadership since the Test and Corporation acts that excluded them from membership in the town corporation did not cover it.[19] Church and civic activity gave

Kendal's Dissenters a sense of pride that made Lonsdale's control over local and county politics steadily more irritating.

Economic development and population growth enhanced a local identity shaped by religious and civic institutions. Wool dominated the local economy, as Kendal's motto *Pannus mihi Panis* (Wool is my Bread) confirms. As an important transportation and market centre, the town supported several minor industries that made it a magnet for labour.[20] Trade in woollen cloth generated considerable traffic between Kendal and surrounding towns, and then on to Glasgow or London. Although Yorkshire had eclipsed Westmorland in producing woollens by the late eighteenth century, water-powered mills opened in and around Kendal during the Napoleonic Wars. Despite its relative isolation, Kendal and Westmorland as a whole played a significant part in domestic, foreign, and colonial trade.[21] Just as Kendal's size and population of roughly 10,000 gave it a country feel, cottage industries dotted the surrounding area and even the most rugged fellside had its mines and quarries. Westmorland's inhabitants joined a high level of self-awareness derived from tourism and literary fame with educational levels comparable to lowland Scotland.[22] Deference no longer secured uncontested political control, and the romantic backdrop of lakes and fells concealed aspects of Westmorland society that provided Brougham a venue similar in significant ways to Liverpool.

Regional politics introduced another element into the contest. The 'twin counties' of Westmorland and Cumberland, where a shared Lord Lieutenant and joint assessment for taxation demonstrated ties at the social, administrative, and judicial levels, had a connection seen elsewhere only between Northumberland and Durham.[23] As an example of how landholding patterns crossed borders, a late nineteenth century survey showed that Lonsdale held roughly 28,228 acres in Cumberland and 39,229 acres in Westmorland, while Brougham land in Cumberland amounted to 1,369 acres and 985 acres in Westmorland.[24] Lord Lonsdale's possession of the Lord Lieutenancy underlined the family's influence and gave access to government patronage. Lonsdale divided Cumberland's two parliamentary seats in a fragile truce with the Cavendish and Howard families who led the Whig interest, but the compromise irritated Whig radicals like John Christian Curwen, who backed Brougham and almost mounted a challenge in Cumberland. The way in which politics crossed county borders raised the level of public interest and discussion throughout Northern England.

Plans to challenge the Lowthers in Westmorland gathered momentum late in 1817 after a November meeting among freeholders residing in London. Brougham and his brother James participated from the outset, although the degree of their early commitment remains difficult to gauge. While he described the committee's resolutions in favour of Westmorland's independence as 'fully proper', Thanet originally disclaimed any jealousy of the Lowthers and spoke of a contest with indifference.[25] The *Liverpool Mercury* printed resolutions passed during a meeting on 10 December, and advertisements for a pamphlet listing them appeared soon after.[26] Letters in the *Kendal Chronicle* after 3 January showed enough local interest for Lonsdale to warn his son of a challenge and urge a prompt canvass.[27] Meetings of local notables in Kendal, Kirkby Lonsdale, and Appleby duly affirmed their support for Westmorland's sitting members and organized committees for the next election on 9 and 12 January. The Lowther brothers acknowledged critics with an announcement in the *Kendal Chronicle* and pledged to defend their conduct to the freeholders at the first opportunity.[28]

Talk of a challenge raised Brougham's name as a candidate, but Lord Lowther believed he would step aside in order to stand for Westminster.[29] Darlington, who controlled Brougham's seat at Winchelsea and was Lonsdale's cousin, stated his opposition after receiving a letter from Brougham's backers. He warned Brougham that despite political differences with the Lowthers and the lack of any personal friendship, family ties precluded him from offering a seat to anyone who had failed in contesting the family's position in Westmorland. The letter's apologetic tone hid neither the message nor Darlington's unstated concern about a challenge to the very principle of family influence.[30] Defeat in Westmorland presented Brougham with the prospect of being excluded from Parliament once again. Thanet urged him to delay any definite commitment until local supporters came forward so that a dignified retreat could be made if canvassing proved unsuccessful.[31] A letter published in the *Kendal Chronicle* on 24 January under the signature 'Old Noll' may have been a deliberate test of interest, but another correspondent pointedly asked whether Brougham had accepted the invitation to stand.[32]

James Brougham arrived in Kendal on 26 January to canvass local interest and meet with James Wakefield, a prominent Quaker and country banker, to organize an election committee. He appeared to have overstepped his instructions by openly committing his brother to a contest. Claiming that he came only to consult with friends, James Brougham told a crowd that the cause was not his brother's but their own as well. He set the election's tone by accusing the Lowthers of treating Westmorland as a rotten borough, and asked whether the county was to be treated as Cockermouth or Appleby by having 'its

Members imposed upon it at the pleasure of any great man'.[33] The event dominated Kendal that day, and the *Morning Chronicle* reported an outburst of popular feeling that led the crowd to chair him through the streets like a newly elected MP.[34]

Brougham reproached James for acting precipitately, and urged him to retract the pledge if it could be done without absolute disgrace. Despite those sentiments, Brougham also enclosed a draft statement entitled, 'Why men of no party should support Mr. Brougham', that cited his opposition to the leather tax, a major grievance among farmers, before listing his defeat of the Orders in Council and income tax along with the 1811 Felony Act that made slave trading a crime. The statement concluded that electing Brougham for his native county would give him more weight in Parliament than ever, thus enabling him to prevent any new burdens on the public while diminishing existing ones.[35] Brougham's letter to the freeholders admitted his early hesitation, but pledged that once committed he would never retreat 'until we shall have obtained for ourselves the free choice of an independent representative'.[36] Carefully avoiding party labels that might compromise the public's sense of his independence, Brougham contrasted his record of support for popular concerns with the Lowthers' reputation as sinecurists, borough owners, and defenders of the government.

Although the election's date remained uncertain until the Prince Regent dissolved Parliament on 10 June, Brougham's announcement began the Westmorland contest. Thanet stressed the need for organization; he believed local supporters must feel the cause 'their own in every sense' and set the task of coordinating their efforts as a priority.[37] Brougham supporters followed the Lowthers' lead with meetings in Kendal and Appleby that passed identical resolutions and formed election committees.[38] The committees quickly recognized that translating popular sentiment into votes required Brougham's friends to build a local interest of their own before the poll.

The Lowthers held a clear advantage as an established interest. The extensive delegation to local committees and individual notables that their effort involved, showed its strength. Subcommittees managed canvassing, receiving outvoters at the election, and arranging transportation for supporters. While some members of an interest acted from ideology, friendship, or family loyalty, the rank and file mostly looked to material rewards, and the Lowthers' local influence and government ties helped them provide for their followers.[39] Lack of patronage posed a serious problem for Brougham in this respect.

Wordsworth perceived the influence of social divisions, and warned Lonsdale that the main threat lay in 'the hostility of little people; blind in their prejudices and strong in their passion'. To avoid alienating the Dissenters whose influence he recognized, Wordsworth also urged substituting the phrase 'King and Constitution' for the usual Tory cry of 'Church and King'.[40] Brougham's supporters accused the Lowthers of 'light[ing] up the torch of political and religious animosity' by appropriating 'all the loyalty of the county, and exclusive attachment to the Established Church'. Asserting his support for 'unbounded toleration', Brougham said he was a Church of England man, and insisted that opponents would not care about his religious views if he controlled church patronage.[41] Lord Lowther echoed Wordsworth in claiming Brougham's support came from sectaries, Thanet's dependents, and those discontented over disputes involving enclosures or game laws.[42] Brougham consciously appealed to middle-class Dissenting freeholders by defining who did not support him: resident gentry, resident clergy, and resident placemen.[43]

Both sides devoted considerable attention to propaganda aimed at Westmorland's general population and a wider national audience. The ritual and rhetorical aspects of elections involved all sections of the community and touched on values and concerns beyond electoral politics.[44] Time and money devoted to propaganda in various forms recognized that a substantial proportion of the public remained open to persuasion. Extensive use of the printed word familiarized people with men and issues, while it also politicized voters and observers by drawing them into the drama of the election.[45] Rhetoric thus set the campaign's terms in a way that merits close attention.

Brougham argued that by monopolizing Westmorland's representation the Lowthers had degraded it into a pocket borough for their own aggrandizement. Acknowledging that he considered the legitimate influence of great possessions and family reputations fair and beneficial, Brougham told a London audience

> that wealth must have some bounds, aristocracy some moderation, and that the people were something in the government of England. Westmorland though small, poor and thinly peopled would set an example that should not be soon forgotten, and that should soon be followed by the larger counties of England.[46]

He set 'independence' against the very essence of rotten boroughs by arguing that even the humblest freeholder had a right to representation.

An early attack challenged the Lowthers or their friends to cite even a single vote that reflected their constituents' wishes.[47] Brougham's papers contain a draft circular under the Lowther brothers' names in which they staked their claims on their father's rank and wealth before calling the election 'a borough contest'. Another letter purporting to be from a Lowther partisan warned readers

> that Westmorland must not give itself airs, as if it were a county. It is a borough and no more. It has fewer inhabitants than some boroughs & much fewer voters than many. Therefore it must submit to being treated as Lord L. & his friends please.[48]

Interfering with the freeholder's choice of representative infringed upon 'the rights of one part of the legislature', thereby encroaching 'on the rights of the Crown itself'. Brougham's supporters expressed outrage that 'our opponents virtually pronounce us disloyal for endeavouring to wrest [back] the liberties which the Constitution gives us'.[49] Letters published under the names Common Sense, Old Noll, and Young Noll – the latter two allusions to Oliver Cromwell – created an undercurrent sharply at odds with Lowtherite Toryism.

The Lowther interest exemplified the 'old corruption' against which Whigs and radicals alike railed, and critics of their local ascendancy raised questions about their government ties. Brougham cited Sir Robert Walpole's definition of political gratitude as 'a lively sense of favours to come' and mocked Wordsworth by naming 'those who united the offices of tax gatherers and sinecurists, who collected the taxes by deputy' as Lowther's most active friends.[50] A letter questioned whether a representative from a family disposing of £30,000 or £50,000 in public funds can have the same motive for economy as a disinterested man freely chosen by the public.[51] Lord Lowther and his brother faced questions about their qualifications for salaried civil and military appointments, and a newspaper listed Lowther's sinecures as providing either £2,600 or £3,200 per annum, with a seven-year total of either £18,200 or £21,770.[52] Such points helped frame the election as a contest between Lowther self-interest and the wider public interest.

Concerns about the election's impact on social cohesion ran as a common thread through Lowther rhetoric. 'A French Royalist' writing in the *New Times* tied events in Westmorland with measures to reduce the political role of landed families and loyalist groups, and the paper attacked Brougham's campaign 'to destroy the constitutional principle of family influence'.[53] Like Brougham, the Tory *Courier* saw influence as the election's key issue, but it predictably backed 'the influence of family, the influence of attachment' against the influence of political feelings. Nothing so ephemeral as political feelings, it claimed, could be reasonably calculated upon.[54] Interest brought the stability that derived from affection and a mutual recognition of responsibility. Another Lowther supporter challenged critics to find any institution 'whether it be to instruct the young, amuse the gay, or relieve the indigent that the House of Lowther does not munificently support'.[55] Only factional discontent over the way Lonsdale successfully used his wealth to benefit Westmorland supported Brougham's challenge. He sought nothing less than to overturn social relationships by 'inculcating the pernicious error that wealth, rank, and title are necessarily enemies of liberty'.[56]

Critics attacked Brougham as a political adventurer trading on the joint capital of others to gratify his own ambition. Doubts about the depth of his support led the *Courier* to dismiss the contest as a speculation 'to pit the purses of the Thanets and Lowthers against each other'.[57] Warnings of the dangers from political speculations by ambitious men, particularly lawyers, featured prominently in Burke's critique of the French Revolution and became a staple of loyalist rhetoric in the 1790s. Along with Brougham's involvement in Westminster's turbulent politics, that theme now tied him with radicals like Burdett, William Hone, and Henry Hunt. One Lowther campaign poster purported to be a letter from Hunt announcing the radical's intention to chair Brougham's election committee, and it proclaimed the committee's support for censures on clergy, judges, and ministers, along with universal suffrage, to make property of no account.[58] A newspaper piece broadened the focus beyond Westmorland by calling the Whigs 'the party who have done all the mischief in the country' and insisting that their leaders like Brougham, Romilly, and Holland had paved the way for plebeian ultra radicals like Henry Hunt.[59]

Analogies with France underlined the argument that radicals were only the servile echo of Whigs like Brougham. The article's next sentence claimed that Mirabeau, Lafayette, and Lameth paved the way for Murat, Danton, and Robespierre.[60] After seeing Brougham at Kendal, Dorothy Wordsworth told her brother she 'could have fancied him one of the French Demagogues of the Tribunal of Terror at certain times, when he gathered a particular fierceness into his face'.[61] Her sentiments expressed concerns among Lowther supporters that the Tory press echoed in general terms. Discussing an increase in crime since 1811, the *Courier* complained of the 'want of contentment with our condition' as 'the one great symptom of personal disquietude and general vice'. What it feared as 'the real corruption of the time' found expression in the violence inseparable from a contested election.[62] A paragraph the *New Times* reprinted from the *Carlisle Patriot* warned that a revolutionary faction had appeared up in Westmorland and urged resistance lest 'the horrors which visited France will soon visit you'.[63]

The Tory press devoted particular attention to violent incidents that confirmed their fears and cast Brougham in a bad light. Accounts of James Brougham's visit to Kendal on 26 January accused him of provoking insults to respectable Lowther supporters, and the *Courier* claimed the crowd had assaulted a well-dressed Brougham partisan by mistake. Magistrates warned afterwards against further disturbances of the peace.[64] The 11 February Kendal riot that began when the Lowther brothers arrived to open their personal canvass in the town stood out as the election's most controversial incident.

The Lowthers planned a triumphal entry into the town accompanied by tenants as well as supporters among the gentry and clergy. Brougham's committee urged friends to

> behave with the utmost propriety upon the arrival of Lord Lowther and Colonel Lowther tomorrow that not a shadow of blame be cast upon so good a cause as the glorious emancipation of Westmorland from its long thraldom.

However, a Brougham pamphlet accusing the Lowthers of subsidizing the election dinner with tax money secured from sinecures fuelled a demonstration against the candidates on their arrival. The Lowthers' distribution of ale among the populace created a volatile situation worsened by the presence of Irish canal labourers who offered or were hired to pull Lord Lowther's carriage through the streets. A crowd that included women attacked the procession with dirt and paving stones. The mob destroyed several carriages, forcing the Lowthers to gallop through the streets to safety, and then attacked the inns where the Lowthers entertained supporters.[65] Kendal magistrates afterwards offered a reward for information leading to the conviction of persons for throwing mud or stones during the riot, but nothing came of it.[66] Colonel Lowther complained that their agents had treated too much and allowed 'blackguards' to take advantage of the taverns opened for supporters. He and his brother agreed that canvassing Kendal had become impossible under the present circumstances, but Lord Lowther told his father that withdrawal would appear as shrinking from the cause. He remained in Kendal quietly to canvass nearby villages, while Colonel Lowther turned his efforts elsewhere.[67]

Newspaper coverage predictably differed along party lines. Tory papers accused Brougham of having raised the mob and disturbed local peace with the tumult associated with a contested election. A correspondent lamented that 'all the violence and brutality of both men and women originate[d] in a cold, envious, malignant sentiment of hatred against their superiors'.[68] Brougham used his connections with Barnes of *The Times* and Baines's *Leeds Mercury*, and later gained an unexpected ally in the *Kendal Chronicle* that abandoned its neutrality in reaction to pressure from the Lowthers. The *Morning Chronicle* stressed James Brougham's exhortation to supporters and the role Lowther ale played in creating the situation.[69] The *Leeds Mercury* lamented that rioting violated the freedom of election by impeding the Lowthers' right to canvass, but suggested that Lowther ale, 'fermenting on ungrateful stomachs, rebelled against the donors'. Noting that such a long space between contested elections as 50 years pent up 'popular effervescence', the paper warned that distributing drink only inflamed animosity created by efforts 'to make popular those with whom the people have no sympathy'.[70]

Treating played an important part in canvassing, and canvassing by surrogates or the candidates themselves measured and built support. The combination of persuasion and pressure canvassing involved explains both the role of treating and the reversal of social roles seen in elections.[71] Even though influence gave them leverage over a freeholder's choice, candidates and leaders of an interest still bid for support. James Losh, the Durham attorney and reformer who corresponded often with Brougham, pledged to use his claims on a non-resident freeholder in Newcastle and mentioned others over whom John Lambton, Brougham's fellow radical Whig, might have influence.[72] Thanet likewise urged Brougham to use Lambton's help to secure non-resident votes in Durham and neighbouring areas.[73] He feared the clergy and gentry supporting the Lowthers would have an advantage in pressuring resident freeholders.

The Lowthers had a remarkably well-organized system for delegating tasks to committees in each part of the county. Canvassers kept track of which freeholders had received visits and promised votes, and Lowther used the records to tabulate support.[74] Thanet also paid close attention to the details of canvassing, including badges and ribbons for canvassing agents to indicate their standing as official representatives of Brougham's committee. Earlier contests had established 'Blues and

Yellows' as synonyms for Whig and Tory; the Lowthers claimed yellow from their family crest, and blue, originally drawn from the Duke of Portland's arms, devolved upon Brougham and the Whigs.[75] Canvassing parties usually included large numbers to demonstrate a candidate's support, and, if possible, they included a canvasser with some sort of leverage over the person whose vote they sought. That person would step forward to assist the candidate or leader of the canvassing party. A crowd at a freeholder's door created an intimidating effect, and the larger number of respectable gentlemen present, the greater the impression.[76] Not surprisingly, many freeholders avoided canvassing parties when they could.

Thanet's concern about what he called 'bullying' by the Lowthers and their use of resident clergy to extend their influence underlined the pressure canvassing often involved.[77] Failure to exert influence showed another side to canvassing. A freeholder's rejection of an appeal backed by strong social pressure underlined the interest's weakness, and few patrons wished to advertise their failure lest others desert them. Candidates rarely treated dissident freeholders differently from those who followed a patron's wishes, and, despite close press scrutiny and calls from Brougham's supporters for reports of any threats, Westmorland saw no reprisals. Contemporary sensitivity over any hint of intimidation or threats suggested 'that they were regarded as illegitimate departures from conventional standards'.[78]

Persuasion remained the real task, and Lord Lowther rightly told his father that securing the election required activity and riding about.[79] Lowther's own efforts crossed county borders to entertain 50 non-resident freeholders in Lancaster.[80] He particularly saw the need to conciliate voters. Noting that the next best thing to granting a man's favour was listening to his story, Lowther asked his father to remind his brother Henry 'that he must listen to the complaints and stories of the freeholders'.[81] Letters preceded the canvass, and convention dictated that local notables receive a handwritten request for their support while freeholders from the middling orders would get printed letters signed by the candidate. The Lowthers kept a book of standard announcements with eleven different letters tailored to the recipient's station that would arrive before printed announcements sent to all freeholders appeared in the post. Canvassers used letters of support their candidate had received to sway the undecided or hesitant and invited respectable supporters to join the canvass itself.[82] The practice showed both the organization that elections involved and their personal nature.

Brougham thought an aggressive personal canvass could bring him enough votes to beat one of the Lowthers. A biographer aptly described the campaign as a forerunner to William Gladstone's Midlothian crusades in 1879 and 1880, and Brougham consciously used it as a platform to extend political discourse beyond Parliament and the capital.[83] His Westmorland canvass linked national issues with local rivalries in an effort to open the county's politics and improve the Whigs' position in the party contest at Westminster. The canvass was an opportunity to draw the public into a broader political role along the lines Brougham had described in the November 1812 issue of the *Edinburgh Review*. His national reputation impressed ordinary freeholders and important backers alike, and James Brougham arranged for the distribution of London newspapers that gave fuller reports of parliamentary business than the local weeklies.[84]

Brougham arrived in Kendal during a blizzard on 23 March to open his personal canvass. Trumpeters with the King's arms and 24 horsemen riding four abreast led a procession including flags, banners, and a band. Despite rumours of violence from Lowther partisans, no altercations occurred as Brougham addressed supporters from a window. Men, women, and children listened while snow fell. The address echoed Brougham's February speech to London supporters pledging to fight for Westmorland's independence. Oppression, Brougham warned, begets resistance, and once roused the spirit of independence would soon triumph. Praising the county's example in defying Lonsdale, Brougham denied being a Jacobin and described the real Jacobins as those who would undermine the constitution by corruption. He stressed the point by quoting Wordsworth to describe the Lowther creed as 'they should take who has the power/and they should keep, who can'.[85]

Brougham's Kendal speech responded directly to Wordsworth's criticism. The poet had defended the Lowthers in letters to the *Kendal Chronicle* signed a 'A Friend to Truth' that questioned Brougham's motives. His activity goaded Brougham, and accounts of the speech suggest that Wordsworth 'was uppermost in Brougham's mind'.[86] Brougham distinguished between Lonsdale and 'agents who skulk in the dark...those contemptible creatures who asperse and misrepresent us', accusing them of acting merely to keep their places.[87] Brougham alluded directly to Wordsworth in a passage excised from the *Carlisle Patriot*'s account:

> The Lowthers' principal literary advocate is a worthy gentleman with a good place in the revenue department, of whose writings I

wish to say nothing but that his readers (I speak of his prose and politics) have harder work of it than he has – without being quite so well rewarded for their pains.[88]

An endorsement from Thomas Clarkson, the abolitionist leader, appeared in the *Kendal Chronicle* with coverage of Brougham's visit. Asked by a fellow abolitionist to aid Brougham, Clarkson immediately concluded that 'Brougham must be supported – we cannot do without him'. Though he disliked giving the impression of opposing Lonsdale, whose moral character he valued, Clarkson believed 'private civilities are only entitled to private rewards'. The confusion between public and private obligations created a want of discrimination in elections that Clarkson thought injurious to the country. The letter concluded with a list of Brougham's efforts to help slaves and promote education.[89] Dorothy Wordsworth saw the letter as 'a feather in their caps' and thought nothing else yet produced by Brougham's friends merited attention. Lowther supporters reacted with outrage amplified by the appearance of a letter defending Clarkson in the Lowtherite *Carlisle Patriot*.[90] Clarkson's letter highlighted Brougham's national standing and drew attention to his leadership on a popular issue at a key point in the canvass.

Brougham complained that he could not secure a public confrontation that would have placed his opponent at a disadvantage.[91] Lowther jibes in the press reflected their concern over his reception in the county. Brougham expressed surprise on being met near Lake Windemere with colours flying, a band, and a large crowd that drew his carriage two miles in procession. He delivered 'a very regular speech such as might have been made in Parliament' and told Lady Holland that 'it answered all the better for not being of an ordinary cast'. A few days later his party met a horseman on the ridge above Windermere who brought them to a large crowd that led a procession with a carriage. Local gentry brought their sons to learn Whig principles and the speeches concluded with a late dinner.[92] At Appleby, he cited yeomanry from the neighbourhood who accompanied him as a refutation of the Lowthers' claim that they held complete support among local proprietors.[93] Mackintosh thought that 'the absolute novelty of such proceedings should leave a deep and lasting impression in those lonely vales, which may be perhaps too strong for influence'.[94]

Lowther complained that Brougham gave 'a speech of an hour long at every village and ale house where he can assemble a mob', though he later wrote that Brougham's speeches worked to their favour, angering local gentlemen and making them much more active partisans.[95] Wordsworth told Lonsdale that the press had 'softened' Brougham's speeches, especially the Kendal one, and omitted some of their most offensive passages altogether.[96] The *Carlisle Patriot*, which the Lowthers controlled, ran a satirical piece on the canvass that likened Brougham to a rabid dog 'supposedly of the Westmorland breed, but on inquiry we find he is of the Scotch species'. It noted that 'two years ago he made a desperate attack on the Prince Regent', and claimed those recently bitten by him were 'leaving their homes...roaring and foaming at the mouth...attacking their best friends and neighbours...and showing many other horrible symptoms of mental disease'.[97]

Thomas DeQuincey and Wordsworth made more formidable attacks with pamphlets responding to Brougham's speeches. DeQuincey entered Westmorland politics through his relationship with Wordsworth, and he sought the editorship of the *Westmorland Gazette*, established after the *Kendal Chronicle* openly backed Brougham. The paper first appeared on 23 May, and DeQuincey replaced its first editor on 11 July to hold the position for eleven months.[98] He wrote election broadsides even before taking over the *Westmorland Gazette*, and DeQuincey's *Close Comments on A Straggling Speech* appeared in April as a reply to Brougham's canvass.

DeQuincey compared the 23 March speech to the snow that fell on Brougham's arrival, as 'it fell as fast, and was not at all weightier', but called its tone 'warm – it was even inflammatory'. The heat came from Brougham's attacks on Lonsdale and Wordsworth, which DeQuincey called 'a jacobinaical harangue'. Brougham's dismissal of the charge, he continued,

> must not be allowed to depend upon [his] definition of a jacobin – whether we shall account him one of that class. A jacobin is understood to be one who arms the passions of the mob and their ignorance against the property of the State and the government of the State: for his own safety he may stop short of treason, as defined by law; and yet, for public mischief and danger, he may go far beyond the evil of any treason that is punishable and formally known as such.

No supposed reverence towards the personal head of state could hide Brougham's efforts to undermine 'the affections of the people to their immediate superiors and the just influence of rank and property', which underlay all supremacy.[99] The pamphlet repeated that he acted only as Thanet's 'cat's-paw', brought forward to secure Lonsdale's rival a triumph or at least avoid a mortifying defeat. Brougham, his local supporters, and fellow Whigs stood open to the same charges he had made against the Lowthers, and DeQuincey dismissed the talk as a screen for ambition.

The pamphlet coincided with Wordsworth's *Two Addresses to the Freeholders of Westmorland*, which stands out as one of the most articulate early-nineteenth century expressions of English conservatism. Wordsworth felt Brougham's public attack keenly, and DeQuincey appealed to that sensitivity to revive their strained friendship. A radical who had changed his views after Napoleon's invasion of Switzerland, Wordsworth's attitude towards aristocracy shifted along with his family's relationship with the Lowthers. His father, John Wordsworth, had been a law agent and steward to 'Wicked Jimmy', the 1st Earl, whose refusal to pay a £5,000 debt impoverished Wordsworth's family. On succeeding his uncle, Sir William Lowther settled the debt with full interest and earned Wordsworth's gratitude.[99] Lonsdale also helped Wordsworth secure a post as Distributor of Stamps for Westmorland at a time in 1813 when the cost of educating a growing family burdened the poet.

Wordsworth's relationship with the Lowthers changed at a point when his concern about the poor and the duty of the ruling classes to dispense charity increasingly shaped his views. After 1810, he feared that a new political economy based upon profit and self-interest had broken old bonds of responsibility, leaving the poor as the first victims of social change. Lonsdale's acts of charity and personal behaviour toward members of all classes epitomized Wordsworth's ideal of paternalistic nobility, and his support for the Lowthers involved far more than self-interest. Similarly, Brougham, as demagogue and proponent of political economy, represented all Wordsworth feared about modernity.[101]

Like Brougham, Wordsworth saw the election in national terms, and his pamphlet engaged Brougham's wider agenda while speaking to local concerns. The first address asked whether the Lowthers had abused their influence: did the county really lie in submission to them? Westmorland's present representatives owed their places to the fact that '*no one else has presented himself*, or for some years back, has been likely to present himself, with pretensions, the reasonableness of which could enter into competition with theirs'.[102] Wordsworth reiterated the Lowthers' insistence that they did not impose themselves as the county's representatives, but merely responded to circumstances they would rather have avoided. The real choice lay between the government that had defeated Napoleon and delivered the country from various crises, and an opposition that earlier had lost power through its own errors and infatuation with the French Revolution.

The second address examined what discernment and consistency could be seen among those who selected Brougham as their champion. Wordsworth believed that the Whigs failed to prize English ways, 'especially as contrasted with those of France'. He attributed the fact that hardly a single distinguished clergyman could be found among the personal friends of Whig leaders to their repugnance at associating with men of grave character and decorous manners.[103] Although the Whigs had tolerated too much Brougham's efforts to 'ingraft certain sour cuttings from the wild wood of ultra reform' on their party, Wordsworth denied that he could be fairly classed among them. On the contrary, Brougham stood first among those economists who used retrenchment as a means of weakening the government and fuelling radical agitation. Wordsworth feared social conflict, and his argument reflected the general Tory view that popular alienation had grown since Napoleon's defeat. Indifference to the government's achievement in securing victory had produced a litany of complaints that Brougham and his cohorts manipulated for their own ends.

The Westmorland contest demonstrated the point. Brougham lacked the property to provide the standing expected of a county's representative, and raised cries of oppression solely to spark a contest. Wordsworth argued that the shade of rank and property gave freedom the safest shelter. Customary practice and statute alike demonstrated the constitution's intent that counties would elect substantial landowners to represent them. Brougham, who had little property in Westmorland, only broke the lethargy of the county's people with 'an officious and impertinent call from the dirty alleys and obscure courts of the Metropolis'.[104] Wordsworth depicted Brougham as an outsider driven by factionalism and ambition, in sharp contrast with the Lowthers, who enjoyed wide support across class lines and based their claim on local attachments. Brougham's candidacy attacked the foundations of English politics, and Wordsworth closed by warning his fellow Westmerians not to follow Middlesex's earlier example from the 1770s of electing a demagogic outsider like John Wilkes.

Charges that Brougham sought to undermine family influence and doubts about his standing among the Whigs touched on sore points. Lowther campaign literature responded to Brougham's rhetoric by noting his ties with Whig families that commanded their own political interests like the Cavendishes, Russells, and Howards. A handbill listed

Lonsdale alongside Whig magnates in defending aristocratic influence over the Commons. DeQuincey specifically warned Brougham against provoking Earl Spencer, whose son Lord Althorp had held the same office during the Talents ministry as Lord Lowther held now.[105]

In fact, Brougham proved unable to rally outside support for his Westmorland campaign beyond Lambton, and his failure seemed to confirm doubts about Brougham's standing within the party. Remarking facetiously that the election was a 'rebellion [against] legitimate authority', Brougham complained that Holland 'won't touch the subject', and noted that, despite Thanet's plea, Lord Derby declined interfering, as did the Duke of Devonshire and Grey.[106] Brougham also resented James Perry's supposed failure to defend him effectively in the *Morning Chronicle* against Lowther charges, and pledged he never again would write for the paper.[107] As during the campaign against the Orders in Council and the Liverpool election, Brougham lamented how readily his party distanced itself from popular appeals.

Brougham's determined attack on the Lowthers certainly dismayed many fellow Whigs. The eagerness with which Brougham's Westmorland committees disavowed party animus as their motive and Brougham's own emphasis on 'independence' gave them an excuse for neutrality. Brougham's failure to cast the challenge in direct party terms enabled opponents to present it as an assault on aristocratic leadership.[108] Conflicting loyalties also played a part. Sir Philip Musgrave, who had ties with Canning, withheld support, much to Thanet's outrage. Devonshire held property in Westmorland that brought some political interest, but since the land had been bought from Lonsdale, the Duke and Lord George Cavendish refused to use any advantage it brought against the Lowthers. Thanet also noted that Lord George had been a friend of Lonsdale. After approaching several Whig magnates for support, he lamented the 'beastly' conduct of our friends', but urged Brougham to refrain from complaint. Thanet later suggested that Lonsdale had told the Cavendishes 'that his interest was to be attacked in Westmorland & Cumberland, and by this artful addition he obtained perhaps something more than a wish to concur with him in preserving the Peace of one County'.[109]

The Cavendish interest in Cumberland had brought earlier challenges to the Lowthers, and they had joined the Howards in accepting a compromise there. Viscount Morpeth, heir to the Earl of Carlisle, represented Cumberland's Whig interest as a member for the county. Brother-in-law to Devonshire, Morpeth had represented the county since his father secured an agreement with Lonsdale to divide control of its two seats. Though an active Whig, Morpeth avoided local conflicts with the Lowthers, who found him the most agreeable among the Whigs representing constituencies in the county.[110] The compromise and Morpeth's handling of it angered other local Whigs. Brougham's supporter John Christian Curwen urged Morpeth in 1818 to join him in a bid to oust Lonsdale's nominee and brother, Sir John Lowther. Morpeth refused, and Whig leaders strove to avoid a contest that would see him squeezed out of his seat by Curwen and Lowther. The situation placed Brougham in an awkward spot. Morpeth had declined to help him, and a Cumberland contest would weaken the Lowthers' ability to enforce their authority in Westmorland. Deliberately injuring Morpeth, however, would alienate Whig magnates and perhaps sever Brougham's party ties. Though Brougham complained to Lady Holland of pressure from his supporters, since 'the least movement in Cumberland lets me walk over the course here', he persuaded Curwen to step aside.[111] Lady Morpeth praised Brougham for opposing a contest when the diversion would have helped him, but the move dismayed Lowther opponents in both counties whose support he needed.[112]

Concerns about Lowther efforts to exclude freeholders from voting by manipulating the land tax returns underlined Brougham's need for support. On 27 May, he complained to the House of Commons that a letter of 9 May sent by John Thompson, clerk of the commissioners for assessing the land tax, instructed assessors not to make out any further assessments until further notice. Brougham argued that the circular operated directly against bona fide voters by preventing them from registering their assessment, and called it 'one of the grossest attempts to defraud men of their right of voting' ever brought before the House.[113] The county franchise required possession of freehold property valued for the land tax assessment at a minimum of 40 shillings per annum. That property qualification covered leaseholders for life, annuitants, holders of rent charges and mortgages on freehold, as well as placeholders in government service and holders of ecclesiastical benefices. Candidates could challenge freeholders at the poll to swear to their eligibility, and votes might be rejected or reserved pending adjudication.[114] Realizing the danger of losing votes in a close election, Brougham's committee already had warned supporters to check the land assessments.[115] A halt in assessments would deny freeholders the chance to correct any discrepancies and ensure their eligibility.

Stephen Lushington replied for the Treasury that 'no such order had been signed or sanctioned by the treasury', but noted applications in

April on some cottages whose ownership stood in question. Brougham questioned the propriety of tax officials inquiring into freeholders' property titles or voting rights. Lord Lowther quickly denied any personal knowledge of the matter. Sir James Graham, the Lowther member for Carlisle, thought the inquiry normal when previously unassessed freeholders came forward so eagerly, but shared Brougham's desire to see the whole correspondence on the topic.[116] Brougham later produced a document signed by two commissioners who had delayed meeting from 13 April to 23 May, and then ended assessments until 27 June. One of them, Christopher Wilson, also chaired the Lowther election committee for Kendal, while the other, John Hudson, served on it. Brougham proffered no formal charge, but hoped the gentlemen in future would confine themselves to assessing the taxes 'without assuming a discretion highly detrimental to one of the parties interested and calculated to disenfranchise a large body of qualified voters'. Denying that Lord Lowther or his brother countenanced such 'a weak act', Brougham attributed it to the zeal of inferior agents whose actions seldom helped those they served.[117]

Lord Lowther simply noted the novelty of 'individuals soliciting to be taxed', and defended the Secretary to the Commissioners as a respectable individual accused unfairly.[118] Calling Brougham's charge an 'electioneering puff', the *Carlisle Patriot* rejected it as grasping at straws. The *Westmorland Gazette*, established as a Lowtherite voice against the *Kendal Chronicle*, insisted that Brougham sought to enfranchise supporters by paying their land tax, and praised the commissioners' actions. Brougham indeed had pressed Charles Wynn, a Grenvillite, to move a bill that would have enabled more of Brougham's friends to vote by removing the assessment as a qualification for voting.[119] Yet, the Lowthers had a notorious reputation for manipulating voting eligibility, and Brougham gave the matter enough publicity to limit further such activity.

The Prince Regent's dissolution of Parliament on 10 June began the election in earnest, and observers read his personal appearance in Westminster for the event as a rebuke to the Commons for voting against grants to the royal dukes.[120] Brougham and the Lowthers mounted a final canvass through Westmorland before the poll opened in Appleby on 30 June. Nominations and speeches from the candidates began the official proceedings, and the deputy sheriff declared for Brougham and Colonel Lowther after the show of hands amongst the crowd that customarily demonstrated popular support before the poll. Lambton, who attended to support Brougham after his own election in Durham, described 300 people in attendance with only 25 for Lord Lowther and 30 for his brother.[121] But the crowd did not represent each side's real strength because polling itself required individual freeholders to declare their votes openly. Lord Lowther demanded a poll, and Brougham led by the day's end with 270 votes to Lord Lowther's 262 and his brother's 252. Brougham fell behind on the second day by 559 to Colonel Lowther's 589 and Lord Lowther's 605. The gap soon widened, and the poll closed on the fourth day with Lowther leading at 1211, against Colonel Lowther's 1157 and Brougham's 889.[122]

Lord Lowther's friend John Wilson Croker thought Brougham's early lead reflected a combination of organization and the fact that his supporters gave plumper votes, where both votes went to a single candidate, while Lowther supporters largely split their votes between the brothers. Overall, Brougham received 820 plumpers and split 60 votes with another candidate, against 1145 votes split between the Lowthers and 18 plumpers for both.[123] Brougham's reliance on plumpers indicated a polarized electorate that left him at a disadvantage. Once the tide turned against him, he accused the Lowthers of bringing up supporters in carts and wagons. Hired constables, many brought in from Liverpool, accompanied the well-marshalled Lowther freeholders. Even in the lead, Brougham complained that his opponents used 'all the arts of legal chicanery' to challenge votes on frivolous grounds. He served as his own counsel before the Assessor's Court against four Lowther attorneys, including Fletcher Raincock, who had represented Brougham during the 1812 Liverpool election. While various grounds for disqualifying votes could be offered, lack of clear title to a freehold was most likely to cause dispute.[124] Brougham finally attributed his loss to Lowther money and the disqualification of votes over the land tax. Lambton agreed, noting that 200 of the 1100 votes tendered for Brougham were disqualified, but expected victory at the next contest.[125]

Brougham's defeat opened a prolonged struggle in Westmorland. At the final close of the poll on Friday, 3 July, Brougham praised his supporters for their unbought votes and pledged to challenge the Lowthers at every election while he lived. 'If I die', he continued,

they will not then be sure of their prey, they will not have riveted your chains; the fire of independence will not be extinguished, and a flame will break forth from my ashes which will utterly consume your Oppressors.[126]

While concession speeches during the period generally sought to restore community bonds strained by the election, Brougham broke with convention by criticizing Lowther efforts to deprive him of votes and the presence of 'bludgeon-men' and 'hired clamourers'. A meeting afterward in the yard of Appleby Castle endorsed resolutions organizing a grand association to secure the independence of Westmorland and Cumberland. It appointed standing committees to promote the cause, and Brougham's supporters pledged to enfranchise votes and secure their own qualifications as freeholders to avoid future challenges to votes. Friends from outside the county would be named honorary members to make common cause against the Lowthers.[127]

While the *Courier* mocked Brougham's final speech as a specimen of 'auto-bombast' and dismissed his efforts as 'a fruitless attempt to subvert the fair and legitimate influence of property, honorably and benevolently administered', others took Brougham's intentions more seriously.[128] The *Westmorland Gazette* warned 'the Lowther party constantly to avert in a spirit of enlightened foresight' to the danger that the whole battle may be fought again. Ministering to Brougham's vanity and ambition, his supporters adopted a model of association that the paper considered 'nearer to the compacts of Irish insurgents than anything...yet witnessed among Englishmen and professing friends of the Constitution'.[129] Exposing and guarding against that threat became the *Gazette*'s main preoccupation under DeQuincey's editorship.

The 1818 Westmorland election brought local tensions into the open and raised political awareness. Thomas Grenville urged his brother, Lord Grenville, 'that our laurels may be worn with meekness and modesty' in order to avoid creating resentment. 'If Lord Lonsdale's family had attended to these considerations', Grenville continued, 'neither his power nor his purse would have been attacked'.[130] Though well aware of the point, Brougham looked beyond county politics in challenging the Lowthers. As Brougham asked Lord Grey:

> was there ever a case in which the *ministers* as such were more implicated than in our attack on [Lonsdale's] party influence? Does he not always use it in the most constant & yet the *meanest* & *shabbiest* way against us?[131]

Congratulating Grey on the elections, Sydney Smith thought Brougham 'made an excellent stand', and wrote that 'if Lord Thanet will back him again, he will probably carry his point'.[132]

Observers generally concurred with Smith's view that the Whigs gained from the 1818 general election, and the results gave a stronger indication of public sentiment than those from 1812. An exceptionally high number of English constituencies saw contests in 1818: more large and medium boroughs than at any point since 1790, and counties and small boroughs matched earlier peak numbers from 1807 and 1804. The number of overall contested English seats rose by over half from 1812.[133] Ministers had 411 seats against 196 Whigs, a net gain for both sides over the 1812 Parliament. The Grenvillites, who had broken with the Whigs in 1817, held 11 seats, and the loss of five English counties underlined Tory dependency upon Scots and Irish support.[134]

The *Leeds Mercury* proclaimed that 'ministers have been least successful where they are best known', and calculated a shift of 34 votes away from the government. Canning and William Huskisson concluded from the returns that the ministry had lost touch with public feeling, and Huskisson feared the impression would hurt the government's standing with the next Parliament.[135] Brougham had told Holland even before his canvass ended that 'the elections have done a world of good, both by beating the government and destroying our worst enemies, Hunt & co'.[136] His efforts and Sir Samuel Romilly's victory in the radical stronghold of Westminster challenged the radicals' claim to represent the public's true voice.

Plans for more concerted leadership marked another promising development for the next parliament. Since George Ponsonby's death in July 1817, the Whigs had lacked a recognized leader in the Commons. A younger member of the extended Ponsonby family, John William Ponsonby, Viscount Duncannon, became the Whigs' whip in the Commons, even though he made no reported speech in Parliament until 1829.[137] In March 1818, Holland had lamented the lack of initiative among Whigs in the Commons despite opportunities to challenge the government and 'less personal indisposition to us in the country than now'.[138] That changed when a group met in July at Duncannon's behest and agreed to send Tierney a formal requisition. Brougham wrote from Westmorland endorsing the idea and implicitly renouncing his own claims to the leadership.[139] The Whigs who signed the requisition wrote that their party would quickly lose the advantages won in the general election without an acknowledged leader. Only Tierney could fill that situation, and his friends concluded that their chances depended upon his being a 'rallying point in the ensuing session of Parliament'.[140]

Although Grey retained the overall lead, the recognition of Tierney's position in the Commons amounted to the first election of a party leader and drew some resistance. Creevey ridiculed the idea of electing or naming a party leader by 'a kind of Luddite test...which having once signed, you are bound to your captain for better or worse'. He insisted on the contrary that leadership must be asserted rather than created. Like Fox, 'a man must make himself such leader by his talents, by his courage, and above all by the excellence and consistency of his public principles'.[141] Lambton, whose objections carried far greater weight than Creevey's, angrily insisted he would not 'submit to the cavalier mode of dictation assumed by the meeting with whom it originated'. Rejecting what he called a cabal, Lambton would 'acknowledge no leader in the House of Commons, who has not been regularly proposed at a general meeting of the party convened...when every man may have his option of attending or expressing his opinion'.[142] Brougham finally persuaded Lambton to give Tierney his support, largely on the grounds that refusal would undermine opposition to the government and the decision reflected a genuine consensus.[143]

Party unity remained essential to effective opposition. Brougham and other Whigs shared Tierney's view that the party had to 'satisfy others that we are as ready to build as to pull down, and that if they help us to overthrow the present administration we can at once supply them with another'. Hopes of gaining support remained futile until 'at least the foundations on which a new cabinet may be built could be distinctly shown'.[144] Brougham might have added that the party must also distinguish itself from both Tories and radicals by addressing public calls for reform. His article on the state of parties in the June *Edinburgh Review* attacked the doctrinaire approach radicals brought to reform, while emphasizing that the Whigs had opposed consistently

> every dangerous stretch of power and unnecessary expenditure of the revenue – defending the cause of liberty and of national independence abroad – reducing the standing army at home – compelling the ministers to adopt measures beneficial to trade and to relinquish an enormous amount of taxes the most burdensome and oppressive.

Just as importantly, nobody could 'seriously maintain that the independence of the Empire or the stability of the Throne would be endangered by their accession to power'.[145] Brougham's 1818 election campaign challenged Tories and radicals alike at their weakest point, extending political debate to include significant interests hitherto left out. Though defeated, the prospect of another contest and his party's overall gains in 1818 strengthened Brougham's hope of bringing the Whigs into power.

4
Social Tension and Party Politics in 1819

The year 1819 marked an important point in the halting process by which the Whigs recovered their vitality. The political scene that year also highlighted the symbiotic relationship between the parliamentary contest at Westminster and public opinion in the country. With support from a better organized and more enthusiastic Whig cohort in the Commons, Tierney mounted a systematic effort to translate popular discontent into a stronger position for his followers. The struggle between government and opposition led ministers in turn to seek a decisive expression of confidence from Parliament, but neither side gained a clear advantage. Social tensions heightened by faltering economic growth from June 1819 came to a head in the Peterloo riot on 16 August. Although threats of unrest strengthened the government's hand as they had done in 1817, Whigs responded with more confidence than before and appealed to respectable opinion through a series of county meetings. They abandoned earlier inhibitions to work with local interests and reform groups in a move that contributed to a gradual shift in popular sentiment to their favour over the next decade.

Brougham set out the stakes for the next parliamentary session with an *Edinburgh Review* article in June 1818 that argued Liverpool's government had lost public confidence and should be replaced by the Whigs. 'Can anything', Brougham insisted, 'be more absurd than to oppose a ministry, and seek its downfall, for the mere sake of destroying it, without putting any other in its place?' The only legitimate object of constitutional opposition could be to establish a ministry on purer principles, composed of more trustworthy men.[1] Despite the Grenvillite secession, Brougham argued that the Whigs embodied the strongest force for civil and religious liberty, not to mention a generally enlightened and liberal policy, ever seen in English history. Only the delusions practised by radical agitators kept in office a ministry that embarrassed its firmest supporters. The Whigs' past failure to contest 'the faction of the Cobbetts and Hunts' had helped ministers by dividing the opposition and raising public suspicion about Whig motives.[2] Whig electoral successes in 1818 had dispelled such fears, and public alienation from both radicals and the government gave the party a chance to lead.

Talk of Whig gains in the 1818 election had raised hopes while impressing on the party's leaders the need to follow up with a strong showing in Parliament. Tierney warned Holland that a failure to make a good display after all the discussion of future prospects would have a very prejudicial effect.[3] By January, he expressed a confidence in the party's prospects at odds with his usual hesitancy. Sir Robert Wilson remarked that with good 'attendance [Tierney] flatters himself victory is certain'.[4] Grey's son-in-law, John Lambton, reported Tierney's doubt 'that so strong a party as ours could exist & not turn ministers out unless it fell to pieces of itself'. Lambton himself spoke warmly of additions to the Whig cohort in the Commons, and, with Holland's encouragement, he planned a weekly party dinner to maintain morale and coordinate tactics.[5]

Although his wife's illness kept him away from London, Grey presented the Whig's case against the administration on 31 December at the Fox Dinner in Newcastle. After discussing the country's economic malaise and the weight of taxation, Grey asked what solution the present government offered. Only a rigid and unsparing system of retrenchment and economy could end distress, and Grey urged the public to support the Whigs in promoting those changes. He spoke particularly of the need for reducing the military establishment to avoid financial difficulties or high taxes as well as to protect the constitution against military despotism. Such retrenchments 'cannot be denied with safety and must not be omitted in this interval of peace'. After the public's rejection of Lord Liverpool's ministry in the recent election, Grey looked to Parliament's opening with sanguine hopes for cooperation between Whigs and responsible men outside Parliament.[6] The speech presented a Whig agenda familiar from earlier attempts to engage popular opinion in the 1790s, and it gave further proof that Whigs abandoned the defensiveness that Brougham had lamented so bitterly during the 1812 election. The party now demonstrated its willingness to look beyond metropolitan preoccupation and work with respectable opinion in the country. Appealing to provincial liberals as Grey had done in Newcastle distanced the Whigs from ministers and plebeian radicals alike. Grey and others anticipated that the 1819 session would allow the Whigs to articulate their agenda, and they sought an issue that would capture attention while highlighting their differences with government.[7]

Securing a decisive engagement during the forthcoming session proved more elusive than either Whigs or ministers had hoped. Parliament met on 14 January, but the Prince Regent's speech left little room for debate since it referred largely to questions on which discussion had been exhausted, and the Whigs offered no amendments.[8] Holland thought the government would disarm critics 'by adopting the measures the latter would be likely to recommend'.[9] Early debates emphasized financial issues, particularly Tierney's motion for an inquiry into public credit on 2 February. Since both sides had agreed on holding an inquiry, Tierney's effort aimed at indicting ministers before independent MPs over their economic policy since Waterloo. Debate over Brougham's exclusion from the subsequent committee further displayed Whig solidarity on 8 February. A later Whig effort to charge the Duke of York's allowance to the Privy Purse rather than the taxpayer-subsidized consolidated fund provided another opportunity to attack ministerial extravagance in debates on 22 and 23 February. Debates in March and April on criminal law reform and matters related to corruption in Scottish burghs raised broad concerns on constitutional liberty and humanitarian reform that fitted well with Whig principles while challenging the government's authority.

William Huskisson told his wife after the debate on 2 February that ministers had strict instructions to avoid issues at stake lest the question be seen as anything other than a party vote. Vansittart lamented that Tierney had acted under vulgar party feeling so early in the session and declared it unnecessary to enter into details when the House unanimously sought a full inquiry.[10] Debate closed with a party vote of 168 in favour and 277 against, and the government majority of 109 reflected a dangerously low attendance that boded ill for the future.[11] Lambton reckoned it a good division for the Whigs on a straight question of confidence, and he told Grey that the government had expected to have 315 against 150 for the Whigs. Tierney spoke well, while the government seemed weak in its response.[12] Against the sparse Tory attendance, Tierney noted the absence of 34 Whigs, only one of whom sent what he called 'a shabby excuse'. He took the chair at an enthusiastic Whig dinner the next day where the members present resolved to hold a fortnightly dinner during the parliamentary session.[13]

Brougham's exclusion from the committee despite his knowledge and interest in economic affairs, sparked a debate on 8 February. Castlereagh insisted that 'it would be very invidious to argue on individual members' and thought it best 'to adhere strictly to the old plan'. Canning also opposed including Brougham because 'such addition would be contrary to precedent'. However, John Calcraft, a Whig known for his commitment to retrenchment, cited several precedents in proposing the motion, and Charles Wynn, a leading Grenvillite, gave others.[14] Drawing upon Castlereagh's phrase, Tierney claimed that objecting to Brougham's appointment on his merits was 'something more than invidious, it was extremely difficult'. Nobody stood 'more eminently qualified to assist in the elucidation of any question connected with political economy'. Lord Morpeth, citing his vote in 1797 to appoint Charles James Fox to a similar committee despite differences of opinion between them, also urged Brougham's appointment 'from a conviction of his peculiar aptitude for the situation.[15] The debate again displayed Whig solidarity, and cheers broke out on the opposition bench as the tellers announced 133 votes in favour of Brougham. A government majority of 42 on a party line vote gave ministers little consolation.[16]

These two early February debates on the Bank committee encouraged the Whigs and set ministers on their guard. Poor performances in debate by ministers cast doubts on their ability to address peacetime economic concerns. Wynn saw the unwillingness among new members to be considered reliable government supporters and 'to receive notes or answer whip' as the new Parliament's most striking feature.[17] Indeed, 157 members, nearly a quarter of the Commons, lacked previous parliamentary experience.[18] Slack attendance by office holders gave an excuse for absences by country gentlemen and fringe government supporters. The government's majority varied according to attendance, and the precarious situation further weakened Lord Liverpool's parliamentary authority. By contrast, Whig unity raised both the party's own morale and its standing in the Commons. Tierney told Grey in late February that 'everybody is in good humour and ready to do what they are desired'. Convinced that the session had gone well, he remained willing to await opportunities in an increasingly favourable climate.[19]

Financial matters provided the most effective material for opposition, but other Whig initiatives, particularly on legal reform, encroached uncomfortably on administrative prerogatives. Before his suicide in November 1818, Sir Samuel Romilly had led Whig efforts to reform the criminal law and address social problems related to crime, and by early

1819 all shades of opinion agreed on the need to address the issue. Castlereagh offered several proposals for inquiries, including one for a general committee on jails and other means of confining and reforming offenders. Sir James Mackintosh's motion on 2 March for a more narrowly focused committee passed over stiff government opposition by 19 votes.[20] While not a party question, voting on the motion largely followed party lines with substantial defections among government supporters.

Outside Parliament, the Westminister election to fill Romilly's seat drew much attention during the session. George Lamb's victory on 3 March raised Whig morale, while sharply rebuking Westminster's strong radical interest. Even though Romilly only appeared before the voters after his 1818 election, his candidacy had forced the radicals to withdraw their second candidate for the borough, Douglas Kinnaird, to avoid drawing votes from Sir Francis Burdett.[21] Romilly's suicide left his fellow Whigs despondent, and it seemed likely that Hobhouse, who maintained a good relationship with Lambton, Sir Robert Wilson, and other Whigs with radical ties would take the seat. Hobhouse made a challenge inevitable, however, by openly charging the Whigs with betraying their commitment to reform. Brougham and James Perry of the *Morning Chronicle* had already stirred Whig animosity against Hobhouse, and his criticism gave other Whigs a pretext to back a separate candidate of their own. Francis Place, who managed Hobhouse's election campaign, concurrently published a series of attacks on Fox and past Whig involvement in Westminster elections that seemed calculated to split Hobhouse from the Whigs. Such charges only gave the *Morning Chronicle* material against the radicals, and Lamb defeated Hobhouse by 4,465 to 3,861 on 3 March.[22] Although the ultra-radical John Cartwright also stood and received a token 38 votes, the public saw the election as a straight Whig–Radical contest that set Whigs apart from the more turbulent radicals.

Whig pressure on the government continued with a close division on Lord Archibald Hamilton's motion on 1 April for papers regarding corruption charges in the burgh of Aberdeen. The government won a slender majority of five in the vote of 105 to 110, and cheers from the Whig benches greeted the result. Hamilton then pledged to bring the question before the Law Officers after the Easter holiday.[23] Scottish affairs attracted little interest in an English-dominated House of Commons, but a successful campaign for burgh reform that had begun in 1817 encouraged reformers to petition against an essentially self-electing system of municipal government. Popular efforts to secure a poll election for the burgh in Aberdeen, which was bankrupt and disenfranchised at the 1818 election, lay behind Hamilton's motion. The government resisted the effort because the issue threatened its control over Scottish seats, and growing independence among Scottish reformers produced a spate of new petitions.[24]

When Parliament met after the Easter recess, Hamilton offered a motion on 6 May to refer petitions on Scottish burghs to a secret committee. He denied using the issue as a pretext for raising the general question of parliamentary reform. Hamilton sought only a reform of the internal management of the burghs, a necessary measure, albeit a radical and comprehensive one.[25] As with Mackintosh's committee on the criminal law, Hamilton threatened to take a controversial issue typically initiated by ministers out of the government's control. The issues at hand in both cases involved Foxite principles and appealed to liberal reformers outside Parliament. Canning saw the implications of Hamilton's proposal, which he described as a sweeping measure that if adopted in one area must be followed up in others.[26] Whig leaders left the debate largely to Hamilton and backbenchers, and the 149 to 144 division in a thinly attended House gave the government an alarming defeat. The next day during a meeting at Liverpool's house, Canning demanded that the government raise a 'vital question' to assert its control over the Commons.[27]

That question came when Tierney proposed a committee on the state of the nation. In a break with his generally cautious desire to wait for circumstances rather than risk hasty action, Tierney framed a clear choice designed to test firm support on both sides; his attempt to separate sheep from goats accordingly drew a flock of record size. Emphasizing how ministers had been 'cuffed and kicked about' since February, Tierney described them as having 'sunk into objects of compassion and contempt'. Votes on law reform and Scottish burghs had forced the government to accept motions it bitterly opposed. Ministers seemed 'governed by no principle, and attached to no system', and, since the government had failed either to bring forward measures of its own or defeat those proposed by the opposition, Tierney argued that 'it was almost left to their antagonists to govern the country'.[28] Two errors blunted the impact of Tierney's speech. Addressing so many issues distracted attention from his strongest charges involving the government's economic policy. More seriously, he failed to make clear whether the motion was a question of confidence and thereby raised doubts over whether he really sought to drive the government from office.[29]

Castlereagh replied that after eight years the government's record could not be so far from memory as to require a committee of inquiry. Calling the debate 'a grand field day' for parading the Whig troops, he eagerly cast the motion as a question of confidence.[30] Canning also described it as 'an acknowledged and constitutional mode of ascertaining the sense of Parliament on the conduct of the administration of the country' and demanded a clear verdict. He closed the debate with the standard Tory argument that while ministers had brought the country safely through the war, the Whigs had offered only 'a succession of theories refuted by facts [and] prophecies falsified by experience'.[31]

The division of 178 to 357 dashed Tierney's hopes, giving the government a majority of 179. A strong Whig muster failed to compensate for defections and abstentions among waverers and independents, and support came largely from MPs who generally voted with the opposition.[32] Having pressed their case against the government to its limit, the Whigs fell short when it became clear that defeat would remove ministers from office. Holland, who thought Tierney approached debates as trials of strength rather than manifestations of principle, understood that the motion required the Commons to endorse the Whigs as well as reject the government.[33] Tierney had forced a party vote on a House of Commons that one independent member described as having 'as little of party spirit in its composition as any Parliament that had ever sat'.[34] Such uncommitted members either avoided the choice by abstention or voted for the government.

The debate marked the peak of Whig efforts during the 1819 session. Subsequent votes saw the Whigs' morale and discipline fade, and the *Courier* mocked that 'even a detachment of His Majesty's Horse Guards could not now rescue them from the overpowering popularity of their fall'.[35] The government deliberately framed subsequent resolutions stating its financial requirements as a question of confidence and secured a majority of almost 200, despite imposing £3,000,000 in new taxes and devoting the entire sinking fund to pay current expenses. Significantly, however, the government resisted a private proposal to revive the income tax by John Charles Herries, a leading Treasury official who did not then sit in Parliament.[36]

Newspaper commentary on the Whigs' failed offensive after the session had closed on 12 July looked back to Brougham's June 1818 *Edinburgh Review* essay. Noting how people in ancient times had been so credulous 'as to listen perpetually to the same stupid oracles, by which they were perpetually deceived', the *New Times* mocked that the *Edinburgh Review* had been proven wrong in all its predictions over the past 15 years. Whig bravado failed to conceal the fact that public sentiment did not support the great system of their practical policy. Far from rejecting ministers, the public simply concluded that the principles by which the government had led Britain through the crisis of war remained its best support in peace.[37]

The *Courier* drew attention to the *Edinburgh Review*'s past analysis before discussing the Whigs' current state. Emboldened by a few successes that they had won through their adversaries' inattention, pride and elation had then drawn the Whigs into a direct assault on the government and its failure withered 'all the laurels which accident had bound upon their brows'. In a cut at Foxite francophilia, the *Courier* likened Tierney's motion to Napoleon's Russian campaign as the commencement of disasters from which the party might never recover. Excessive belief in their own importance, mismanagement, and public indifference handicapped the Whigs. Why else had they vainly struggled for nearly half a century, with only a few transient glimpses of office, 'to exchange the pastures of popularity for the more fattening ones of place and profit?'[38]

Repeated failure to unseat the government had only produced a total disregard of order, subordination, and discipline among the Whigs. Hinting strongly that Brougham had written the article, the *Courier* insisted that he believed himself the Whig's inevitable leader and only accepted Tierney's lead with reluctance. Now that defeat reduced the Whigs 'to the condition of a Mahratta confederacy' lacking principles or acknowledged leaders, Brougham had 'recovered from a politic illness' to take the field again with hopes of supplanting Tierney. While the next chapter remained unsure, Whigs could not achieve as stragglers what they had failed to accomplish as a party.[39]

The *Courier*'s veiled accusation that Brougham had given Tierney the lead in order to profit from his likely failure reflected his low profile during the past session. Brougham deferred to Tierney in 1819 much as he had done for the first part of the 1818 session. Although he closed the 25 February debate on the Windsor Establishment, Brougham paired off for the vote on Tierney's state of the nation motion and generally avoided speaking on economic issues. Lambton described Brougham as 'below concert pitch' in a 5 February letter to Grey that attributed Brougham's reticence to criticism for speaking too often last year, and he wished that Brougham not hold back too much further.[40] Charles Greville, a keen observer, thought that the Whigs did particularly well in the debate to include Brougham on the Bank committee because the government and its supporters were caught off guard, having assumed that an attack in the December *Quarterly Review* hurt Brougham so much that 'he would not be able to lift up his head again'.[41]

Yet on 25 January the *Courier* ran a parody likening Brougham to a steam packet that 'leaves her moorings at Billingsgate every day during the session'. It further described 'the Brougham' as

> true American built, her engine has been manufactured by Scotch and French philosophers, her boiler is heated by disappointed ambition, she emits an unexampled quantity of vapour, and for noise and smell has no competitor.

In an allusion to Brougham's 1817 attack on the Prince Regent, the *Courier* described the 'boat' as having new 'safety valves' that made it unlikely she would again 'burst her boiler and scald her friends'.[42]

Taken with his lower profile during the session, the paragraph suggests a shift in the tone rather than the tempo of Brougham's activity. Mackintosh's consultation with Lord Holland prior to raising the question of criminal law reform to ensure that Brougham had not chosen to undertake the subject himself pointed to his continuing political involvement.[43] Brougham, at least for the moment, realized the importance of acting with sufficient temper to avoid diverting attention from the matter at hand, as he had done by attacking the Prince Regent in 1816. Although he gave Tierney the lead in raising economic issues, Brougham spoke often during the session on humanitarian issues, including the state of convict ships and the chimney sweepers bill. Brougham's impromptu reply to Peel in a debate over a government measure to reform charitable abuses enlivened the closing days of a parliamentary session that had fallen short of Whig expectations.

Tierney's emphasis on economic issues during the session pointed to the problems that soon would lead to public unrest. Peterloo and the controversy it sparked showed a significant change from 1817 when the Whigs had been squeezed politically between the government and metropolitan radicals. Economic issues may have given Whigs their best case against the government, but the social tensions created by the economic cycle often created unrest and fears of mob violence. Minsters easily cast themselves as defenders of the social order against unrest or even revolution and depicted Whig opponents as a thin end of the radical wedge. In 1819, however, the Whigs avoided internal divisions and set Peterloo within a Foxite narrative of resistance to arbitrary power. Led by Lord Fitzwilliam, they staked a claim as spokesmen for provincial interests and public opinion in a way that suited Brougham's broader efforts to build support among liberal interests in the country, marking a significant point in their revival.

The trade cycle had improved in 1818, ending the immediate post-war depression and reducing the social tension that had characterized the previous two years. By June 1819, however, the situation had changed as imports fell by over £6 million, exports by £9 million, and re-exports by under £1 million.[44] Living standards had collapsed among working men as real wages fell and prices remained constant, and conditions were particularly acute in the Manchester area.[45] By late June, the *Leeds Mercury* reported agitation in the manufacturing districts prompted by the lack of work and low wages. Unemployment gave Henry Hunt and other radical agitators a ready audience, and the paper reported meetings that linked political topics with distress and saw violent language from speakers, though not among the local workmen attending them.[46] Tension grew steadily through the summer months. *The Times* insisted that the ease with which agitators led the unemployed from discussing their distress to 'talk sedition and to threaten the overthrow of the state' indicated their incapacity to remedy current ills. Such political meetings, it warned, reduced compassion for the unemployed and would inspire equally brave men to oppose and repress them.[47] The *Leeds Mercury* argued that 'the danger of the country arises from the ultras on both sides – the Ultra Royalists and the Ultra Reformers'. These groups played into each other's hands, and the *Leeds Mercury* encouraged moderate men to 'interpose themselves with counsel and assistance to avoid a choice between revolution or military despotism'.[48]

Baines's unsigned articles in the *Leeds Mercury* underlined the recurring fear among Whigs and their liberal supporters in the provinces of being squeezed out by Tories and radicals. Tories responded to public meetings by raising alarms about social unrest, while radicals seized on unemployment as an opportunity for agitation. Whig leaders and their press allies persistently criticized mass meetings as an imprudent response to distress. As Lord Lieutenant of the West Riding of Yorkshire, Earl Fitzwilliam, an elderly Whig magnate and disciple of Edmund Burke, took a close interest in the question. While no friend to radicalism, Fitzwilliam denied that meetings demonstrated widespread disaffection with the present social order and explained their high attendance by the 'want of occupation among the people'. In a widely publicized letter to the Lord Lieutenant of nearby Cheshire, he firmly rejected the idea of arming one class against another and criticized those who exaggerated the popular disaffection.[49] The *Morning Chronicle* praised Fitzwilliam's view and lamented 'the rash zeal' with which both radical agitators and the Tory press set classes against one another.[50] In attacking the *Courier* as a servile government organ, the *Times* similarly condemned the suppression of popular discontent and argued that repression would simply drive back the symptoms of a malady that could only be cured by economical government.[51]

Tension peaked on 12 August when yeoman cavalry dispersed a public meeting called by Henry Hunt at St Peter's Fields near Manchester. An earlier meeting at Birmingham had named Sir Charles Wolsey the city's 'legislative attorney' or representative in defiance of the law against electing a member of Parliament without the King's writ. Radicals spoke of their efforts having an impact not on Parliament, but on public opinion in the country, and critics saw mass meetings as efforts to create a rival forum to Parliament for discussing issues.[52] By doing so, radicalism presented a fundamental challenge to the governing order. Rumours that the assembly in Manchester would follow Birmingham's example with Wolsey led the local magistrates to order Hunt's arrest and the dispersal of the crowd gathered to hear him. The yeomanry charged the crowd during a moment of confusion that left 4 people dead and 400 injured.[53] Peterloo, as the incident became known in an ironic comparison with Wellington's 1815 victory, sparked public outrage. The government only worsened the situation by conveying the Prince Regent's thanks to the magistrates for their prompt action.[54]

Many newspapers shifted almost overnight from condemning agitators and challenging the wisdom of holding mass meetings to decrying the assault on the liberties of Englishmen. Sir Francis Burdett and other radicals quickly organized meetings to register their anger at the event. Even conservative Whigs who had worried about the threat agitators posed to public order believed the magistrates had mishandled the situation. The Duke of Devonshire told his wife that, with every disposition to excuse the magistrates, he could only conclude they had erred in seizing Hunt and relying on yeomanry instead of disciplined regular soldiers with no private or local enmities. Several Lancashire Whigs, including Lord Derby and George Philips, a factory owner and MP, blamed the magistrates despite their own awareness of tensions between workers and employers in the Manchester area. On a broader note, Brougham and Francis Jeffrey viewed Peterloo as a sign of a dangerous separation by the upper and middle classes of the community from the working classes.[55] The consensus in outlook among Whigs did not, however, extend to their practical response.

Similarities between the current situation and events in the winter of 1816–17, when unrest culminating in the Spa Fields Riot had encouraged the government to suppress agitation, made the Whigs cautious. That period had seen tensions emerge with Grenville that weakened the Whigs and undercut their accomplishments in 1816. Grey now thought the party would benefit from seizing the middle ground by condemning the conduct of Hunt and other ultra-radicals who operated beyond Parliament while strongly resisting any measure to curtail constitutional liberties. Such a position would rally moderate and reasonable men, including 'a great proportion of the property of the country'. It also would encourage the people to see Whigs as their natural leaders. Bitter experience with public meetings and the current state of the country, however, led him to urge delay until Parliament met.[56] Grey remained deeply suspicious of radical leaders, asking Sir Robert Wilson whether there was 'one among them with whom you would trust yourselves in the dark' or if he could doubt at all 'the wickedness of their intentions?'[57]

Holland, however, warned that delay would leave the country 'to two outrageous parties, the legitimate Tories on one side and the violent reformers on the other'.[58] Tierney thought it both the Whigs' duty and in their interest to 'mark our opinions on the recent conduct of government and do our share' of urging the public to petition the Regent and Parliament. If left alone, the radicals would be sure to spoil a good cause and alarm those gentlemen who might otherwise join the Whigs when the issue was taken up in Parliament. Noting talk of calling a Middlesex meeting, Tierney thought it expedient for Whigs with ties in the county to attend, and he hoped that its success might encourage similar meetings elsewhere.[59]

Fitzwilliam gave the decisive lead by organizing a Yorkshire meeting to petition the government for an inquiry. The *Leeds Mercury* had called on 28 August for 'some true British Nobleman' to present the facts of Peterloo to the Prince Regent. A lightly veiled reference to Fitzwilliam spoke of a 'venerable man whose years, whose talents, whose public virtues, whose unsullied life, whose rank in the magistracy and the peerage would eminently qualify him for the acceptable performance of this great public duty'.[60]

Demands for a parliamentary inquiry at a York Guildhall meeting on 20 September by Lawrence Dundas, a Yorkshire Whig with close ties to Fitzwilliam, gave the first public hint of the peer's views before his open call for a county meeting.[61] Fitzwilliam's leadership precluded opponents from tainting the Yorkshire meeting with extremism, and he carefully emphasized the question's implications for constitutional liberties. He also told Holland that, while avoiding any prejudgement of the case or provocative images suggesting atrocities, the meeting would call for Parliament to meet for an inquiry. The requisition Fitzwilliam drafted to call the meeting noted events 'which, not hitherto satisfactorily explained, appear to affect important rights of the people' and stated the meeting's purpose as preventing 'any invasion of the acknowledged rights of the people (if such shall appear to have occurred)'.[62] That deliberately moderate language gave Whigs in other counties a model.

The *Leeds Mercury* announced a requisition signed by local peers and gentry asking the county's High Sheriff to convene a county meeting on 2 October and noted rumours that James Archibald Stuart Wortley, Yorkshire's Tory MP elected in 1818, would oppose an inquiry.[63] The meeting occurred in York on 14 October, with between 20,000 and 30,000 in attendance, along with Fitzwilliam, his son, and other Whig notables. The Duke of Norfolk moved the resolutions in a brief speech that lamented the haste with which ministers had given the Crown's approval of the magistrates' behaviour. While Stuart Wortley opposed calling for an inquiry, he agreed on the importance of the people's right to meet and discuss their grievances. When the crowd interrupted his speech, Edward Baines and Lord Milton, Fitzwilliam's son, insisted that they hear him. The crowd also shouted down James Mitchell, a radical described as 'an itinerant political orator', when he called for parliamentary reform. Another gentleman intervened to urge the meeting not to raise extraneous questions. Baines then accused Mitchell of being a provocateur and warned the crowd against betraying their cause through disunion. Thomas Wooler, who had earlier declined to support Mitchell's motion, rejected Baines's charge but urged Mitchell to speak no further.[64] Whigs and their supporters clearly controlled the meeting and set a moderate tone. By allowing dissenting views on all sides to be aired while showing no sympathy for radicals, they cast it as a demonstration of respectable opinion in Yorkshire.

The meeting drew wide coverage, including attacks from the Tory press that rehearsed old themes. The *Courier* asked how many qualified freeholders were among the crowd and suggested that by playing to public opinion, the Whigs would find themselves political bankrupts denied credit with either radicals or the respectable public. The *New Times* called it a meeting of radical reformers, who obligingly permitted a few noblemen and gentlemen to occupy the hustings and move the resolutions.[65] Despite Stuart Wortley's efforts, most government supporters boycotted the meeting, partly to avoid a public defeat, and their separate gathering to pass a resolution of loyalty to the Crown only emphasized their isolation.

Fitzwilliam's leadership encouraged other Whigs, and plans for meetings were revived in Middlesex, Hertfordshire, and Essex. Grey, who met Fitzwilliam in Doncaster along with Lambton, told Holland that the Yorkshire requisitions ended 'all my doubts & difficulties, & I can no longer have any hesitation in saying that we ought to do all we can to give effect to the example which they have set us, & promote similar meetings in other localities'. While noting problems in Northumbria and Durham, Grey pledged to do his best to surmount them.[66] Lord Carnarvon, a Whig peer who before had taken an alarmist view, began organizing a Hampshire meeting with Tierney's support.[67] Tierney also expressed great satisfaction with Fitzwilliam's action and thought that Yorkshire's lead had more effect than any other arrangement could produce.[68]

Brougham cautiously had begun planning Westmorland and Cumberland meetings in early September, and Fitzwilliam's requisition quickened his pace. On 11 September, he told Lady Holland that requisitions for a Westmorland meeting were under way, though it remained uncertain whether it would be held. Several of those who had signed the requisition had 'advertised to "post those persons as liars who circulated a report that they were connected in any way with radical reform"'.[69] By 19 September, Brougham opposed 'any middle course of petition, remonstrance, & etc.', declaring his preference for organizing public meetings, even if they drew few participants, and attending those called by others. Brougham thought repression less likely if peaceful and orderly meetings showed there was 'no risk if the people & constitution are only let alone'. He also saw meetings as a way to limit divisions between social classes and thought that by participating the Whigs would at least do their 'best to keep well with the people without encouraging their delusions'.[70]

At a dinner for the Friends to the Independence of Westmorland on 24 September, Brougham publicly called for a full inquiry by Parliament into Peterloo. His speech sounded a cautious note in expressing doubts about the wisdom of the Manchester magistrates, and by extension the ministers who supported them, along with the radical leaders who had called the meeting. While defending the right of public assembly, he also opposed

> moving great bodies of the people from their homes to attend meetings at a distance – nor could he see why the good men of

such considerable places such as Bolton should not meet at home, and leave the Manchester folks to meet at Manchester. Such assemblages as were not necessary might be fairly deemed inconvenient; and though there was nothing unlawful in them, they had better be avoided.[71]

Brougham told Grey that Westmorland definitely would meet, and he expressed hopes for meetings in Cumberland and Liverpool as well. Westmorland would adopt the Yorkshire resolutions with only superficial changes to avoid the appearance of having copied them.[72]

The Cumberland meeting assembled on 13 October, the day before Fitzwilliam's Yorkshire meeting. Thomas Salkeld, the county's High Sheriff, opened the meeting by describing the requisition as 'numerously and respectably signed' and urged participants to act with 'temper and moderation, and not wander from the immediate object of the meeting'. The requisition stated the right of subjects to meet and discuss matters of public concern and condemned military interference with lawful meetings as 'an invasion of the most sacred privileges of the people'. While condemning popular violence, the meeting also opposed all encroachments on the constitution and called for an inquiry into the recent proceedings in Manchester. J.C. Curwen told the assembly that their representatives in the House of Commons needed public support to make their concerns heard, and the meeting agreed to a resolution asking the Prince Regent to summon Parliament for an inquiry.[73] Despite his role in organizing the meeting, Brougham only spoke briefly at the end to thank the participants and deny personal attacks. He thought the Cumberland meeting a great success, not least because it eclipsed an effort by local radicals and forced them to defer to the Whigs.

Thomas Wybergh, one of Brougham's leading friends among the local gentry, began the Westmorland meeting in Kendal on 21 October with resolutions drawn from the Cumberland meeting. He outlined the events at Manchester, with sarcastic jibes at coverage in the *Courier* and other ministerial papers, concluding that without further investigation any minister might use the precedent to 'cry havoc, and let slip the dogs of war'. William Crakenthorp, who had played a key part in Brougham's 1818 campaign, seconded the resolutions. Although he disapproved of the Manchester meeting's illegal dispersal, Crackenthorp echoed Brougham's earlier words about the impropriety of large meetings and wished that people had met in their own neighbourhoods. Civil liberty remained the real issue, however, and he urged listeners to protest lest the right of meeting to petition be lost or tied down with restrictions.

As before in Cumberland, Brougham spoke last. The meeting had 'very properly instructed' Westmorland's parliamentary representatives to support the petition, but their absence seemed strange, and he assumed silence betokened acquiescence. Noting the number of leading men who supported the Cumberland and Yorkshire meetings, Brougham was convinced that those meetings reflected public senti-ment against the Manchester magistrates' actions and concerns over the security of popular liberties. The meeting carried the resolutions along with a motion that the county's members, Lord and Colonel Lowther, present them with Brougham's assistance.[74] Despite Wordsworth's view that plebeian freeholders found the speeches in Kendal unpalatable, the meeting brought supporters together and again distinguished Whig views from those of ultra-radicals like Hunt. Drawing that distinction before the public was a key aspect of these county meetings.

The Whig campaign in the counties predictably drew a sharp response. The government dismissed Fitzwilliam as Lord Lieutenant and *Custos Rotolorum* of the West Riding within a fortnight of the Yorkshire meeting. Henry, Viscount Lascelles, Lord Harewood's eldest son and a Tory who had represented Yorkshire for several years, was appointed Lord Lieutenant in his place.[75] Fitzwilliam's political martyrdom angered Whigs of all stripes and enhanced party unity. Lord Althrop privately admitted his delight at the dismissal for its effect in bringing the party together.[76] The *Morning Chronicle* saw the move as proclaiming that only tame acquiescence in the government of the day's every wish or senti-ment could escape its displeasure. *The Times* denounced what it saw as a high-handed act of reprisal and ridiculed suggestions that Fitzwilliam had encouraged discontent by asking if ministers 'affect to fear the friend of Burke?'.[77] A Yorkshire meeting convened on 18 November to vote their thanks for Fitzwilliam, and Lord Althrop attended to eulogize the earl despite his own claim to only a distant connection with the county. Noting that many Yorkshire Whigs had resigned their positions in protest, Edward Baines spoke of the need for 'discreet and good men' in a troubled time, and urged others to remain at their posts unless driven from them by ministers.[78]

Newspapers announced a special session of Parliament called for 23 November, which the *Morning Chronicle* expected to result in an inquiry into the government's reaction to Peterloo as well as the event itself.[79] Fitzwilliam's initiative and similar Whig meetings forced the government's hand. Unwilling to join the Whigs in proselytizing the country, ministers instead sought to defend their position in Parliament and strengthen the laws to deal with unrest. Lord Eldon believed that only Parliament could respond to what he saw as an utterly new degree of unrest, while Liverpool feared that meetings would continue unless Parliament were recalled.[80] Despite the independent efforts of Tory editors and writers, ministers made no attempt of their own to make their case through the press, and local supporters held back from public meetings for fear of embarrassment. Fitzwilliam's dismissal aimed partly at rallying Tory opinion that faltered in the face of county meetings and earlier radical pressure. The challenge from radicals had pressed the government into vigorous action to support public order and it expected to rally loyalist support and force Whigs onto the defensive as it had done in 1817.[81]

Parliament met on 23 November to hear the Regent's Speech outlining the government's view of events. Grey acknowledged the situation's gravity, while urging conciliation instead of repression.[82] Castlereagh subsequently announced legislation in response to unrest that was later called the Six Acts. Several of the 'gagging acts', as critics described them, prohibited unauthorized military training, restricted public meetings, and authorized magistrates in disturbed areas to search for and seize arms gathered for illegal use. The Seditious Meetings Act forbade meetings to discuss religious or political issues without a requisition signed by seven householders, and prohibited persons from outside the area from attending. Other measures raised penalties for seditious and blasphemous libels, reduced delays in prosecuting offences, and imposed newspaper duties on cheap pamphlets blamed for popular discontent. Ministers had taken great care in framing their proposals with aid from the law officers, and Liverpool told Canning in October that even Brougham and Lord Erskine had expressed concern about mass meetings.[83] The government crafted these measures carefully to avoid challenges on constitutional grounds and win support from independents.

The main vote specifically over Peterloo came on 30 November, with Lord Althorp's motion before the Commons for a select committee to inquire into the state of the nation. Althorp saw the only grounds on which the House could agree to the proposed measures were 'perfect confidence in His Majesty's ministers' or belief that papers laid before Parliament gave a complete view of the country's state. Since no one could decide so serious a question merely on a principle of confidence, he insisted that the Commons should satisfy itself first that the facts justified Castlereagh's proposals.[84] Althorp then described recent events that showed much disagreement between reasonable observers and denied that unproven assertions could be taken for evidence.

Charles Bragge Bathurst, a friend and protégé of the Home Secretary, Lord Sidmouth, regretted that Althorp and the Whigs would pursue such a line of conduct when the country 'requir[ed] the united efforts of the House to restore it to tranquility'.[85] Lord Lascelles defended the government's measures as 'necessary for the protection of the sound and loyal part of the community' against radical disaffection.[86] His speech prompted Lord Milton, Fitzwilliam's son, to respond that both the Manchester magistrates and the cabinet had acted in ways that called into question the most important rights. The meeting's legality did not affect the fact that, even if illegal, 'it was to be dispersed according to law'. Milton repeated Althrop's call for an inquiry 'due to public feeling as well as public justice'. Unlike Lascelles, he feared that danger 'rather menaced the people than emanated from them'.[87]

Despite their ability to muster a clear majority, ministers took a defensive tone in the debate. Government supporters argued that Whig calls for inquiry and conciliation played into the hands of disaffected radicals. Amidst calls for a vote, Castlereagh gave an impromptu speech that criticized Althorp's motion as a delaying tactic and accused the Whigs of 'only wait[ing] for an opportunity of trying their strength'. Disappointed in his early hopes for Whig support, Castlereagh insisted that the both the House and the country had sufficient good sense and spirit to save both, not in spite of the Whigs, but without their assistance.[88] Tierney replied sharply to remarks that he saw as having no object beside 'exciting a strong and acrimonious party spirit' by blaming public discontent squarely on the Tory policies that had brought debt and taxation. Parliament, Tierney insisted, was bound to consider the causes of distress before passing severe laws or further restricting the country's liberty.[89]

Nevertheless, Althrop's motion failed by 173 in a division of 150 to 323 that indicated a polarized House of Commons unlikely to respond to Whig appeals. Despite strengthening an effort to enhance their appeal by deferring to Althorp and Milton, eldest sons of two of the most conservative Whig peers, Spencer and Fitzwilliam, Whigs could expect neither defections nor poor attendance to assist them in the division lobbies. Although Brougham did not speak during the debate on Althorp's motion, he had made a case in an earlier debate along the lines of Milton's argument that authorities must act according to the law. The division on Tierney's motion to amend the reply to the address indicated the Commons' desire for an investigation into Peterloo and foreshadowed the vote on Althorp's motion.[90] Ministers relied on their majority to secure the legislation's passage, while conceding minor points in order to deny the Whigs grounds for sustained attack. The Whigs used the debates to set out their position and pitched their arguments beyond the Commons itself to reach opinion in the country.

Whig reactions to the Six Acts were part of their broader case that conciliating the disaffected public required reform and economic retrenchment. Brougham led Whig resistance to the government's specific measures, carefully picking at the arguments given to justify them. Whigs opposed the Seizure of Arms Act on the grounds that it abridged the right to self-defence. The Training Prevention Bill drew little opposition, and Brougham acknowledged that it simply adopted more specific penalties against a practice already illegal under common law. They only accepted the Misdemeanors Bill after the government conceded a Whig amendment preventing unreasonable delays in trials from either prosecutors or the accused.[91]

The acts restricting assembly and the press drew the strongest Whig opposition. Complaining that 'all the bills lately introduced into Parliament tended to abridge the liberties of the subject', Brougham particularly attacked the proposal to curtail blasphemous and seditious libels by extending the stamp tax on newspapers. Liberty of the press was 'the great pillar of the constitution', and Brougham's argument built on his earlier legal work and speeches.[92] More broadly, he argued that reckless speeches and articles did not justify abrogating popular rights. Other Whigs also insisted that restrictions on public meetings and the press aimed at repressing, if not stifling popular opinion. Debates underlined the fundamental Whig argument that radical subversion provided no cause for government measures, which themselves subverted the constitution.[93]

While unable to defeat the Six Acts, the Whigs forced modifications and turned the debate to their long term advantage. Both at county meetings after Peterloo and in subsequent parliamentary debate, Brougham and other Whigs marked out a position distinct from those of ministers and plebeian radicals who rejected parliamentary channels for expressing grievances. The Whigs' commitment to liberty as an absolute good in itself made Peterloo an effective issue for cooperating with reformers, especially when Fitzwilliam took the lead in organizing public meetings. Provincial liberals who remained committed to petitioning and other ways of working through parliamentary channels drew closer to the Whigs who had accepted Brougham's strategy of using outside support to bolster their position at Westminster. Whigs and provincial liberals shared a dislike of special repressive measures beyond the ordinary process of law that brought the two groups together.[94] Where Brougham had earlier faced resistence from his fellow Whigs, he now pushed an agenda that the party shared. Loyalist appeals to order and the fear of revolution no longer cowed Whigs as they had done in 1817 and earlier.

Grey's disappointment over the Whigs' performance during the short session at the close of 1819 overlooked the party's wider gains. Sir Robert Wilson justly claimed that 'the conduct of opposition is universally applauded and, though the country has lost some of its liberties, I think it has approached its redemption by the union which has been promoted between the public and the Whigs'.[95] Cooperation in organizing public meetings and opposition in parliament brought Whigs together, and the struggle against the government itself bolstered their confidence. Whig leaders accepted the need for concerted appeals to provincial opinion, and they mounted a more effective challenge in 1819 than for many years past while gaining support from 'out of doors'. The question of whether Brougham and his colleagues would seize the advantage from the government, however, remained open.

5
Public Opinion and the Limits of Opposition: 1820–26

George III's death on 29 January 1820 began a year of political upheaval that tested Liverpool's government before finally demonstrating the limits of opposition. The election required within six months of a sovereign's demise gave the Whigs a welcome opportunity to build on their gains in 1818. George IV's accession also raised the contentious political question of resolving his failed marriage to Caroline of Brunswick, and the popular agitation that accompanied the Queen's trial in 1820 revived the previous summer's tensions before Peterloo and directly challenged the government's authority. Brougham used the crisis in an unsuccessful attempt to drive Liverpool from office, and it brought the Whigs closest to gaining power since 1812. It also raised Brougham's reputation as Queen Caroline's attorney and confirmed his standing as the Whigs' indispensable, though deeply controversial, lead spokesman in the House of Commons.

Legislation from the early eighteenth century provided that Parliament could continue in session for only six months after the sovereign's demise. Observers had realized that George III's poor health made it likely that his death could force two elections in quick succession, and Brougham proposed a measure in March 1817 to avoid that contingency.[1] The requirement for a dissolution on a new sovereign's accession remained in force, however, and Parliament met on 30 January 1820, to hear official notice of George III's death. A short adjournment followed two days later. Newspapers predicted an election would be held soon after the funeral. Castlereagh confirmed rumours on 18 February when he announced the King would call a new Parliament once the Mutiny Act and several other measures that otherwise would expire were extended. He expected a prompt dissolution to allow the new Parliament to meet by 25 April, and the session closed on 28 February.[2]

Brougham sparked the election's first controversy with the timing of the announcement that he would again stand for Westmorland. His letter in the black-bordered newspaper editions reporting the King's death welcomed the election as a chance for Westmorland to assert its independence and called it 'on every account a subject of sincere congratulation'.[3] Although Brougham later added the phrase 'except on the melancholy occasion of it', opponents seized on his words. The *Westmorland Gazette* accused 'the rash and rude dictator of the mobocracy of Westmorland' of rejoicing in his sovereign's death and published Brougham's letter as 'a specimen of rashness, vanity, and want of feeling'. Colonel Henry Lowther, regretting that it forced him to intrude 'on the general sorrow', announced that he and his brother Lord Lowther would stand for re-election.[4] Lowther's prompt response showed the importance of his candidacy since an outsider standing against an interest that held both seats in a constituency had only to defeat one incumbent. The traditional unwillingness among voters to give one candidate both their votes and a desire to deflect pressure from both sides often led freeholders to split their support between the senior incumbent and the outsider. Most of Brougham's split votes in 1818 had been with Lord Lowther, which made the real contest one between Brougham and Colonel Lowther for second place.[5]

The 1820 Westmorland election received less attention from London papers and the provincial press outside the region than the 1818 contest. Local newspaper coverage underlined the degree to which the 1820 election marked another chapter in a continuing struggle between Whig blues and Lowther yellows. 'An Old Freeholder' noted in the 26 February *Kendal Chronicle* that neither side had changed its principles and derided the Lowthers for claiming support on the inclusion of Westmorland as a disturbed area under the Six Acts. He insisted further that the county needed at least one MP who would attend to his constituents' wishes. Another correspondent, who claimed to have voted for the Lowthers in 1818 after a promise that one brother would withdraw at the next election, declared his intention to resist an encroachment that plainly seemed to be perpetuated.[6] The extent of Lonsdale's influence, and his efforts to maintain it, remained the central issue.

The poll opened in Appleby on Wednesday, 15 March, after contingents from both sides arrived in the town, and the Lowthers held the lead by the day's close.[7] That evening saw clashes between rival partisans when Brougham visited freeholders at inns where the Lowthers entertained supporters. The tide turned on Thursday after Brougham's supporters prevented the Lowtherites gaining an advantage by taking control of the hustings.[8] Leading after the second day with 473 votes against 469 for Lord Lowther and 438 for the colonel, Brougham chided his opponents for attempting to crowd the husting with freeholders 'pent up like so many cattle'. Lord Lowther retorted that Thanet had brought freeholders to Appleby in his carriages to aid Brougham.[9] Lord Lowther told his father that the Blues had more voters, above 300 still unpolled after Saturday, and better organization than they had anticipated. Morale among Lowther partisans languished as Brougham led the poll for two days running.[10]

Enthusiasm among Brougham's supporters grew when news of the Cumberland election arrived on Saturday. The Cumberland poll opened on Friday, 17 March, with the nominations of Lord Lonsdale's brother Sir John Lowther and Lord Morpeth. A certain Mr Dykes, who had promoted Curwen's abortive candidacy in 1818, publicly challenged Morpeth to show that his election had not been secured by a compromise with the Lowthers, and then nominated Curwen when Morpeth failed to refute the charge. Curwen stepped forward to represent Cumberland's independent freeholders with encouragement from Westmorland's Blues. Sir John Lowther and Curwen won the show of hands, and the poll Morpeth demanded gave Lowther 166 votes, Curwen 148, and Morpeth 92. The crowd jeered Lowther, and Curwen congratulated supporters for showing that Cumberland was not a close borough like Cockermouth. Morpeth left the town that evening and officially withdrew from the poll the next day.[11]

The chance that Colonel Lowther might be squeezed into third place encouraged Thanet's hope that Lowtherite freeholders would plump for Lord Lowther to exclude Brougham from 'the post of honour'. Both parties 'exerted themselves to the utmost for Monday's poll' and talk among Lowther supporters of challenging the result suggested they feared defeat.[12] On Tuesday morning, Lord Lowther complained that Brougham's strength in the East Ward where Thanet's interest lay prevented them from regaining the lead, but the balance turned when the Lowthers took the lead by 17 votes. The gap widened to over 60 on Wednesday, and Brougham conceded defeat at the close of that day's poll.

Thanking the Westmorland freeholders, Brougham chided the Lowthers for bringing all their friends, along with servants and other dependants, to the poll to gain only a narrow win. While the election's short notice had denied him 'the great advantages which result from a minute and personal canvass through the county', he challenged anyone to deny 'that we have a majority of the resident freeholders'. Convinced of having gained everything but the return, Brougham pledged to stand again. Crackenthorp then promised to be the first to call on him at the next election.[13] Thanet believed they had made a good fight and lamented Brougham's disappointment at the result. He described their party as 'in high spirits resolved more than ever to fight again & again' and concluded that with more time they would have won handsomely.[14]

Lowther noted Morpeth's low spirits after the contest and thought 'many of his friends would now be happy to join our party'.[15] Morpeth's defeat aroused a controversy among the Whigs that showed the persistence of factionalism and distaste for aggressive opposition. Thanet told Holland that Cumberland's Whigs had wished to join another candidate with Morpeth and only abandoned the plan a few weeks earlier as a concession to him. However, the Lowthers' attacks on Curwen and others among Brougham's supporters in Cumberland spurred the Westmorland Blues to intervene against Sir John Lowther. No friend to Curwen himself, Thanet claimed that Morpeth had placed himself in an awkward position by refusing to support 'factious Blues on any occasion', and he should be congratulated on escaping from it now by defeat.[16]

Brougham spoke little of his bitterness over support some Whig magnates gave the Lowthers, but viewed the indifference their conduct showed toward Thanet with contempt. Nobody could have blocked a contest as Brougham had done in 1818, but Morpeth might have kept his seat without a contest by repudiating the Lowthers on the hustings.[17] Despite his regret over Morpeth being out of Parliament and Brougham's having failed to ensure that Morpeth would withdraw to avoid a contest, Grey saw the dispute as a misunderstanding rather than a fault by Brougham or Thanet.[18]

Brougham held his seat for Winchelsea, and the Whigs did well overall. An analysis based upon voting patterns in the Parliament elected in 1820 calculated that the government could rely upon 250 firm supporters and 99 others who occasionally defected, while the opposition mustered 154 regular votes and 66 waverers. That assessment gave ministers an 8-seat gain from 1818 against an opposition increase of 25.[19] Preliminary calculations at the time also suggested a consolidation of previous Whig gains. The *Morning Chronicle* reported on 14 April that 15 new opposition or independent MPs would replace the same number of government supporters. Brougham spoke privately of 14 Whig seats and Duncannon estimated 4 or 5 in England and an even balance in Scotland or Ireland.[20]

Since the predictions could only be confirmed by divisions in the Commons, their accuracy remained uncertain. Brougham's motion on the droits of the Crown brought a division on 5 May that mustered 155 opposition votes against a government total of 273.[21] After the previous year's experience, ministers worried about managing a Parliament with many new members whose loyalties could not easily be judged. Huskisson lamented to Charles Arbuthnot, the chief government whip, that the election had deprived ministers of their 'best and steadiest' supporters. Disaffection fuelled by economic distress and the threat to civil liberties by Peterloo and the Six Acts shaped the election results and encouraged the Whigs to increase their pressure on the government.[22]

The Queen Caroline affair revived public agitation and marked the most serious crisis of Lord Liverpool's administration. While economic questions or public scandals caused tensions among backbenchers and country gentlemen, this question threatened to alienate George IV as well. George IV's disastrous marriage to Caroline ended in a separation soon after their daughter's birth, and her subsequent indiscretions had brought an embarrassing inquiry in 1805. Brougham later became Caroline's counsel after advising her daughter Princess Charlotte during her quarrels with the Prince Regent over her own marriage. Opportunistic hopes of cultivating a future Queen had drawn Brougham to Charlotte's side, but Grey, who had responded cautiously to her request for advice, doubted any advantage could be secured and wished Brougham would hold back as well.[23] The situation had echoes of an older eighteenth century opposition tactic of cultivating a reversionary interest with the heir to the throne in hopes of gaining power on their accession. Princess Charlotte's death in 1817 and Caroline's self-imposed exile after 1814 seemed to close the question, though, as her attorney, Brougham knew of Caroline's indiscretions.[24] By raising Caroline to the throne as putative Queen consort, however, George III's death caused what the *Morning Chronicle* aptly called 'the curious and delicate emergency' of resolving her fate.[25]

Liverpool sought a compromise that would satisfy both parties and avoid a politically disastrous conflict. The cabinet had resisted demands for a divorce since 1816 on the grounds that conduct by both parties would make public scandal the inevitable result of a legal proceeding that might well fail. Liverpool warned Eldon in 1820 that both the character of the monarchy and the future of the government depended upon avoiding hostile discussion involving Caroline in Parliament. George IV precipitated the crisis after his father's death by demanding the removal of Caroline's name from the liturgy, a move that implied further action.[26] The government's refusal in mid-February 1820 to begin divorce proceedings aroused his ire and marked the first of a series of disputes that threatened to drive Liverpool from office. Speculation and discreet approaches from court officials prompted Whig leaders to consider their terms for accepting office. Though regretting his absence from London, Grey told Holland he disliked leaving the impression 'of a discreditable eagerness to avail myself of any chance of coming into office' and very likely incurring 'all the ridicule of disappointed hopes and expectations'.[27]

A few days later, Grey decided that the Whigs could not form a government in the event of renewed quarrels between King and cabinet. Despite these doubts, however, Grey outlined terms for accepting office. Prudence and honour alike dictated reducing expenditures 'to the lowest scale, which the well understood dignity of the crown and the real exigencies of the public service require'. The King should surrender the Crown's hereditary revenues as his father had done. Grey told Holland to state his views freely on conciliating the public by 'measures favourable to the popular rights' and general retrenchment, along with his insistence on Catholic Emancipation and repealing the Six Acts. He also feared a Whig government would be undermined as the Talents had been, since its programme would arouse 'the secret enmity of the court' without the compensation of strong public support.[28] Although the product of speculation, Grey's terms set out much of the party's programme for the remainder of the decade.

Having brought George IV privately to accept a settlement short of divorce, Liverpool approached Brougham with terms. Earlier discussions had held Caroline back from precipitating a confrontation by arriving in England to press her case directly, and Brougham urged her to confer with him before crossing the Channel. After considerable delays, Brougham and Lord Hutchinson met Caroline at St Omer on 3 June. Hutchinson offered £50,000 per annum on condition she stay out of Britain and not use any title attached to the royal family. He also stated that the government would abandon all compromise if she crossed the channel. Brougham urged her to accept, warning she would antagonize the government by courting popular favour like a parliamentary candidate. Nevertheless, Caroline instructed him to reject Hutchinson's proposal the next day.[29]

Her refusal showed the limits of Brougham's influence, despite his later claims to the contrary. Noting speculation that Brougham had betrayed the Queen for his own advancement, Croker later reported talk that he had acted dishonourably toward her. Liverpool, who had accepted Brougham's good faith, felt aggrieved and now doubted his motives.[30] Canning had warned against unnecessarily antagonizing Brougham with arguments over his precedence as the Queen's Attorney General, and Liverpool urged that case to Eldon, the Lord Chancellor. Liverpool also asked Hutchinson to comment on a narrative outlining their talks that Liverpool had prepared in case Brougham later challenged the government's conduct. That Brougham felt obliged to insist on his own sincerity on several occasions during their talks reveals much about his reputation.[31] As an outsider to the negotiations, Grey complained that Brougham's conduct reminded him of Richard Brinsley Sheridan and, to a lesser extent, Samuel Whitbread, both of whom combined talent and eloquence with reckless bad judgement. He thought a compromise would discredit all parties to it while leaving the appearance that Brougham had betrayed his client's interests.[32]

Caroline's return to England on 5 June after having refused Hutchinson's offer overshadowed all other public business. The crisis that the cabinet had sought to avoid at all costs now began as they resolved to present evidence before a parliamentary inquiry. Brougham submitted her message to the Commons, stating that measures against her had forced Caroline to defend her character and just rights.[33] Castlereagh denied approaching the case 'with a tone of prosecution or persecution', but the House of Commons rejected his proposal for an inquiry. Brougham urged them to 'recollect that prevention was better than cure' and avoid further conflict through a private and conciliatory arrangement.[34] Tierney accused the cabinet of trying to escape responsibility, no matter where it ultimately might fall. He further irked Castlereagh by asking where the faction known as the 'King's friends' had gone. Privately, Tierney concluded that ministers had disavowed the King.[35] With support from Tory county MPs like Stuart Wortley and Sir Edward Knatchbull, Wilberforce moved a week's adjournment for negotiations that passed without a division.[36]

After the debate, George IV approached the Whigs again through his legal advisor Sir John Leach and Lords Hutchinson and Donoughmore. Lansdowne reported that Donoughmore spoke of the delicate situation between the King and his cabinet over the Queen's case, and intimated that if Grey, Holland, and Grenville were willing to take office, the King 'was prepared to dismiss his present administration instantly'.

Although no conditions would bind the new ministry, Lansdowne doubted a government able to carry any important measure against opposition could be formed on a narrow party basis.[37] Tierney reported a similar offer in stronger terms and also that the King no longer felt any personal hostility toward Grey.[38] Lansdowne, Tierney, and Holland replied cautiously, and Grey made no move in response. Once more, George IV acceded to the cabinet's wishes after failing to find alternative ministers to replace it.

The Queen's refusal to accept any arrangement that even implied wrongdoing and her further demand through Brougham for a tacit rebuttal of past insinuations blocked an accommodation. Wilberforce led Parliament's last attempt to force a compromise with a motion on 22 June urging the Queen to make concessions. Discussion of the Queen's earlier exclusion from the liturgy turned the vote into a party question as Whigs rallied to her side, but despite a division of 391 to 124 she ensured a trial by rejecting the Commons' plea.[39] The government accordingly brought a Bill of Pains and Penalties with a divorce clause before the House of Lords.

The trial that began on 17 August consolidated Caroline's support among Whigs and radicals. Brougham's opening speech warned the Lords that passing a judgement against the Queen would turn popular sentiment against them by further alienating the people and urged them to pause before they rendered such shocks to the nation.[40] The impossibility of refuting the government's case in detail forced Brougham to base his defence on discrediting the government's witnesses in cross-examination. Substantial testimony came from Italian and German servants who required translators, and Brougham's exposure of inconsistencies in their testimony brought laughter. His humiliation on 23 August of Theodoro Majocci, who failed to remember much of what he had previously told the prosecution, made *non mi ricordo* a catchphrase for the trial.[41]

Procedural rules prevented Brougham from arguing recrimination in his client's defence or even naming the King. He caused an uproar at one point by asking one of the government's agents the name of their client. As the House disallowed the question, Brougham insisted that Queen Caroline must know her accuser in order to present her defence. Speaking of the unknown plaintiff, Brougham alluded to George IV with a slight mis-quotation of John Milton's lines on Satan:

> This shape,
> If shape it could be called that shape has none
> Distinguishable in member, joint, or limb;

Or substance might be called that shadow seemed,
For each seemed either...

What seemed his head
The likeness of a kingly crown had on.[42]

The attack played to an audience beyond Westminster in a attempt to force Liverpool to retreat, and its cruel, personal tone explained George IV's subsequent aversion to Brougham. Grey, who maintained a detached demeanour throughout the proceedings, argued that justice and expediency alike compelled the Lords to reject the bill. Many witnesses had impeached themselves by contradictory testimony, and, since the case against the Queen had not been proven conclusively, it would be unjust to exact the bill's harsh penalties.[43] Although the measure passed on 6 November, the government declined to proceed in the face of public clamour and risk being defeated in the Commons.

Demonstrations in London that degenerated into rioting and a wave of petitioning meetings through the country underlined the government's unpopularity. The trial spawned caricatures and pamphlets that lampooned ministers and the King while often praising Brougham as the Queen's champion. Radicals fuelled the agitation, particularly in the capital. Southwark petitioners demanded the government's dismissal in October, and Westminster and the City of London's common council held meetings for the same purpose. Whig leaders also joined the effort, with Fitzwilliam supporting a Yorkshire meeting called to show the county's united opposition to the government.[44] A sharp drop in the circulation of Tory newspapers critical of Caroline showed that even the government's friends baulked at the trial. The one exception, Theodore Hook's *John Bull*, kept up circulation by outrageous and libel-inducing attacks on the Queen and her supporters that even alienated many Tories including the fastidious Robert Southey.[45]

Anti-government sentiment never translated into firm support for its replacement by a Whig ministry, even though it again highlighted provincial discontent and showed the potential impact of public opinion. Queen Caroline's trial sparked a general popular expression of contempt toward authority that had little political impact beyond raising fears among the propertied classes. Thomas Babington Macaulay later described the protests in support of the Queen as a union of the middling and lower orders that forced Liverpool's withdrawal of the Bill of Pains and Penalties so as to avoid a public convulsion.[46] They mobilized popular sentiment with an exceptional amount of activity for the period before 1830. Grey's comment to Holland that he 'could carry anything with the middling & lower classes of freeholders' in Northumberland despite resistance among Tory squires echoed the point. The Queen Caroline affair marked an important point for the Whigs by indicating the existence of a large body of respectable, as well as radical, opinion in the country that would oppose a government willing to sacrifice moral principles to the whims of a profligate monarch.[47] However, it also became clear that personal scandals alone could not sustain a political movement. No agenda beyond immediate protest held public sentiment together. The temporary alliance behind Caroline thus collapsed soon after the trial that had brought it into being.

The very nature of the case produced an apolitical discourse lamenting the plight of a woman scorned. Petitions from women supporting the Queen's cause and much of her defenders' rhetoric played on personal aspects of her case rather than its constitutional or political implications.[48] The scene differed greatly from scandals around the French court in the 1780s that had alienated public opinion from the monarchy. Queen Caroline's trial saw the radical parable of court and ministerial corruption 'deluged by royalist melodrama and romance', and a tidal wave of gossip and bathos swept away the underlying issue of the monarchy's legitimacy.[49] William Hazlitt lamented that 'the cant of loyalty, the cant of gallantry, and the cant of freedom mixed all together in delightful and inextricable confusion' turned the public from more serious matters. Brougham's cross-examination of the government's witnesses provided fodder for pamphleteers and cartoonists who quickly cast the hapless Italians as the villains rather than George IV or his ministers.[50] When the public grew tired of the melodrama, sentiment in favour of the Queen faded. A piece of doggerel expressed the consensus by January 1821:

> Most gracious Queen, we thee implore
> To go away and sin, no more;
> But if that effort be too great,
> To go away at any rate.[51]

As in the earlier cases of the Orders in Council and income tax, the House of Commons wanted a change of policy rather than personnel. Liverpool complied by withdrawing the Bill of Pains and Penalties. On 25 November, Lord Grenville refused the King's direct request that he form a government, forcing George IV to choose between Liverpool and the Whigs.[52] Grey told Holland that 'it is quite impossible for the King and his ministers to separate however much they loath one another'. Brougham saw no change possible until the government itself broke up, and this conclusion guided his subsequent political strategy. Thomas Wishaw reminded Sidney Smith that 'we live in a Tory country and that the great majority of well-informed and respectable persons whose sentiments ought to have weight in politics think very differently from ourselves'.[53] A change in administration, therefore, would require profound changes in public sentiment as much as in parliament itself. Smith himself dismissed the hope of Whigs ever coming into power. He complained to Lady Grey that:

> The kingdom is in the hands of an Oligarchy, who see what a good thing they have got of it, and are too cunning and too well aware of the tameability of mankind to give it up. Lord Castlereagh smiles when Tierney prophesies resistance; his Lordship knows very well that he has the people under, for ninety-nine purposes out of a hundred, and that he can keep them where he has got them.[54]

Such bitterness reflected the frustration of a party excluded from power for a generation.

Lord Liverpool held a precarious position in the trial's aftermath, having aroused George IV's hatred and still facing opposition from Whigs and radicals along with the prospect of 'a crossfire from Canning, Peel, and the Grenville connection'.[55] Political desperation led him to begin rebuilding the cabinet to gain debating strength in the Commons and co-opt potentially threatening factions. The Grenvillite rump joined the government in January 1822 when Wynn entered the cabinet and the Marquess of Buckingham, who led the faction after Grenville's retirement, won a dukedom for his support. Since Grenville himself refused to offer support, Liverpool received less from the bargain than he had hoped.[56]

Peel joined the cabinet at the same time as Wynn. Further additions came later in 1822. Although Canning had carefully avoided any hint of intrigue, many of his former cabinet colleagues distrusted him and feared he might threaten them at the head of a faction. Castlereagh's suicide in August 1822 made Canning indispensable as leader in the House of Commons, despite the King's opposition to an appointment that brought other changes. Frederick Robinson replaced the inept Vansittart as Chancellor of the Exchequer, and, while Huskisson did not join the cabinet itself until November 1823, he helped the government as President of the Board of Trade. Liverpool's reshuffle decisively strengthened the government and ended any doubts about its future.[57]

Economic growth after 1820 aided Liverpool further by reducing unrest. Social tension measured by a comparison of the trade cycle and wheat prices had peaked in 1819, and it fell steadily before reaching the lowest level of the decade in 1822. Prosperity undercut efforts to revive the agitation that faded after Queen Caroline's acquittal, and the government reduced taxes and removed restrictions on trade in order to mute critics. Some of the changes drew on proposals by Brougham and other Whigs, and Brougham drew a sharp retort from Canning in early 1825 for congratulating ministers on following his advice. The government's implementation of reforms backed by the Whigs meant that when economic problems returned in 1826, the loudest complaints would come from government supporters and Tory opponents of Canning and Huskisson.[58] For the moment, however, Liverpool's cabinet worked primarily to assuage complaints from the landed interest and win over other economic interest groups.

Above all, they sought to avoid repeating the situation in 1816 in which ministers found themselves cast as defenders of speculators and fundholders against a united phalanx of landowners, merchants, and manufacturers that had forced them to abandon the income tax. Drawing attention to the degree to which a rentier element, whose economic interests diverged from those of the landed and mercantile classes alike, provided the social basis for the Pitt/Liverpool/Peel regime could only damage the government.[59] Such an image would distance the government from both its core loyalist constituency and opinion in the country more generally. An 1822 pamphlet entitled 'The State of the Nation' prepared under ministerial supervision showed the government's increasing sensitivity to public opinion. The Queen Caroline affair had emphasized its limited influence over the press, as well as the need to respond to critics. With its heavy stress on economic matters, the pamphlet that went through at least seven editions mounted a careful defence of Liverpool's policies. Despite the difficulty of measuring its effect, newspaper reaction suggested that Liverpool's tentative effort at public relations drew some notice among the political and professional classes it addressed.[60]

Although it took Liverpool time to solidify his government's position, Whig defeats in several key votes early in 1821 showed that ministers could rely on a firm majority in the House of Commons despite lingering public pressure. The *Morning Chronicle* noted that speeches made little difference without 'means as powerful as a property tax' to support the Whigs' challenge.[61] Through the rest of the 1821 session, politics largely shifted from the party contest that had characterized 1816–20 to a narrower focus on specific policy questions. Liverpool's strong position indeed made occasional defections among wavering government supporters and independent country members more likely since they did not risk prompting a change in administration. Fragmentation and weak leadership among the Whigs also led individuals to promote their own agenda in the hope that the party would follow.

Efforts to advance parliamentary reform showed how debate could help forge a Whig consensus. Parliamentary reform had hurt the Whigs in the past by dividing the party and prompting charges of radicalism. As Peel noted, however, public sentiment by 1820 had shifted toward favouring a degree of reform. Grey also had told Fitzwilliam in April 1820 that nine-tenths of the lower and middle classes desired reform, and the decision by Whigs to raise the question encouraged a further shift in public attitudes.[62] Concerns that new interests lacked an effective voice at Westminster influenced debate in the 1820s, and these broader implications made parliamentary reform appealing for Whigs. Lord John Russell had raised the issue in December 1819 by proposing the transfer of seats from corrupt boroughs to populous areas without representation. While conceding the essential argument, Castlereagh opposed the establishment of a general rule for transferring seats from disenfranchised boroughs and instead asked Russell to bring forward a motion for the specific case.[63] The seats for Grampound, a notorious Cornish borough, eventually went to Yorkshire in 1821 after the Lords blocked a bill backed by Whigs and independent county members transferring them to Leeds.[64] England's largest county, where geography, population, and the prestige at stake combined to make contested elections ruinously expensive, now returned four representatives.

Differences among the Whigs on parliamentary reform faded as public sentiment changed. Lambton had called for sweeping reform in a motion on 17 April 1821, that failed when moderate Whigs abstained from voting in a thinly attended House.[65] Russell then tried unsuccessfully on 9 May to establish the general principle of giving seats from disenfranchised boroughs to places that had greatly increased in wealth and population.[66] Whigs mended their differences, and in 1822 Russell set another measure before the Commons in a judicious speech for reform. Noting the impact of demographic and economic changes, he urged that large towns and the interests they represented be given representation lest the Commons become a self-selecting corporation detached from the wider community.[67] Canning replied that many leading Whigs, including Brougham and Tierney, sat for small boroughs closed to popular influence. His real argument, however, stressed the dangers of change: 'If this House is not all that theory could wish it', Canning still 'would rather rest satisfied with its present state' than risk losing 'so much that is excellent' in its constitution. Although defeated by 155 to 124, Russell's motion won broad support among radicals and independent county members as well as Whigs.[68] Lambton, along with Brougham, Althorp, and Milton backed Russell, and Fitzwilliam came to accept his measured approach. The resulting consensus now allowed Whigs to pre-empt radicals as Brougham had hoped by presenting themselves as the advocates of a viable reform programme.

   Leadership in the House of Commons remained a problem. Tierney was a spent force by the end of the 1819 session, and Althorp had consulted Lambton in May 1820 on 'the best way to get Brougham quietly seated in his place'. Lambton, however, noted difficulties because of lingering prejudices against him.[69] Wishaw had predicted in 1817 that Brougham would effectively lead the Whigs, but warned that 'many of them will not act cordially under such a leader'.[70] Queen Caroline's trial had only deepened suspicions. Fearing then 'the irregularity of his mind & the consequent uncertainty of his conduct', an exasperated Grey lamented the prospect of acting with Brougham 'in any confidential and responsible situation'.[71] Even a friend like the Durham radical James Losh thought Brougham 'often causes himself to be feared when he might be loved and excites obstinate resistance where he would otherwise find respect and attention'.[72] Objections to Brougham fundamentally lay in his erratic temperament and his emphasis on agitation outside Parliament that many Whigs still resisted as a threat to their authority.

   Brougham nonetheless remained both the best Whig speaker in the Commons and Tierney's likely successor. Milton was disqualified by the probability he soon would succeed his ageing father, Lord Fitzwilliam, and Althorp's reticence led him to decline accepting the leadership alone until the decade's end. Grey, Lansdowne, and Holland agreed that no government could be formed without Brougham, and in August 1822 Grey directly invited him to lead the House of Commons if the Whigs gained power.[73] Insisting that he could not abandon his legal work without financial hardship, Brougham demurred. He further noted that his refusal of office would avoid quarrels and thus keep his friends on the Whig Mountain within the party.[74] Grey bluntly told him that 'the lead there must *really* & *effectively*, if not nominally, be in your hands, & this it can only be by your being a member of the government'.[75] The same logic applied in opposition, and Brougham's refusal to accept the formal lead in the Commons contributed to the party's ongoing weakness.

Spared the burdens of acting as the official Whig leader in the Commons, Brougham had the time to turn his legal work and journalism to the party's advantage. He continued his earlier project outlined in 1812 of extending debate beyond Parliament and raising specific questions that often engaged broader issues and involved political reform and public opinion. As a source of Crown and ministerial patronage, the Established Church represented to many Whigs a key element of the 'Old Corruption' that kept them from power. Like that of the Crown, the power of the church seemed indistinguishable from that of executive government.[76] On another level, clergy support for local corporations that excluded Dissenters made the Anglican church a bulwark of the regime. Moreover, Whigs rejected intolerance, whether in penal laws or milder disqualifying statutes, as a key part of their 'principle of moderation & liberality in both religion & government'.[77] This principle served as an important link between the cosmopolitan High Whiggery with its interest in culture and focus on affairs in the capital and the growing force of provincial Dissent. Bonds of sympathy that later held Victorian liberalism together emerged during the 1820s as Whigs and provincial liberal groups pressed their opposition to what they perceived as the complacency, exclusiveness, and inefficacy of the Established Church.[78]

Religious questions such as Addington's proposal in 1810 to license Dissenting ministers, missionary activity in India, Catholic Emancipation, and repeal of the Test and Corporation Acts produced more petitions than any other questions during the early nineteenth century, including the Orders in Council and income tax. Chapels provided the centre for social life among their members, and Dissenting ministers mobilized their congregations politically with great effectiveness. Brougham won support from Dissenters during his Liverpool and Westmorland campaigns, and he consciously defined his Westmorland candidacy as a challenge to the authority of resident clergy allied with the Lowthers. Generally speaking, the government's weakness during the early 1820s lay in matters of religion, not representation, and religious questions accordingly emerged as the main object of demands for legislative social change. Concessions did not so much appease Dissenters as whet their appetite for further agitation.[79] Along with other Whigs,

Brougham assiduously cultivated Dissenters through efforts on key issues that directly affected them.

The requirement under the Marriage Act of 1753 that Dissenters be married by a clergyman of the Church of England according to the Book of Common Prayer touched directly on the Whig principle of toleration. Although Jews and Quakers remained exempt from the law, it forced Unitarians in particular to accept doctrines they rejected in order to have a lawful marriage. The rule aroused great bitterness among Dissenters and their latitudinarian friends among the Anglican establishment. Sydney Smith, a clergyman with close ties to Grey, Brougham, and the Hollands, urged its repeal in the March 1821 *Edinburgh Review*.[80] The question came before Parliament the next year, and Brougham presented a petition to the Commons from Kendal Unitarians asking for a change in the law that would allow Dissenting ministers to marry those of their own faith legally. Although Parliament denied relief, Brougham and the Whigs effectively contrasted their support for Dissenters against the government's commitment to the Anglican establishment.[81]

Brougham attacked the clergy's political role in two widely discussed legal cases. He successfully prosecuted the Reverend Richard Blacow in September 1821 for a libellous sermon denouncing the Queen as an adulteress. The *Liverpool Mercury*, which had become a leading advocate for Dissenters and Catholic Emancipation, denounced Blacow as 'a frantic bigot, a modern Sacheverell' and 'one of the numerous horde of interested expectants' who had vilified the late Queen.[82] Like Henry Sacheverell, who had been tried in 1710 for a sermon denouncing occasional conformity and toleration, Whigs and provincial liberals saw Blacow as the epitome of those Tory clergymen who turned prescriptive theology to the service of a political party in hopes of preferment.

Brougham defended John Ambrose Williams against a libel charge brought in November 1821 by the Durham clergy. As editor of the *Durham Chronicle*, a Whig newspaper supported by Lambton, Williams had denounced their refusal to toll church bells on Queen Caroline's death. His article, published three days after her death on 10 August 1820, described the Durham clergy's denial of the customary sign of mourning as indicative of a general spirit of hypocrisy:

> It is such conduct which renders the very name of our established clergy odious till it stinks in the nostrils; that makes our churches look like dead sepulchers, rather than temples of the living God; that raises up conventicles in every corner, and increases the brood

of wild fanatics and enthusiasts; that causes our beneficed digni-
taries to be regarded as usurpers of their possessions; that deprives
them of all pastoral influence and respect; that in short has left
them no support or prop in the attachment or veneration of the
people. Sensible of the decline of their spiritual and moral influence,
they cling to temporal power, and lose in their officiousness in
political matters, even the semblance of the character of ministers of
religion. It is impossible that such a system can last.[83]

Williams singled out the Durham clergy, which alone had denied
Caroline the customary mark of respect, and he took pains to distin-
guish between the church and the abuses that defaced it. Even so,
James Scarlett, the Attorney-General for the County Palatine of
Durham, obtained a rule on 14 November 1821 authorizing a criminal
proceeding against Williams. After hearing arguments from Scarlett
and Brougham, the Court of King's Bench referred the case to the
Durham assizes in August 1822.

The *Morning Chronicle* perceptively warned that the prosecution
would subject the church to a more severe test than it had experienced
for many years.[84] Williams' charges gained a much wider audience, and
the case drew attention to the clergy's wealth and political influence.
The Times called it 'a fearful thing to see the resources of that highly
endowed cathedral employed against the printer of a provincial
paper'.[85] Brougham later told Creevey that the real issue involved the
much broader question of clerical abuses, and he claimed to have
devoted as much effort to Williams' defence as to that of Queen
Caroline.[86] The Established Church had exceptional authority in the
County Palatine of Durham, but that circumstance was an extreme
version of the usual practices by which Anglican elites kept Dissenters
from effective participation in local government. Religious exclusion
provided a counterpart to political exclusion that had become increasingly controversial. Self-conscious Dissent grew in different areas from
those where the older society remained dominant, and those regions
also were centres of new economic interests that believed themselves
denied the representation merited by their importance.[87] The relationship between religion and political exclusion at the local and national
levels made issues that involved the church all the more pointed.
A Tory critic later charged that securing Williams' acquittal was
secondary to exciting public hostility toward the clergy.[88]

Brougham's speech to the jury conceded nothing except his own
disagreement with aspersions that Williams' article cast on Dissenters.

If upheld, the libel charge would remove from discussion 'all the institutions of the country, whether sacred or secular, and the actions of those who administer them'. Brougham claimed a general right to question both ministers of the church and the foundations of the establishment itself. Only by living up to its calling could the clergy preserve the church's place in the people's hearts. Brougham closed his argument by urging the jury not to render a conviction that would destroy the free press of this country and with it freedom itself.[89]

Brougham's deliberately confrontational defence failed as the jury convicted Williams. The *Morning Chronicle* repeated its earlier insistence that 'natural indignation against persecution and persecutors' would prompt inquiry into abuses in the church. A conviction in the face of Brougham's forceful argument only showed that 'county trials for libel are an absolute mockery' in which juries serve merely as 'a cloak for the judge'. *The Times* accused the Durham clergy of seizing 'an instrument, not of elucidation, but of vengeance', strengthened by the arbitrary way in which juries interpreted the law of libel. Asking whether the church could rest comfortably on such ground, the paper stated that by taking 'opinion, not blind power for their support, [the clergy] must stand or fall by their own facts'.[90]

The prosecution later dropped the case when Brougham moved a rule to show why judgement should not be arrested, but articles on the Williams trial and other church matters in the November *Edinburgh Review* raised the issue again. Sydney Smith attacked an effort by the Bishop of Peterborough to enforce orthodoxy on the clergy of his diocese that only caused complaint and 'provided a stalking horse to bad men for the introduction of revolutionary opinions, mischievous ridicule, and irreligious feelings'.[91] In a harsher article on the Williams case, Brougham reiterated his defence and linked the case with the clergy's general political involvement. The prosecution of Williams, the Durham clergy's electioneering, and Blacow's sermon against Queen Caroline illustrated the degree to which the Established Church set the cultivation of worldly power above its true calling.[92] Brougham challenged the Tory commitment to the Established Church, while bidding for support from its critics. He pressed the Whig argument for general reform of church and state that appealed to provincial Dissenters excluded from both. A writer recognized Brougham's hand in the effort by describing him 'as the leader of an assailing party' rather than a single enemy.[93] Brougham and his supporters shifted the debate to avoid charges of irreligion that had hurt Whigs before, and criticizing church abuses allowed Brougham to appeal for support among

Dissenters while continuing his earlier campaign against corruption and misuse of charitable endowments.

Brougham's leadership in the anti-slavery movement engaged another cause dear to many Dissenters. A Tory writer's description of abolitionism as 'a cause uniting at once the appearance of piety and the reality of faction' underlined the role of politicized Dissent in the campaign.[94] Groups established to oppose the slave trade in the 1780s and 1790s developed extensive networks with committees of correspondence that distributed literature, coordinated policies, and collected evidence. Abolition of the slave trade in 1807 led the movement into quiescence for over a decade by satisfying its primary demand. Criminal law reform drew attention to ending slavery itself after 1818 and revived the coalition that had persisted in skeletal form.

Despite the role played by Whigs like Brougham, Mackintosh, and William Smith, slavery was not a party issue. Whigs saw it as part of a broader reform agenda, while Dissenters, along with some Anglicans like Wilberforce who often sided with the government, viewed slavery instead as an evil to be stopped by political action. Public pressure grew after 1822 with a campaign that brought 225 petitions by late August 1823. The Anti-Slavery Society had 230 correspondents and 800 towns 'in connection'. Women and children took an active part in boycotts of West Indian sugar. Organizing such campaigns built formidable networks in the provinces and gave activists important experience in mobilizing opinion at different levels. Slavery became an issue of growing importance during the 1820s with strong centres of provincial activity that often included members of liberal groups sympathetic to the Whigs like Baines's friends in Yorkshire. Local networks expressed frustration over the lack of progress toward abolition by national leadership, prompting further agitation.[95]

The Smith case in 1824 captured public attention and showed that Brougham remained among the most effective voices against slavery. A military court in Demerara had sentenced Reverend John Smith, an Independent minister sent to the colony in 1816 by the London Missionary Society, for involvement in a slave revolt in 1823. Smith died in prison the next year before an appeal could be made or the sentence executed. Brougham brought the Smith case before the public with an article in the March 1824 *Edinburgh Review* that indicted both the trial and slavery in general. Sir James Mackintosh presented a petition from the London Missionary Society on the Smith case to the House of Commons on 13 April 1824, that drew further attention.[96] The *Morning Chronicle* wrote that a missionary could not read scripture to slaves 'without subjecting himself to the charge of inciting to insurrection'. Slave holders, the paper continued, saw Christianity and slavery as irreconcilable and thus 'looked with a very unfriendly eye on the former'. *The Times* insisted that even the official account made it impossible to believe the charges made against Smith.[97]

Brougham offered a motion on 1 June that expressed the Commons' alarm over Smith's treatment and requested the King to secure 'a just and humane administration of law' in Demerara. His speech outlined the indictment from his March article. Along with denouncing those responsible for Smith's fate, Brougham emphasized the cruel punishment inflicted on rebellious slaves who were either shot on capture or 'torn apart by the lash' with sentences of 600 or 700 strokes. He insisted that authorities had conceded implicitly that converting slaves to Christianity introduced them to freedom. Slavery thus demanded that missionaries like Smith be banished and the slaves be kept in ignorance.[98] Debate on Brougham's motion continued over three nights, and Canning tried to deflect pressure on 11 June by moving the previous question. He complained that Brougham's motion obliged the Commons either to contend 'for the perfection and propriety of every part of the proceedings' in Demerara or to assign Smith 'the honours of a martyr'. The debate had answered every purpose of public justice that could be presently attained and closing the question now would best fulfil the House's duty.[99] Brougham criticized Canning for implicitly stating that blame existed on both sides and trying to avoid the real issue of Smith's unjust conviction. Discussion on a matter like the Smith case meant nothing without a vote 'to promulgate with authority what is admitted to be universally felt'.[100]

Although defeated by 47 votes, Brougham's motion, as he insisted during the debate, drew support from across the political spectrum.[101] *The Times* claimed that the minority included almost everyone distinguished for reputation, public influence, and talent who was not a regular government supporter. A leading article in the *Leeds Mercury*, which covered the debate in detail, saw Canning's tactic as an admission that the allegations in Brougham's motion were correct.[102] Smith's trial, and the circumstances surrounding it, galvanized abolitionist sentiment in Britain. Brougham used it effectively to promote both abolition and his own political reputation. His work publicizing the case enhanced his credentials as a leading opponent of slavery and brought support from the anti-slavery movement's local supporters. By emphasizing Smith's role as a missionary to the slaves and the religious aspects of the case, Brougham again bid for support among Dissenters while challenging the perception of Whig indifference toward religion.

Brougham also took an increasing part in the longstanding debates on Catholic Emancipation that revived in the 1820s, and by 1826 the *Morning Chronicle* likened the measure's opponents to defenders of slavery.[103] Politicians with Irish ties or experience generally led in promoting Catholic Emancipation, a measure with strong support within the government as well as among Whigs and radicals. Brougham only raised the issue directly in 1824, after pledging his support to Daniel O'Connell when he presented a petition on behalf of Irish Catholics.[104] He saw the question as an effective way to divide the government and challenged Canning in early 1825 to show his commitment to Catholic Emancipation by resigning unless the government adopted the policy. Foreshadowing Grey's later attack in 1827, Brougham insisted that Canning's willingness to apply liberal principles to Ireland over his colleagues' opposition marked the real proof of the Foreign Secretary's sincerity. Canning risked little when his colleagues cared more for keeping power than adhering to their principles, and Brougham mocked the idea that Lord Eldon, leader of anti-Catholic diehards, would leave office if Canning forced the question. It was a vain fear, he taunted, as the adoption of liberal policies on financial and foreign matters had not yet brought Eldon's resignation.[105] Catholic Emancipation, which earlier kept the Whigs from office, now became a wedge dividing their Tory opponents.

Althorp urged restraint until the government's intentions on Ireland became clear, but a measure to restrict the Catholic Association Daniel O'Connell had founded in 1823 brought strong Whig opposition.[106] Catholic Emancipation itself tallied closely with Whig opposition to policies of exclusion and monopoly. Specific efforts to suppress the Catholic Association also saw the government resort to special measures of repression beyond the ordinary process of law that Whigs and liberals both opposed.[107] Brougham declared himself the Association's defender and insisted that its members had the same right as any other group to organize, raise funds, and discuss public matters. The real threat arose from the government's failure to assuage Irish grievances. Along with the Whigs, 'every liberal-minded man in the country' supported Catholic Emancipation, and Brougham lamented Canning's membership in a 'cabinet professing a contrary doctrine, not, indeed in name, but certainly in substance and effect'.[108] Persistent anti-Catholicism among the public in England and Wales made gaining support difficult. Whigs claimed that the just demands of toleration and the need to conciliate Ireland made removing Catholic disabilities essential, but many retained a thinly veiled disdain for Catholic doctrines and the church's hierarchy. Noting the priesthood's role in Irish politics, Brougham warned Holland against 'the old error of unnecessarily quarrelling with those whom we must necessarily have for our allies' by criticizing their religion.[109] Coalition building played as great a part in the manner in which Whigs engaged the Catholic question as their sense of justice.

Parliamentary elections remained a central part of Brougham's strategy for broadening Whig support, and he worked hard at building his own interest in Westmorland after 1820. While critics mocked his determination to continue the campaign against the Lowthers, Brougham turned out enough support in 1820 to justify another attempt. Over the next few years, he worked to identify himself with Westmorland through involvement with local groups, including the Mechanics' Institute established in Kendal. Although Brougham's support in the county extended beyond Thanet's personal following, the peer's death in January 1825 inflicted a major setback. Lowther described the new Earl as a shy, reserved man with mild Tory sympathies and thought him likely to remain in France where his brother had died.[110] Thanet's financial support and personal activity had been a major asset before, and it seemed doubtful whether his brother Charles would show an equal commitment. While eventually refusing to abandon Brougham, he provided little support beyond the family's political influence, but keeping that influence alive required money and personal attention that Thanet would not or could not give. Holland told Lansdowne in July 1825 that Brougham's 'Westmorland affairs are in a fine unintelligible confusion'. Where Spaniards likened 'a business awkward to meddle with' to the long war in sixteenth-century Flanders, Holland quipped that '"It is a Westmorland" will be a proverb among electioneers'.[111]

By mid-1825, national attention turned increasingly toward prospects for the next general election. Lowther reported a Whig meeting at Lord Darlington's house in July where Brougham secured his party's support for another Westmorland campaign.[112] The challenge for Liverpool's government involved choosing the most opportune moment to put their case before the country. Social tensions grew in 1826 as the economy declined after several prosperous years. Prices fell sharply in 1825, and the collapse of a speculative boom late that year brought a financial crisis that drew capital out of circulation through a run on banks. Manufacturing stagnated in 1826, and the drop in wages, particularly among textile workers, produced serious hardship and rioting in Lancashire. Tierney had predicted widespread problems in December 1825 that would hurt trade and agriculture over the coming year, and Grey warned of a return to distress as a result of a drop in agricultural rents and monetary instability.[113]

Despite the renewed concern over the economy, the Catholic question dominated the 1826 election. Internal differences on economic policy among both Whigs and ministers made the issue less clear than in earlier years. A measure to end Catholic disabilities passed the Commons on 10 May 1825, and, arguably, only a decisive attack by the Duke of York, the heir presumptive to the throne, had defeated it in the House of Lords on May 18. The fact that Liverpool had virtually conceded the measure before York and a faction of ultra Tory peers blocked it ensured that the question would remain unsettled.[114] Although the consensus in Parliament supported Emancipation, public opinion in England and Wales remained staunchly anti-Catholic. Among large segments of Tory opinion, anti-Catholicism increased in the 1820s, posing difficulties for Canning and other advocates of emancipation.[115] Along with economic questions like reforming the Corn Laws, Catholic Emancipation did more to highlight differences within Liverpool's government than between it and the opposition.

Both the issues at hand and the earlier collapse of the party contest in the House of Commons made the electioneering that slowly began in the Spring of 1826 less party-oriented than it had been in 1818 and 1820. Brougham declared his candidacy on 3 May with a letter written in response to a requisition signed by his leading supporters.[116] He had taken every opportunity over the past year to advertise his support in Westmorland, and publishing the requisition in local and national newspapers provided another chance to convince waverers that he would win. Tory papers like the *Courier* and *New Times* predictably doubted Brougham's prospects and dismissed his candidacy as an act of pique. Although they had delayed an earlier canvass to limit expense, a letter on 13 May announced that both Lowthers would stand.[117] Their committee then stepped up its work in preparation for the candidates' personal canvass.

Brougham's illness and the closing days of the parliamentary session kept him in London, which delayed his personal canvass. On behalf of Brougham's Kendal committee, John Wakefield told freeholders in a published letter that representatives including Tufton, Crackenthorp, and James and William Brougham would soon visit them. A week later, Brougham apologized for the delay in his own arrival and noted that the Lowthers had opened an aggressive canvass 'long before any step whatever could be taken by our friends'. Wakefield also urged freeholders to remain patient and withhold their votes until canvassers visited them.[118] Sustaining enthusiasm, particularly outside Kendal, posed an acute problem. Wordsworth thought the Lowthers had a pronounced lead, and suggested that resident freeholders had turned from Brougham as earlier passions abated and 'the natural ties of interest resumed their power'. The inability of Brougham's friends to cover previous election debts and his ardent public support for Catholic Emancipation also hurt his prospects.[119]

The Catholic question permeated the 1826 election, particularly in Westmorland where the contest pitted ultra Tories against the leading Whig liberal. Lord Lowther and Colonel Lowther circulated a declaration by former supporters of Brougham who had changed their allegiance as a result of his position on the Catholic question. They called upon 'every true Protestant, be he Churchman, Methodist, or Dissenter [to exert] himself for the protection and safeguard of the Protestant interest'. With the aid of the Reverend John Adamthwaite, a former Brougham supporter, Lowther secured 40 signatures for the published version. While not fatal to Brougham's hopes, Lowther expected it to inflict a severe blow.[120] *The Times*, doubtless at Brougham's instigation, dismissed the statement 'as a very knavish fabrication or a gross perversion of the facts'. Many of the seceders, it alleged, had been 'deceived as to the object of the paper which they signed; others never had been or intended to become supporters of the learned gentleman; and of others the names had actually been forged by his enemies!'.[121]

The poll opened in Appleby on 22 June, but only a few freeholders voted since a dispute over the numbers of assessors the Lowthers could employ took up most of the day. With ten and nine votes against Brougham's six, Lord Lowther and Colonel Lowther established an early lead that they sustained throughout the contest. Rioting briefly interrupted polling on Saturday 24 June, but the restoration of order allowed the candidates to address the crowd. Brougham urged his supporters to greater efforts as more friends would join them on Monday. While Lowther partisans might be kept penned like cattle, Brougham praised the Blues for coming to the poll 'as freemen, fairly determined to fight the cause of their country'. Describing the Lowther arrangements to feed and lodge their supporters, Brougham compared them to the Italian witnesses conscripted during Queen Caroline's trial.[122]

After his canvass in late May, Colonel Lowther had earlier predicted a drop in Brougham's support since plebeian voters had disposed of their freeholds and few new ones had been created.[123] Brougham's standing in the poll confirmed the suspicion, and he spent much of Thursday 29 June mustering freeholders in Kendal to make up the difference. On 28 June, the Lowthers had demanded that freeholders take the long oath, which involved abjuring the Pope, to exclude Catholics whose votes previously had been accepted. For his part, Brougham used the bribery oath to dissuade Lowther freeholders. He and supporters bitterly attacked the Lowthers' use of mushroom votes created since 1820.[124] By 30 June, a Lowther agent reported that the party now polled three to one against Brougham, who only kept the poll open to increase his opponents' expenses. The 'mushroom system' Brougham had introduced after the first contest 'has turned quite against him and made him quite crazy'.[125]

Brougham conceded defeat on 30 June, privately complaining that his supporters lost heart as they saw the Lowthers' growing lead. Men who 'would have walked barefoot' to the poll now thought it 'useless contending agt. 1,500 mushrooms & would hardly have come if we had had (as our opponents had) a post chaise for each voter at his door'. Brougham kept the poll open until he matched his total from 1820, and others 'came by chance & of themselves'.[126] The final tally gave him 1,377 votes against 2,097 for Lord Lowther and Colonel Lowther's 2,020. Brougham again received mostly plumpers, splitting only 90 votes with Lord Lowther, while his opponents largely split votes between themselves.[127] The *Kendal Chronicle* denounced Lord Lonsdale for securing his control over the seats by creating mushroom voters and exploiting dependents. The *Manchester Guardian* lamented seeing clergymen 'who should be especially zealous in laying up treasures in heaven, joining with anxious wistfulness the trained bands of those who have the dispensing of treasures on earth'.[128]

Although Brougham's position on the Catholic question did more harm than good, his real problem lay in money and organization. The Lowthers devoted great energy and expense to creating new voters between elections, while Brougham's supporters fell behind as they failed to sustain earlier efforts that had helped them in 1820. Money and organization facilitated Lowther canvassing and provided the transport and hospitality that brought freeholders to the poll. William Vizard, Brougham's solicitor, saw little hope of recovery after 1826, since the Blues could never match Lonsdale's purse. The Lowthers' determination to deny Brougham a Westmorland seat at all costs underlined the point.[129] The 1826 election had cost the Lowthers just under £30,000, while they had paid roughly £25,000 in 1818. Lowther had counselled his father to consider selling a borough seat to meet what he had feared would be an ongoing expense, and his correspondence after the 1826 contest discussed ways to limit future costs.[130]

Despite his failure to win election for Westmorland, Brougham seriously challenged the Lowther interest and put Lord Lonsdale to great expense. Brougham's three campaigns thoroughly politicized Westmorland by questioning the legitimacy of Lonsdale's local hegemony, thereby shifting county politics from a rivalry between aristocratic interests over patronage to an ideologically charged party conflict. A survey of the three Westmorland elections shows consistent party support among freeholders. New voters raised Brougham's total vote between 1818 and 1820 and accounted for 81 per cent of Colonel Lowther's increased margin in 1826. Virulent rhetoric on both sides polarized the electorate, and the Lowther interest's tactics for maintaining their supporters' consistency also hardened their opponents' determination.[131] The novelty of having three successive contested elections alone raised political awareness, and Brougham's reputation and agenda sharpened the effect. By presenting himself as the defender of Westmorland's independence, Brougham attracted a committed local following while adding to his national reputation as an advocate of reform.

The election nationally turned on the Catholic question and local concerns that together produced an inconclusive result. Peel thought there never had been an election less characterized by differences bearing on the government's general policy. Opponents of Catholic Emancipation gained a slight edge in England and Wales, while losing ground in Ireland, and the net outcome favoured the anti-Catholic cause slightly.[132] Economic concerns quickly drove election reports from the newspapers, ending the period of relative calm that had benefited ministers since 1822. Instead of reviving party conflict, however, the political tensions heightened by distress fuelled divisions within the cabinet. Having failed before to drive Liverpool from power, the Whigs had little chance of gaining office without a decisive split among the government and its supporters. Brougham's work to promote a liberal agenda outside Parliament over recent years raised issues that divided ministers while appealing to the Whigs' natural constituency in the county. Whether it would bring the Whigs back to power or simply lead the government to adopt some conciliatory measures to forestall their opponents had become the central question.

6
A Revolution in Parties: 1827–30

Opposition parties in Britain rarely drive governments from office, but rather seize upon an administration's own failure to hold power. The Whigs realized in the late 1820s that they could gain office only after Liverpool's government and the Tory phalanx that sustained it had collapsed. The Tory ascendancy cracked when a stroke on 17 February 1827 left Liverpool 'if not actually, at least politically dead'.[1] The *Morning Chronicle* rightly deemed it 'extremely unlikely that he will ever again submit to the toils and anxieties from which it is understood he has long been anxious to free himself'.[2] The consequent scramble for power revived factionalism among Tories and Whigs alike, throwing politics into confusion for the next several years. Holland shrewdly predicted a 'revolution in parties' that would produce either 'a liberal ministry with an intolerant court opposition, or an intolerant court ministry with a liberal opposition'.[3] Brougham urged coalition with Canning to secure a liberal government, but Grey opposed a union he thought inconsistent with Whig principles. Differences thus emerged among Whigs just as the Tories fell into their own factional quarrels.

The opportunities Liverpool's stroke opened for the Whigs raised difficult questions. How far could the Whigs compromise their principles or accept the role of junior partners in a coalition? Balancing tactical decisions with a broader strategic effort sparked bitter disputes. Brougham favoured short-term compromises with George Canning and his successor Lord Goderich that he believed would allow Whigs gradually to dominate the coalition, and even draw the Canningites into their own ranks. Regardless of how offices might be apportioned within a coalition, Brougham thought public sentiment would give the Whigs a dominant role in policy. Some Whigs who supported coalition saw the situation in an earlier political context where parties bid for support from factions to secure a majority in the Commons. Grey and other critics of the coalition, however, thought the Whigs would lose by associating with Canning. They feared that a compromise in principle would diminish their public standing. The situation in 1827 appeared to resemble earlier overtures in 1809 and 1812 that had aimed at securing Whig support for Tory measures, and Grey again objected to the prospect of sustaining one or other Tory faction in office. These quarrels among the Whigs had a deep effect on Brougham's later standing within the party and on politics generally.

Liverpool's unassailable position in Parliament after 1822 had not hidden tensions within his government completely. Divisions went beyond the delicate balance maintained between supporters and opponents of Catholic Emancipation. Canning's sharp wit, along with old animosities and current suspicions about his influence over Liverpool, alienated cabinet colleagues, and Huskisson aroused feelings bordering on hatred within both the government and among the Tory press. Canning's eagerness to cultivate public opinion as Brougham long had done by 'going round the country *speechifying* & discussing the acts & intentions of the govt.' irritated both colleagues and the court.[4] While siding with ultra Tories on the Catholic question, Liverpool had supported Canning against Wellington on foreign policy and he promoted economic reforms associated with Huskisson and Frederick Robinson, the future Lord Goderich. The abandonment of legitimist diplomacy and mercantilist financial and commercial policies had outraged many high or ultra Tories no less than the cabinet's neutrality on Catholic Emancipation and threats that neutrality might give way to open support. Internal conflicts in 1824, and more seriously in 1825 and early 1826, threatened to break up the administration.[5] Liverpool's political management and his ability to bridge factional differences made him hard to replace. Croker warned in 1824 that Liverpool's retirement would produce 'what is vulgarly called a blow-up', and events in 1827 proved him right.[6]

Observers had predicted a Canningite overture to Lansdowne and other leading Whigs even before Liverpool's stroke. Holland told Grey in September 1825 that Lansdowne agreed more with 'Huskisson & etc.' on foreign and trade policy, particularly reforming the Corn Laws, than 'with you & I who do not care about or perhaps understand such matters so much & well'.[7] Their indifference to economic questions indicates a serious problem that Whigs had faced in appealing beyond the aristocratic world of metropolitan politics and engaging new interests in the country. Grey laid the basis for future events in February 1826, when he informed Lansdowne that he wished to step aside and now looked to the younger Whig peer 'as the person best qualified to undertake the direction of the party'.[8] The Whigs thus entered 1827 without clearly defined leadership.

Brougham's behaviour also prompted speculation. Canning had privately expressed his appreciation early in 1826 for Whig support, naming Brougham specifically, and Lord John Russell had remarked on Brougham's 'moderate and conciliatory' tone.[9] Brougham's personal attacks on George IV since 1812 and his part in defending Queen Caroline made it unlikely the King would tolerate his appointment to office. Still, Brougham saw Canning as a wedge to split the Tory party and implement a Whig agenda by stealth. Lansdowne and others also wished to pull Canning in a liberal direction. Brougham used his influence with *The Times* to suggest on February 20 that

> from the general principle of liberality evinced by Mr. Canning...a union with the Marquess of Lansdowne might be accomplished, that gentleman stipulating only for ministerial support of the Catholic question, and not requiring the admission of many of his friends as a *sine qua non*. His friends also, it is said, that is the Whigs as a body, are ready to make this sacrifice of personal aggrandizement to public principle.[10]

A few days later Brougham told Holland's advisor John Allen that the Whigs had long 'suffered [Canning] & his part of the govt when we could have turned them out or left them to the mercies of their colleagues of the Ultra persuasion'. If Canning chose to play 'the shabby game of place hunting and consents to a divided and neutralized government', Brougham then urged the formation of a tight body of the opposition to continue their pressure on the 'illiberal' part of the government. Such a policy would neither unite the government nor deprive Whigs of votes from radicals or passive members of their own party.[11] Instead, it would force Canning to rely on support from Whig liberals.

Peel and Canning advised George IV to delay any changes involving the appointment of a new Prime Minister before controversial votes on Catholic Emancipation and the Corn Laws. A delay in settling the government's leadership seemed advantageous for the first few weeks of the 1827 parliamentary session that had opened in February. During a brief rally of lucidity on 23 March, Liverpool asked who had succeeded him and then told his wife that he could never resume the burdens of office.[12] With no reliable knowledge of changes in the government, Tierney proposed on 30 March that funds be withheld until the Commons knew who would be Prime Minister.[13] Although Tierney's motion failed by 153 votes, Canning told the King that Peel and Robinson agreed that the leadership must now be settled promptly. *The Times* concluded that Canning would soon be named as Liverpool's successor, but questioned whether his ultra colleagues would accept the appointment.[14]

George IV delayed selecting a Prime Minister during the first week of April. Appointing Canning to form a government on the same principles as Liverpool's with those cabinet members who chose to stay while leaving him to replace others who left, seemed the best way of preserving continuity. Stephen Lushington, a government whip in the Commons, saw the alternatives as either an exclusively Protestant government of mediocre men led by Peel, or a coalition of Whigs and Tories committed to Catholic Emancipation.[15] Canning insisted on having either the premiership or its substance under the nominal leadership of a sympathetic peer, while Peel concluded that he could not serve under a premier committed to Catholic Emancipation regardless of whether or not the cabinet remained neutral on the question. On 9 April 1827, Canning rejected the proposition that he and Peel serve under Wellington. George IV summoned Canning to form a government the next day, and his appointment prompted a substantial number of ministers to resign along with Peel and Wellington.[16]

The refusal of so many members of Liverpool's government to serve under Canning made an overture to the Whigs inevitable, and Brougham played a major part in establishing the coalition. Before leaving London in early March for legal business on the Northern Circuit, Brougham told Sir Robert Wilson that he expected Canning to become Prime Minister with Whig support and he would not impede the junction by demanding office for himself.[17] Rumours that Canning would compromise with the ultras to gain office led Brougham to warn Wilson that those Whigs otherwise disposed to aid Canning would bitterly oppose him if he took office under such circumstances. Wilson forwarded the message to Canning through intermediaries and requested a subsequent letter from Brougham that he could give Canning.[18] Brougham replied that such earlier feelings of distrust for Canning as persisted among the Whigs would end once the party was 'thoroughly convinced he is disposed to risk what he ought in order to do his duty and obtain his just rights'. Insisting that his only interest was to secure 'government on liberal & moderate principles', Brougham pledged his support without any demands for office that would excite the King's prejudices against him.[19]

Wilson forwarded Brougham's letter to Canning, having informed Lansdowne of its sentiments and his own activity. Lansdowne replied that it confirmed Brougham's earlier conversations with him and conformed perfectly with his own views.[20] Canning used Brougham's letter to convince George IV on 10 April 1827 that he could form a government without Peel or Wellington. According to the diarist Charles Greville, Canning told the King, 'your Father broke the domination of the Whigs; I hope Y[our] M[ajesty] will not endure that of the Tories'. George IV predictably replied, ' No, I'll be damned if I do'.[21]

Canning approached the Duke of Devonshire and Lord Carlisle on 12 April in hopes of gaining the support of individual Whigs without the compromises entailed in a coalition.[22] The two peers favoured Whig support for Canning's administration, but deferred the question to Lansdowne, who met with Canning on 19 April 1827. After meeting with Brougham, Darlington urged Lansdowne not to allow personal dislike of Canning among Whigs to hinder a coalition that would benefit the country and tend strongly to promote their general political views.[23] Brougham warned Lansdowne that the ultras may recover 'from their very unusual fit of resignation, and if we have in the meantime been cold or thrown impediments in Canning's way, he may be driven to take them back'.[24] Croker indeed told his friend Lord Lowther, who stood on the brink of resigning, that Canning's appointment of pro-Catholics would be 'not his fault, but yours'.[25]

Holland took a more circumspect view than Brougham, urging Lansdowne to secure some commitment from Canning on the Catholic question to avoid a misunderstanding later that would break up the government.[26] A substantial group of other Whigs, including Althorp and Lord Tavistock, opposed a formal junction with Canning, but offered support for his general policy from the opposition benches. Grey emphatically rejected any thought of a coalition with a government constituted on the same basis regarding the Catholic question as Liverpool's. He believed the appointment of John Singleton Copley, an opponent of Emancipation, as Lord Chancellor indicated the cabinet's true character. Grey further regarded Canning's offer of a few cabinet places without the leadership of the House of Lords as insulting to Lansdowne.[27]

The Catholic question, and Irish appointments in particular, posed the main barrier to an agreement. Conscious of Whig differences with

142

Illustration 6.1 'The Three Georges—The Patron—The Sovereign—and the Patriot' by GW depicts St George, George IV, and George Canning as the king's champion slaying the dragon of Tory conspiracy whose heads feature Wellington and Eldon. A group of Whigs in the background declare their readiness to offer support. Reproduced with kind permission of the British Museum.

Canning over parliamentary reform and repealing the Test and Corporation Acts, Lansdowne took great care to avoid concessions that would damage either his or the Whigs' credibility. He also faced pressure to gain an appropriate share of government patronage. Those factors made Lansdowne very hesitant in accepting Canning's terms. The new cabinet's balance of opinion rendered meaningless Canning's pledge to George IV that he would discourage further parliamentary debate of the Catholic question and keep the cabinet officially neutral on the issue as it had been under Liverpool.[28] Lansdowne sought the appointment of an Irish administration favouring Catholic Emancipation as a sign of the government's future intentions. Canning resisted on the grounds it would upset relations with the King by forcing an added concession, and talks ended on 20 April 1827.

Brougham had complained earlier that day to Althorp that by insisting on minor points Lansdowne would bring back the ultras and preclude a solution to the Catholic question.[29] When news arrived from Lansdowne House, Brougham and Wilson organized a Whig meeting at Brooks's Club. The situation aroused Brougham's long-standing resentment over the idea that the Whig party was merely the creature of a few aristocratic families. As he later told Jack Campbell with more than a little vanity, 'my support in the House of Commons is of much more consequence than Lansdowne's in the House of Lords', and Lord Dudley reported to Canning that most Whigs in the Commons followed Brougham's view.[30] In presenting Canning's terms and Lansdowne's offer before the Whigs at Brooks's club, Brougham spoke in terms calculated 'to make the very stones mutiny', and the meeting essentially deprived Lansdowne of the party leadership. Lord Essex complained to Wilson that questions raised about forming a government had ended 'in a few individuals meeting at a club to settle a business of this nature', when residences of Whig nobles such as 'Devonshire House, Bedford House, and Lansdowne of Burlington House...are the places where men of high principles and character should be assembled to advise their sovereign of matters in which the country is so deeply involved'.[31] Other Whigs who had not been at Brooks's shared Brougham's view, however, and Lansdowne complained of being overwhelmed with letters reproaching his terms regarding the Irish government. The much harassed marquess agreed to a renewal of talks before leaving London for his country estate at Bowood.[32]

Devonshire and Carlisle again met with Canning on 21 April 1827, and a subsequent meeting between Canning and Lansdowne on 27 April brought a tentative agreement. Lansdowne had waived his insistence on a pro-Catholic Lord Lieutenant in Ireland, and William Lamb's appointment as Chief Secretary helped resolve the issue. Under the provisional arrangement of 27 April, Devonshire and James Scarlett, the Whig lawyer, agreed to take office immediately, while Lansdowne, Carlisle, and Tierney would support the government independently until they joined the cabinet after the parliamentary session closed. Tensions between Canning and the Whigs brought changes on 9 May when Lansdowne moved earlier than expected to join the cabinet, without portfolio, along with Carlisle and Tierney, in an effort to assuage Whig concerns. After Parliament had been prorogued in early July, Lansdowne became Home Secretary and other appointments completed Canning's government.[33]

Brougham had promoted the coalition through *The Times* in the weeks before the 27 April agreement. After the ultras resigned as a group, *The Times* described the consequent junction between Canning and the Whigs as 'so apposite and natural, that we are surprised it has not already been cemented'. It later attributed delays to 'the indifference of moderate Whigs to place, and the aversion of the more ardent ones to it' without Catholic Emancipation.[34] The *Morning Chronicle*, whose editor had been amazed on 11 April 1827 that 'seven seats in the cabinet remained empty because no one would accept of them', also backed the coalition. It later warned against the folly of fastidiously withholding support so as to weaken those who would do good, albeit less good than might be wished.[35] Leading provincial papers sympathetic to the Whigs, notably the *Leeds Mercury* and *Manchester Guardian*, echoed their metropolitan counterparts, and much of the party fell in line behind Lansdowne and Brougham. Coalition, they thought, provided the best way to exclude ultra Tories and guarantee a continuation of liberal commercial and foreign policies.[36]

Serious differences persisted on whether and to what degree Whigs should support Canning. Brougham's argument for curtailing ultra influence by doing 'anything to lock the door for ever on Eldon and Co.' led many Whigs to join Canning's government by taking office or simply declaring their adherence.[37] Others saw the coalition as a violation of principle that would break up the Whig party. The arrangement with Canning conceded points that Grey, with general Whig support, had previously considered essential to taking office. This was no small matter for a party that under Fox had defined itself in terms of honourable commitment to principle regardless of the immediate political cost. In so far as it compromised principles that had defined the Whigs as a party, the coalition threatened to lead them into factionalism based on patronage and personalities. While few in the party took as extreme a view against the coalition as Grey, many who finally supported it raised such concerns.

A substantial group of younger Whigs led by Althorp and Milton declined to join a government not wholly committed to Whig principles. They shared Lord Tavistock's view that 'principle alone is the test of men and parties' and thus sought to preserve a strong opposition party.[38] Despite his willingness to support Canning's government, Althorp doubted that Whigs should join any government unless it were formed on 'principles of civil & religious liberty'.[39] Such principles demanded a firm commitment to Catholic Emancipation and repeal of the Test and Corporation Acts. Even so, Althorp crossed the House on 7 May and announced his support for Canning's government on the ground that 'we must choose between a government actuated by liberal and enlightened principles, and one of Toryism in its most odious forms'.[40] That support remained qualified, since Althorp would not bend on principle and mainly sought to hold the Whigs together while keeping the ultras out of power. Althorp and Milton called their group the 'Watchmen', signifying their role as custodians of Whig principles as well as the oversight function of an opposition party, but others described the larger body of Whigs who to varying degrees resisted coalition as 'malignants'.[41]

Lansdowne had clearly piqued Grey by having taken his oft-stated desire of giving up politics at face value and stepped forward as party leader in talks with Canning. Brougham had reminded Lansdowne that Grey's expressions were 'almost annuals' soon forgotten as his spirit revived.[42] However, Grey's deep contempt toward Canning and his fear that the Whigs only would suffer as junior partners of a coalition underlay his intense resistance to the coalition Lansdowne and Brougham had made. He had resisted suggestions by Tierney and Grenville that the Whigs seek support from Canning's faction in 1812 as an alternative to Whitbread's Mountain. Grey's comment that he 'regarded the son of an actress as incapacitated *de facto* for the Premiership of England' underlined the personal distaste for Canning his letters had shown over the past decade. James Abercrombie, who declared himself no defender of Canning, criticized Grey's efforts 'to run down Canning' and 'deprecate him or any other man by vilifying his parentage and reproaching him with the frailties of his mother'.[43] More than personality lay at stake here given the Whigs' preoccupation with questions of honour and consistency. Grey thought Canning the least trustworthy public man of the day, and his experience with Portland and Perceval had led Grey to assume that a coalition would only implicate the Whigs in policies they would otherwise oppose and limit their subsequent flexibility. Cooperation would require strong assurances, and Grey insisted that 'nothing will satisfy me that Canning is sincere and in earnest but his bringing forth [Catholic Emancipation] and staking his power upon it'.[44]

Grey told the House of Lords on 10 May 1827 that he could not risk his character and honour by serving in a government under Canning's lead. Separation from friends 'with whom I have acted throughout the whole of my political life' pained Grey, but 'the exclusion of the Catholic question as a measure of government' precluded his own adherence without betraying the principles on which he had acted since 1807. Grey dissected Canning's record mercilessly, denying that he deserved 'exclusive praise for any act of the late administration'. The possibility that Canning himself, rather than indiscreet friends, had contrasted his record with that of his fellow Tories would only confirm Grey's deep suspicions about Canning's character. With the exception of Catholic Emancipation, Canning had backed his party in undermining civil and religious liberty, and Grey judged his foreign policy a complete failure in abandoning Spain to France. Far from signalling a liberal dawn, the new political alignments had left Grey to pronounce himself 'almost without political connections' beyond adherence to those principles that had guided his career.[45]

Grey's speech drew cheers from the Lords and created a sensation that, according to rumour, led Canning to contemplate accepting a peerage in order to answer Grey's charges personally. Although the Duke of Bedford, Lord George Cavendish, and Creevey joined Grey, he found little further support.[46] The *Leeds Mercury* insisted that Canning deserved praise as the foe of bigotry and illiberality, and the *Morning Chronicle* questioned whether Grey's principles were well-served by perpetuating the recollections of former times or binding public men to past opinions.[47] Holland set out his own position in support of Canning the week after Grey's speech, and he remarked in response to Tory attacks on Canning that 'he considered it derogatory to the dignity of the house and injurious to the service of the country for public men to be flinging dirt at one another'.[48] Grey's offence at Holland's words prompted a break of several months in their correspondence, and the situation also strained Grey's ties with Brougham and Lansdowne.

Part of the disagreement between Grey and Brougham lay in their views of coalition. Grey saw a true coalition as involving more than the appointment of a few Whigs to strengthen a Canningite ministry; he demanded a partnership in which the Whigs received a greater proportion of both power and patronage than Canning offered. Alignments within Parliament and at the court were a paramount consideration for Grey who believed the party must be seen openly to have a leading role. Like the Rockingham Whigs of the early 1780s, he insisted that the King openly accept Whig men and measures before joining Canning. Where Grey focused on the composition of the government, Brougham looked to public sentiment for the framework in which the government could operate. Grey's very Foxite concern with principle as the foundation of public reputation neglected what Brougham saw as the degree to which outside pressure could substitute for formal conditions on taking office. He criticized 'the great men of 1782, [i.e. Fox, Burke, and Sheridan] who preferred saving their party & personal honour' to accepting a junior role under Pitt and Shelburne, and who then turned instead to a coalition with their opponent Lord North. He complained to Allen that the Whigs' unwillingness to mute their pride and shape policy from within a government by taking office had blighted the party's chances for power. The current political situation had rendered old names and associations useless, and Brougham thought the Whigs' future lay in promoting a liberal agenda through Canning's ministry.[49]

Like many other Whigs, including the Watchmen, Grey doubted Brougham's professions of disinterest. Ambition and a reputation for sharp dealing had caught up with him. Brougham spoke of defending Canning from his 'hill fort', as he called the place on the back benches from which Pitt had given Addington's government support. Later in August, Brougham told Holland that his legal career prevented him from taking any offices besides professional law appointments.[50] George IV's refusal to accept Brougham in office was widely known. The insistent tone in which *The Times* and the *Morning Chronicle* stated that Brougham 'placed his motives out of the question' by refusing any appointment, and his portrayal in a caricature depicting Canning as 'Diogenes in Search of an Honest Ministry', however, deceived few in Westminster.[51] Brougham's constant pressure on Canning, along with demands for patronage from other Whigs, placed great strains on the new government. Pestered by Brougham's friends, Canning exclaimed on one occasion, 'Damn him, he shall have my place'.[52] Privately, Brougham expressed great dismay that Scarlett received the Attorney Generalship

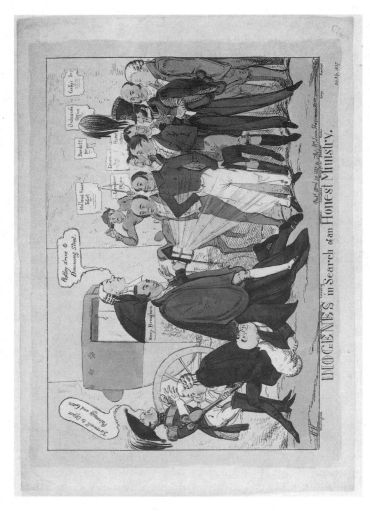

Illustration 6.2   Canning depicted as Diogenes stepping over Eldon and leaving Wellington behind to seek an honest ministry amongst Lansdowne and other Whigs with Brougham's aid. Reproduced with kind permission of the British Museum.

rather than himself. Copley's appointment as Lord Chancellor angered Brougham more because it filled an office he sought than for the Tory's opposition to Catholic Emancipation. Brougham's desire to receive the Mastership of the Rolls, a legal appointment that provided a permanent salary and would allow him to stay in the Commons, became an open secret.

Brougham won a promotion at the bar on 23 May 1827 that solved a problem on the Northern Circuit where senior lawyers could not serve as junior counsel to the more popular Brougham. Where a King's Counsel would have a salary that would require an MP to stand for re-election, Brougham's promotion merely restored the rank he briefly had enjoyed in 1820 as Queen Caroline's attorney. More importantly, it did not require Brougham to receive the appointment directly from the King.[53] Brougham's supposed venality and undisguised ambition had long been a theme for caricaturists, and prints entitled 'Disposing of the Old Stuff' and 'The Broom Sold' portrayed the appointment as a reward for Brougham's work in securing the coalition. Another cartoon depicting Canning distributing the 'Loaves and Fishes' to eager Whig coalitionists made the point more broadly, but the Whigs gained far less patronage than they sought.[54]

Attitudes toward Brougham at Westminster differed sharply from his reputation in the country at large, and this gap had a growing impact on his public role over coming years. Where political allies and opponents alike often saw Brougham as a gifted pest, leaders of provincial opinion praised him as the principal advocate of reform. The *Leeds Mercury*'s chiding of Lord Grey contrasted with its praise for Brougham as a founder of the coalition; Brougham's long efforts to cultivate support among journalists and editors had paid handsome returns. He responded to critics in a widely reported speech in Liverpool on 18 June 1827. Brougham insisted that the basis of Canning's government could not be compared to that of the Fox–North coalition of 1784 since no personal hostilities existed between Canning and his Whig allies, and only on parliamentary reform did they differ. Great public questions had drawn Canningites and Whigs together to marginalize the old Tory regime.[55] Brougham implicitly replied here to Grey's speech before the Lords, and by speaking in the city where he had made his reputation as a public tribune against the Orders in Council he underlined the differences in their views of politics. The *Manchester Guardian* joined the *Leeds Mercury* and other papers in praising Brougham's vindication of his and other Whigs' support for Canning.[56] As part of its report, the *Liverpool Mercury* noted that

150

Illustration 6.3 Brougham's promotion at the bar portrayed in caricature as his reward for securing the coalition, 1827. Reproduced with kind permission of the British Museum.

Brougham's adherence to the ministry placed him in a strong position to promote reform by ending the government's opposition to measures it previously blocked. Remaining out of office had done little to diminish Brougham's standing in the provinces.

The coalition was weaker than Brougham acknowledged, however, and disagreements over patronage contributed to its difficulties. Although secure from opposition in the Commons, the House of Lords' rejection of legislation to modify the Corn Laws brought an embarrassing defeat from an alliance of ultras and Whig malignants. Canning's death on August 8 threatened to throw the administration further into turmoil. Croker thought the King would choose Wellington as Canning's successor, a move that would end Lansdowne's further participation in the government and reunite the Tories.[57] George IV preferred to keep the government together, however, partly from his irritation with the Tories who had resigned rather than serve under Canning, and conditionally offered Goderich, formerly Frederick Robinson, the premiership. Despite the King's effort to proscribe discussion of the Catholic question, the cabinet insisted that it remain open as it had done under Liverpool and Canning.[58]

Deciding on appointments caused much more trouble, and George IV's refusal to allow further Whig appointments added to the strain. While denying any personal objections to Lord Holland, the King refused his nomination as Foreign Secretary to prevent the Government from taking on the label or appearance of a Whig administration. Such a change, George IV insisted, would be fatal to the ministry's stability and contrary to his own principles.[59] The coalition Whigs saw Holland's admission to the cabinet as a test of their influence. The degree of Whig power had been a matter of secondary importance under Canning since they trusted that he would assert and maintain their shared opinions effectively. But under Goderich's weaker lead, many of them now saw cabinet appointments and the consequent distribution of power as vital issues.[60]

The nomination of John Charles Herries, a Treasury official under Liverpool and known opponent of Catholic Emancipation, as Chancellor of the Exchequer seemed a calculated affront. Rumours that Herries had made a fortune by trading on privileged information and his ties with the Rothschilds only raised Whig suspicions and prompted a cabinet revolt in mid-August. Holland, who had long warned Lansdowne to pay close attention to the division of patronage, pronounced Herries unacceptable as a court favourite unconnected with Whigs or Canningites. Radicals and Whig aristocrats aligned with

Grey would join in viewing 'every item proposed by Mr Herries as if it came from a Tory government'. Holland later insisted on 'the utter impossibility of undertaking the business of government in the [Commons] with a finance minister, whose views & principles are unknown to you, & who does not possess the confidence of those upon whose support you mainly rely'.[61] Tierney complained that the appointment exposed the Whigs to censure regardless of their response; staying in the cabinet with Herries would be called a disgraceful abandonment of principle, while resigning would break up the government and let in the Tories.[62]

Brougham sought to preserve the coalition and counselled Lansdowne against resigning over Herries's appointment. Despite his own objections to Herries, Brougham pointed out the difference between trying to block his appointment and breaking up the government rather than accepting it. As he told Abercrombie in a letter forwarded to Lansdowne, avoiding a conflict that would split the government made it more likely that cooperation in office would forge a bond able to sustain a liberal opposition were they driven out later by the Tories.[63] Several attempts to substitute Tierney, Sturgis Bourne, or Lord Palmerston for Herries failed as the King insisted on the appointment. Huskisson and Goderich tried to conciliate Lansdowne, and George IV requested that Lansdowne remain in office as a personal favour.[64]

By demonstrating Goderich's weakness and inability to manage either the King or his cabinet colleagues, the dispute over cabinet appointments foreshadowed the government's collapse in January 1828. While unable to get Holland in or keep Herries out, Lansdowne forced Goderich to give the Whigs several junior offices, honours, and promotions in the peerage. These concessions did not prevent Althrop from comparing the Whigs' position in the government with that of Charles Wynn and the other Grenvillites who earlier had joined Liverpool's cabinet without gaining much place or power. Convinced that he should remain in a state of 'armed neutrality', Althorp thought the coalition Whigs had fatally compromised themselves over Herries's appointment.[65] Grey had predicted in August that a Tory government would soon 'be re-established on its own principles, and almost in its old form' by those Whigs who had forged the coalition only to find themselves compelled to resign in embarrassment. The greatest evil Grey saw at present would be 'the dissolution of the Whig party and the total destruction of its consequence and character'.[66] Lord Rosslyn chided Brougham in October that his influence had only brought arrangements that 'indicated a feeling most hostile to the Catholic question, and adverse to all the expectations which were held out when our friends took office'.[67]

Brougham's stock within the Whig party fell as the coalition he had worked so hard to promote failed. His primary support now lay beyond Westminster among provincial liberals and the press. Goderich told George IV on 8 January 1828 that the cabinet was fatally divided, and the King placed Wellington at the head of a Tory administration that included Canningites, with Peel leading the Commons. Although Brougham had gauged national opinion correctly in the October *Edinburgh Review*, the government's weakness rendered impossible the joint appeal to liberal sentiment by Whigs and Canningites that he had urged.[68] Press and politicians alike saw him as 'the matchmaker between Whigs and Tories', and critics attacked his manoeuvres as a bid for power.[69] Whig defenders of the coalition themselves blamed Grey and Althorp for not aiding Lansdowne, but Brougham drew greater criticism for pressing a policy that had split the party. Differences over tactics had become questions of principle to the detriment of Brougham and Lansdowne. Althorp noted the animosities of the past year with his earnest hope in January 1828 that party feelings would return to where they had been before the coalition damaged the Whigs' public reputation.[70]

A quarrel between Brougham and Grey provided another case where Brougham's recklessness undermined his standing within the party. At first unwilling to widen any breach with Grey, Brougham had complained to Lansdowne in October 1827:

> that Lord Grey's ground of difference resolves itself into the Government being popular and consulting public opinion instead of the feelings of the aristocracy, which he thinks requires support and is resolved to stand by as against the government...it is really as if he had taken up his own party expression of 'his order', and was determined to make it his creed merely because it was attacked.[71]

Brougham gave a conversation between Grey and Darlington, recently created Marquess of Cleveland, as the authority for a claim that the tenor of Grey's personal attacks on Canning seemed to confirm. Grey's opposition to Brougham's popular line in 1827 revived memories of Whig opposition to his tactics during the campaign against the Orders in Council and the Liverpool election in 1812. After an exchange of letters in which Cleveland and Brougham denied any ill intent, Grey declared the case closed and resumed his relationship with Brougham on the same terms as before. Talk of the quarrel among Whigs, however, revived doubts about Brougham's character and led many, including Grey and Creevey, to think him mad.[72]

Although the failure of the Canning and Goderich ministries frustrated Brougham's plans, he continued efforts to promote a liberal reform agenda that would shift the political scene to his party's advantage. The Whigs entered the 1828 parliamentary session as divided as they had been between 1808 and 1812, when conflicts between Foxites, Grenvillites, and Whitbread's Mountain blunted the effectiveness of their opposition. Without an accepted leader in either Lords or Commons, the party adopted a cautious policy of 'armed neutrality' designed to promote liberal policies through an offer of qualified support. The *Courier* greeted Wellington's premiership as a reunion of the old Pittite party and reminded its readers that 'the school of Fox' had never lost its 'original taint of reckless innovation' and after its recent disappointment would resume 'the true *feu d'enfer* colouring'.[73] Some observers saw Canningite participation in the government, along with the exclusion of ultra Tories like Eldon, as a sign of its intentions. Commenting on Wellington's 'mixed and speckled cabinet', the *Times* called for a 'strict though watchful forbearance' until its character could be known.[74] The absence from the House of Commons of ministers forced to stand for re-election as a consequence of their appointment to office delayed a clear reading of the new scene. Speaking on the reply to the King's address, Brougham warned that 'he looked not to the members of the Administration, but to their measures'; if those measures were good, the government would have his firm support.[75] Though other Whigs rejected Brougham's pretensions as a party leader in the Commons, they largely shared his cautious approach to the new government.

Factional divisions that prevented the Whigs from offering themselves as a credible alternative underlined the apparent strength of Wellington's government. The absence of a concerted opposition made the new government's position seem more secure than later events soon would prove. Ministers could not foresee where they might find support or what issues would divide them.[76] The issues that finally arose in 1828–30 drew the Whigs back together as they drove Tories further apart. Moreover, those questions engaged core Whig principles that provided common ground with provincial liberals.

Demands for a repeal of the Test and Corporation Acts that excluded Dissenters from public office gave the Whigs an issue calculated to draw them together after the divisions of the past year and place the government in an awkward position. Lord John Russell gave notice for a motion to address the question on 26 February, and supporters outside Parliament paved the way with petitions and meetings. By separating their cause from Catholic Emancipation, the Dissenters' United Committee blunted resistance from Tory defenders of the Established Church. John Smith denied cooperation between Catholics and Dissenters to obtain relief when presenting a petition on 4 February, and William Smith, chairman of the Dissenter deputies and a Whig member of Whitbread's Mountain, reiterated the point two days later.[77]

Russell explicitly denounced the use of any religious test and insisted that no practical grounds existed for excluding Dissenters from public office. His motion for a committee to consider a measure to repeal the Test and Corporation Acts faced hesitant government opposition. In a speech punctuated by jeering and derision, Huskisson argued that repeal would impede settlement of the Catholic question. He furthermore thought it revolting to continue the disqualification of the first duke of the realm, the Catholic Duke of Norfolk, while removing impediments on Dissenters. Peel dismissed the claim that Dissenters faced an undue burden since an Indemnity Act made the law a dead letter. The petitions recently generated in favour of Russell's motion demonstrated effective organization by a few Dissenters rather than the real sense of public opinion. Peel, however, differed with Huskisson and other Canningites in fearing repeal would encourage a renewed assault on Catholic disabilities.[78]

The strongest opposition came from backbench ultra Tories, led by Sir Robert Inglis, who reacted jealously to any encroachment on the Established Church's prerogatives. Religious toleration permitted other forms of trinitarian Christian worship, but it did not require placing all sects on the same footing with the Church of England or admitting Dissenters to political power. What ultras viewed as the equalization of privilege among Dissenters and Churchmen touched on sensitive constitutional questions involving representation. Defenders viewed agitation for repeal as a clear bid to overthrow the Anglican ascendancy. The *New Times* spoke for Russell's strongest critics when it criticized a motion designed to overthrow 'one of the bulwarks of our establishment' and concluded that, unless a clear infringement on religious freedom could be shown, '*the point where concession must end has been attained*; YOU PASS NO FURTHER'.[79]

Brougham closed the debate with a speech that reiterated his earlier arguments during the Durham clergy case and in *Edinburgh Review* articles on the Established Church. Borrowing Canning's phrase, Brougham asked whether it was no grievance 'to have the mark of the chain remaining, although the fetter itself may have been knocked away?' Adherents of one faith had no moral right to exclude others on the grounds of their beliefs, and evading the law or using indemnity acts to mitigate its effects provided no relief. Even were the practical effects removed, which Brougham denied, Dissenters still had a real grievance:

> Is the stigma nothing? Is it nothing that a Dissenter, wherever he goes, is looked on, and treated as an inferior person to a Churchman? ...Is it nothing to be thus degraded by law and insulted as a body? Is it nothing, even, that the hon. baronet [Peel] should say, as he has said this night 'we will allow you to do so and so?' What is it that gives the hon. baronet the title to use this language...but that the law encourages and entitles him to use it.[80]

The law allowed political participation by Dissenters on sufferance, and the possibility that sufferance might be denied and the Test and Corporation Acts enforced once more added real injury to insult. Brougham rejected the supposition that the church required safeguards beyond its own good works and doctrine, which alone would cement popular attachment and reverence. The only point at issue was whether the Test and Corporation Acts were a sufficient evil to merit parliamentary action. Brougham significantly ended his speech by admitting that penalties against Catholics imposed a far greater burden than disabilities imposed on Dissenters. The principle at the core of his argument also justified Catholic Emancipation, and Brougham would have preferred to see the Catholic question settled first.[81]

Lord John Russell's motion passed by 44 votes with 237 in favour and 193 against. The listing of both the majority and minority when usually only those voting against were given by name underlined the importance of the division.[82] *The Times*, which pointed out the conflict between Peel and Huskisson, described the vote as a thundering event. Following Brougham's line it lamented that Catholic Emancipation had not been carried first and warned against casting the question in party terms. The *Leeds Mercury* argued that government efforts to rally supporters against the measure and cooperation, however awkward, between Peel and liberal Tories led by Huskisson rendered the triumph even greater.[83] Although the vote had only been for a committee to consider repeal legislation, Peel's decision to concede the measure made its passage inevitable. A declaration that the powers of office would not be used to subvert the

Established Church replaced the Test and Corporation Acts in March 1828 at Peel's urging, largely to spare bishops the embarrassment of having conceded openly the church's position in the state.[84]

As Whigs united around a question of principle central to their political identity, the government and its Tory supporters quarrelled. Repealing the Test and Corporation Acts alienated ultras as previous conflicts on other issues had divided Canningites from the core of the government's supporters. Efforts to maintain unity while deflecting the issue only brought charges of inconsistency. The *Leeds Mercury* charged Huskisson with sacrificing his principles to retain a place within Wellington's ministry.[85] Peel, according to the *Morning Chronicle*, resembled an Italian actor obliged to play both the *Doctor* and *Pantaloon*. 'With the same grave air, the same earnest and supplicant tone' in which Peel spoke as a legal and administrative reformer,

> he pours out stores of bigotry and puerile absurdity too rich, one should think even for Oxford Divines, as if he wished to heighten the effect of his wisdom by the contrast of his folly, or the effect of his folly by the contrast of his wisdom.[86]

Resentment in the Tory press against the government's willingness to concede repeal hinted at deeper tensions. The *Courier*, whose editor received a government subsidy and regular briefings, complained bitterly about a liberalism that demanded sacrifices from the Established Church without making any of its own. Catholic Emancipation would soon follow unless the friends of church and state regained their vigour.[87] *John Bull* likewise saw repeal as a precedent, and *The Age* accused Peel of ratting on the Tory commitment to church and King'.[88] The presence of Huskisson and other Tory liberals in Wellington's cabinet heightened ultra suspicions, but brought both compensating expertise and forbearance from the Whigs until May 1828 when a disagreement over legislation to disenfranchise Penryn and East Retford led Huskisson to offer his resignation. Wellington surprised him by accepting it and other Canningites resigned as a group. Opposition from ultras and the Canningite secession together indicated growing divisions within the phalanx of opinion in the country that had sustained Perceval and Liverpool in office. Whigs remained cautiously supportive in hopes that they could expect more concessions. Abercrombie told Brougham later in the year that Wellington lacked the real support of a party, and weakness might force him to yield what a more liberal government might withhold.[89]

Brougham joined other Whig and radical leaders at a dinner on 18 June celebrating repeal of the Test and Corporations Acts that marked his main public appearance of the year as well as a party reunion of sorts. The assembly toasted several Whigs for their efforts to promote repeal, and the speeches in reply made clear that they expected further reforms. Brougham observed that Dissenters 'owed their triumph to the improvement that had taken place in knowledge, to their union, mutual forbearance, and to the prudent concert among men of various opinions'. Their cordial cooperation that neither delay nor powerful opposition could subdue had proven irresistible. The same means had ended the slave trade in 1807 and would soon bring 'the final extirpation of West Indian slavery, and...the ultimate abrogation of tests on all classes of their fellow subjects'.[90] Brougham harnessed Whig principles to a key issue for provincial liberals, and the party clearly saw Catholic Emancipation as their next object with a broader agenda to follow.

Daniel O'Connell's defeat of William Vesey Fitzgerald in the Clare election a few weeks later brought the Catholic question back to the forefront of politics. Vesey Fitzgerald's appointment to replace Huskisson as President of the Board of Trade forced an election, and O'Connell only stepped forward when the Catholic Association, which had pledged to oppose any supporter of Wellington's ministry, failed to persuade a Protestant sympathizer to stand.[91] Although O'Connell could not take a seat in Parliament without swearing oaths against transubstantiation and papal authority, no law prevented him from being returned at the poll. An attempt by the House of Commons to exclude him would bring a reprise on a much larger scale of the controversy surrounding John Wilkes' successive elections for Middlesex in 1768–69. The *New Times* warned that refusing to admit O'Connell would only prompt a compatriot to stand in his place and a general election would see the same scene 'played in fifty places that is now played in one'. The Clare election had established the Catholic Association's influence over the Irish electorate, and only the delay before the next parliamentary session postponed Wellington's choice between coercion and conciliation.

Wellington gave little indication of his intentions before Parliament met in February 1829. The Whigs, however, had adopted a harder line. Althorp feared the government would accompany conciliation 'with some foolish irritating measure' or 'propose some half measure which will continue & perhaps even increase the irritation'. Nevertheless, he believed the Whigs 'ought to take what we can get, but if it is not the whole we must enter our protest that it will not & ought not to satisfy the Catholics'.[92] The *Manchester Guardian* described Peel's silence on the question at a public dinner in Manchester as a sign of the government's willingness to concede Emancipation.[93] Brougham insisted in December that 'unless we hear and see something precise, we must debate and divide until we carry' Catholic Emancipation.[94] As before, however, he remained willing to aid a government committed to a liberal agenda however reluctantly it adopted essentially Whig measures. Grey went further in holding back from any hint of concerted opposition for fear that Wellington might be dissuaded from concessions.[95]

The King's speech, read by the Lord Chancellor on 5 February 1829, removed all doubts about the government's intentions by instructing Parliament to review the laws against Roman Catholics. During the debate that followed on the reply to the address, Wellington directly stated the government's intention to introduce a measure repealing Catholic disabilities. Eldon immediately denounced the plan, as he had earlier condemned repeal of the Test and Corporation Acts, as a dangerous and unconstitutional effort to destroy the indissoluble union between church and state.[96] Sir Robert Inglis, Eldon's ultra counterpart in the Commons, saw concession as 'nothing more or less than the prostration of Protestantism at the feet of the Roman Catholics'. The public, he continued, sought no changes in the constitution, but merely its conservation.[97]

Brougham saw the Catholic question as basically resolved, and he largely set the Whig tone for the session by casting party considerations aside to offer the government full support.

His preference for men,

> ready to profit by experience, above those who live to grow more perversely obstinate, year after year reaping the sad fruits of long life without the important, the melancholy consolation of being able to set off against increasing age, augmented wisdom[98]

hinted at the widening Tory split. Henry Grattan, son of the Irish Whig, praised Peel's change on the Catholic question, and said that, far from deserting his Orange colours, Peel 'had torn down a standard which was inimical to the peace of the country'.[99] Althorp, who shared Whig leadership in the Commons with Brougham, privately declared

> it of the highest importance that ministers should feel confidence in our entire & cordial support & that they should not fancy that we

have the slightest wish to take advantage of their unpopularity with their usual supporters to trip up their heels.[100]

Despite his opposition to the government's foreign policy and other matters, Althorp sought to postpone all such extraneous questions until Catholic Emancipation had passed. Grey told Holland before the 1829 session opened that he feared applying pressure might deter Wellington from concessions.[101] The Whigs shared these sentiments and even accepted the government's decision to disenfranchise Irish forty-shilling freeholders as part of Emancipation.

Wellington's decision to force Catholic Emancipation finally shattered the coalition that had sustained Tory governments in power since 1807. Although the Duke successfully pressured Peel and George IV to accept the measure and secured the requisite majorities in both Houses of Parliament, he failed to bring the Tory party with him as well. Having lost the Canningites through his inability to work with Huskisson, Wellington now drew bitter enmity from the ultras and their supporters in the country who felt deeply betrayed that he and Peel had changed sides on the Catholic question. Peel drew particular ire as former leader of the Protestant cause in the Commons. The Tory press had become more militantly opposed to Catholic Emancipation over the past decade, largely because readers 'refused to buy pro-Catholic Tory periodicals or newspapers'.[102] Wellington's support of Emancipation, along with his refusal to cultivate journalists and general disdain for expressions of public opinion, created an adversarial relationship with the Tory press for the remainder of his administration. With the exception of the declining *Courier*, notorious for its servility to the ministry in power, and *John Bull*, Wellington relied largely on the *Times* which continued to adhere to Brougham's view that liberal measures could be secured best by a non-party government long after the Whig barrister himself had abandoned it.[103]

The revolution in parties that Holland had spoken of earlier arrived in force with the passage of Catholic Emancipation. It split the Tories and drew Whigs and some radicals into cooperation with Wellington's government. Political alignments in Parliament and the country favoured the Whigs as they had not done for decades. Religious questions led directly to political reform, and recent debates had fuelled public interest politics. The *Leeds Mercury* saw settling the Catholic question as a step 'leading to a completely new formation and casting of parties...and, we venture to hope, to the formation of a strong, united, and liberal administration'.[104] Catholic Emancipation, along with repealing the Test and Corporations Acts and reductions in government expenditure, brought Wellington support from liberal opinion in the country. The *Manchester Guardian* cited Wellington's appointment of Scarlett and Rosslyn to the cabinet as signs of his desire to work closely with Grey and the Whigs.[105] Certainly, the government held a weak position that could only be improved by bringing men of stature into the cabinet who could defend the government in Parliament, particularly the Commons, as well as manage departmental business.

Wellington's tactic of 'picking off' individuals failed to draw support that impressed Whigs or Canningites. Althorp concluded in June that the administration was now too weak to govern and asked Brougham about mounting a renewed opposition to drive them from office.[106] Nor did Wellington want additions that would undercut his leadership. He had insisted privately during the Emancipation debates that he could not 'submit to be the puppet of the rump of the Whigs and Mr. Canning' and later told Harriet Arbuthnot that his object after securing Emancipation was to 'reunite the whole Tory party & he [would] not bring any Whigs in'.[107] Tory factionalism deepened, however, as Canningites and ultras alike remained alienated, while the Whigs drew closer together in the closing months of 1829. Rather than continuing their support for Wellington's government, several Whig leaders including Brougham, Althorp, and Grey's son, Howick, sought to reunite the party around their own measures on finance, reform, and foreign policy. Lord John Russell proposed that Brougham and Althorp lead jointly in the Commons and Holland in the Lords.[108] Whig leaders now prepared to revive the opposition challenge again.

Events in 1830 brought the opportunity to unite provincial interests with the Whigs for a decisive effort. A sudden return of economic distress, and the social tensions it created, quickly replaced Catholic Emancipation as the dominant political issue after mid-1829. The situation revived memories of 1819 and Peterloo. A poor harvest in 1828 hurt the landed interest and raised food prices. The collapse of trade and manufacturing the next year extended the problem to all sectors of the economy and sparked discussion in Parliament and the press. Social tension measured by unemployment and high food prices peaked for the decade in 1829, creating a situation that proved worse than that of 1819.[109] Wage cuts by cotton manufacturers prompted strikes and demonstrations around Manchester that echoed in other industrial districts.[110] Although manufacturing and trade began reviving in March 1830, the delayed political impact of distress continued through the year while the situation for agriculture worsened. A wave of county meetings to prepare petitions before the opening of Parliament in February 1830 fuelled agitation and marked another similarity with the year of Peterloo. Grey, recognizing the parallel, sent Holland an amendment he had moved to the address replying to the King's speech in 1819 'as if it had been written for the present occasion'.[111]

Distress brought renewed interest in parliamentary reform, as various interests saw reform as a solution to their economic problems. Religious questions with constitutional implications already had generated momentum behind a further political campaign. Earlier discussions throughout the decade had made the country familiar with arguments for reform and defects in the existing system, and Canningites and ultra Tories both abandoned their opposition to an idea Whigs had long promoted.[112] Lord John Russell's motion for transferring seats to Birmingham, Leeds, and Manchester drew broad support despite failing on 23 February by 48 votes.[113] Turning recent unrest to his advantage, Russell insisted on the need

> to unite, as much as possible, persons representing every kind of property, and connected with every kind of interest in order to remedy the evils that now oppress us, and to avert the dangers that may hereafter threaten the country.[114]

Yet, for all the debates on reform and other questions, Parliament enacted few measures. A Yorkshire newspaper summed up the session with the homely adage, 'much cry and little wool'.[115]

The early months of 1830 drew Whigs together into an active opposition. No longer would they cooperate with Wellington in hopes of implementing their agenda by stealth. Brougham vacated the seat he held from the Marquess of Cleveland, formerly Lord Darlington,when his patron joined Wellington in early 1830, and Whig leaders promptly secured Brougham's election for Knaresborough, the Duke of Devonshire's pocket borough opened by Tierney's death in January.[116] On 13 July, Brougham raised the issue of slavery in a widely reported speech that quickly appeared in a pamphlet. Announcing his intention to promote abolition, Brougham declared that 'the same cloud is gathering that annihilated the slave trade'. While his motion failed by 29 votes, the debate raised slavery as a key election issue and mobilized the abolition movement in the provinces.[117] As Whigs drew together, Grey returned to active politics by attacking ministers as incapable of maintaining the country's honour. Brougham sparked a scene in the

Commons by likening Wellington's political style to Polignac's reactionary ministry in France and fiercely denouncing the cabinet as Wellington's 'flatterers – his mean fawning parasites'.[118]

George IV's death on 26 June forced a general election in which the Whigs and other opposition groups seemed certain to gain seats against Wellington's government. Brougham's opportunity to stand for Yorkshire, Britain's largest and most prestigious constituency, came by chance when the county's two sitting Whig members gave up their seats. Lord Milton and John Marshall both feared the massive expense that even an uncontested election would involve. The Fitzwilliam and Lascelles families each had spent over £100,000 in the 1807 contest, while several candidates held back in 1826 for fear of being ruined by the expense. Even without a contest, Milton and Marshall, a Leeds flax spinner backed by Edward Baines and other liberals in the West Riding, had together paid £53,000. A prudent man would not risk incurring the cost of a contest, and the Tory Lord Wharncliffe impressed on Milton the need for the county's leaders to unite against a system that deterred good candidates.[119] The immediate hesitation among suitable men to step forward in 1830 underlined the problem.

Yorkshire's size prevented the ascendancy of any one interest, and contests there gave a fair indication of public sentiment that drew national attention. Unlike other counties, landed classes and trades linked with agriculture shared power and territory with growing commercial and industrial interests. The gentry and nobility still took a more active part than in non-rural counties like Middlesex, and these factors together made Yorkshire a highly politicized constituency that needed elaborate organization.[120] The Reverend Christopher Wyvill had built a national campaign for parliamentary reform in the 1780s from petitioning meetings in Yorkshire, and his Yorkshire Association helped return Henry Duncombe in 1780 and William Wilberforce in 1784. Wyvill's later activity at the close of the Napoleonic Wars provided an important degree of continuity among reformers.[121] Wilberforce's election at the head of the poll for Yorkshire in 1807 marked a decisive expression of public opposition to the slave trade in a way that underlined the role of local Dissenters in the anti-slavery movement.

The West Riding, which included the industrial towns of Sheffield and Huddersfield as well as Leeds, provided the basis of Yorkshire's liberal interest along with a plurality of its wealth and freeholders. Yorkshire's gain of two additional seats in 1821 provided representation for its growing industrial regions, but giving the seats to the county rather than the towns themselves allowed the landed interest to limit their influence. Milton had strong ties with the West Riding and the Leeds clothiers, and Edward Baines had promoted Marshall's election in 1826 as the area's representative. The 1826 election had cemented an alliance between liberals led by Baines in the West Riding and the Fitzwilliam Whig interest that had begun in 1807 and grew rapidly after the agitation of 1819.[122] Baines spoke for commercial middle-class opinion as owner of the *Leeds Mercury*, and his connections with local businessmen and Dissenting ministers gave him great influence in Yorkshire politics.

Baines had urged Yorkshire freeholders in 1812 to return Brougham or Whitbread in Wilberforce's place without expense as friends of peace and reform.[123] Since then he had been among Brougham's strongest advocates in the press, and the situation in 1830 allowed Baines to promote the idea of electing Brougham for Yorkshire in earnest. A long article in the *Leeds Mercury* noted that since freeholders could now give 'their voluntary and *free* support to the men of their real choice, the county must carefully select the most worthy representative'. After endorsing the Earl of Carlisle's son, Lord Morpeth, who recently had proved his liberal credentials in the Commons, the paper urged Brougham on the ground that Yorkshire deserved a representative 'inferior to none among the Commoners of England'. While not a Yorkshireman, Brougham's years practising law on the Northern Circuit provided a strong local connection. His efforts to secure the independence of neighbouring Westmorland from the Lowther interest's Tory hegemony recommended him further. Moreover, other counties had recently selected outsiders in recognition of their services. By returning Brougham, Yorkshire 'would give an honourable and memorable example of the public coming forward to reward public virtue'.[124]

Leading Yorkshire Whigs already had agreed to support two nominees free from expense, thus removing the only barrier to Morpeth's willingness to stand. On 14 July, before Baines's declaration, Samuel Clapham informed George Strickland, a leading member of the county's Whig gentry and potential candidate, that local anti-slavery societies strongly favoured Brougham. But few of the Whig gentry realized the strength of Brougham's support in the West Riding until a meeting to choose candidates in York on 23 July. Milton expressed some ambivalence, and several gentlemen came forward to provide an alternative. Baines pressed hard for Brougham in a heated discussion, and the Whig gentry united behind J.C. Ramsden. Insisting that religion and humanity rather than politics had drawn him to the meeting, the Reverend Thomas Scales, a Leeds Presbyterian minister and abolitionist, told the meeting that Brougham would be nominated at the poll whatever decision they made. The Leeds delegation's uncompromising position forced the gentry to sink their prejudices and accept Brougham.[125]

Baines's coup brought sharp reactions. The liberal *Sheffield Iris*, which shared his general appreciation of Brougham and finally backed him, wondered before the York meeting whether a local candidate could not be found. Brougham would not, it predicted, 'represent Yorkshire – though he might, as did Mr. Wilberforce, do honour to the name of the county, as identified with a most signal career of general usefulness'.[126] County members had all been Yorkshiremen since the Reformation and no lawyer had been elected since the 1650s. Brougham's candidacy thus broke several precedents that troubled even his supporters. Only after Brougham had entered the field and addressed a public gathering in Sheffield, did the *Iris* waive its objections and endorse him as the man who would consummate Wilberforce's efforts by abolishing slavery.[127]

Tory critics openly attacked Brougham. The *Leeds Intelligencer* accused Yorkshire Whigs of having been 'regularly jockeyed – thrust out – trampled upon – laughed at...[and] compelled to surrender to the Bainesocracy of Leeds'. Even before Brougham's nomination, the *Intelligencer* listed objections to Brougham as an outsider whose other interests would prevent him from promoting the county's welfare. The *Yorkshire Gazette*, which detested 'the word *liberal*, for the party to whom it is applied have nothing English in their conduct or opinions', expressed

> astonishment at the impudent attempt to force a man like Mr. Brougham on the county; whose only claim to the patronage of the freeholders of Yorkshire is, that he has been invariably rejected whenever he 'screwed his courage to the sticking place' for encountering a popular election.[128]

Like the *Sheffield Iris*, the *Gazette* also wondered why Yorkshire, and the West Riding in particular, sent to Westmorland for Brougham instead of nominating a local candidate.

The York meeting on 23 July assured that Brougham and Morpeth would be elected. Only the presence of an eccentric spoiler, Martin Stapylton, brought the contest to a formal poll, and the *Yorkshire Gazette* deplored his 'absurd and ungentlemanly behaviour' in putting the candidates and their friends to unnecessary expense.[129] Baines publicly stated that he acted without Brougham's knowledge, and at first Brougham told Greville privately that he 'would not stand, nor spend a guinea, nor go there, nor even take the least trouble about the concerns of any one of his constituents, if they elected him'.[130] The nomination, he remarked disingenuously to the Duke of Devonshire, brought less satisfaction than if he were younger. Brougham took it with detachment, pleased only 'because it bears a strong testimony to our opinions and principles, and because it gives me (whether I accept or refuse) a great weight to promote those principles in Parliament and the country'.[131]

Whatever Brougham's private thoughts, he readily accepted the formal invitation to stand in the Whig interest with Morpeth. His reply on 23 July thanked the freeholders for the honour of nominating him and pledged never to rest in their service,

> until, by the blessing of God, I have seen an end of the Abuses which bend England to the Ground, and the Mists dispersed from the eyes of the Ignorant, and the Chains drop from the Hands of the Slave![132]

The election gave Brougham a platform to attack Wellington's government and propound his reform agenda for the coming parliamentary session. The Yorkshire canvass brought his tactics from Westmorland to a wider arena with the *Leeds Mercury* echoing his speeches throughout Northern England.

Brougham and Morpeth opened their canvass in Leeds on Tuesday 27 July, with an address at the Coloured Cloth Hall to a crowd numbering over 10,000. The *Leeds Mercury* issued a special edition to cover the event and printed the candidates' speeches again in its regular Saturday paper. Morpeth's attack on the game laws, slavery, and monopolies drew cheers, and he called for parliamentary reform and changes in the Corn Laws. Brougham first addressed his standing as an outsider, reminding listeners that he had spent considerable time in Yorkshire practising law and on other business. He defined the forthcoming election as a referendum on parliamentary reform, Corn Law revision, and abolishing slavery. Despite congratulating Wellington's ministry for passing Catholic Emancipation, Brougham told the crowd that he and Lord John Russell had repealed the Test and Corporation Acts over government opposition. Wellington's willingness to yield showed the government's weakness and inability to lead. Insisting on reform, Brougham demanded amidst cheering an effort to 'emancipate all the middle, the industrious, and all the humble class of our fellow subjects, and let us see England tranquil and in peace and contentment'.[133]

Although he privately told Milton that he had worked to unite the party by preventing Baines and other supporters from replacing Morpeth with his friend George Strickland, Brougham's strident public rhetoric cast doubt in many minds on his claim to promote a close union between the landed and commercial interests.[134] He told crowds at Leeds and elsewhere that he would tolerate no monopoly, neither to the East India Company nor the landed interest. Cooperation, Brougham implied, should be on equal terms, and his praise for the York meeting's 'disposition to join [the commercial classes] and support the objects of your choice' underlined the point.[135] If the tone struck many Whigs as harsh, the substance of Brougham's speech adumbrated the alliance between Whig reformers in Parliament and commercial interests in the provinces that came to define Victorian liberalism.

After visiting Leeds, Brougham and Morpeth continued their canvass together through Huddersfield, Dewsbury, and Heckmond. Morpeth's duties at the county assizes and Brougham's legal business forced them to visit Sheffield and other areas separately. Brougham travelled from York to address supporters in nearby towns after full days in court pleading cases. Campaigning at a frenetic pace, his canvass drew crowds that matched O'Connell's mass meetings in Ireland and comprised the largest political gatherings in England to date. Brougham later declared the canvass

> by much the hardest work I ever went through; but good health, temperance, and the stake I was playing for carried me through. I not only survived, but during the whole of this laborious time, I never in my life felt better, or more capable of further exertion, had such been called for.[136]

Speaking in Sheffield on 29 July, Brougham replied to a question about events in France by insisting that England had no business interfering and praising the French people's spirit in defending their liberties against Charles X and Polignac.[137] Although news of the revolution in Paris arrived too late to influence the 1830 general election, it dominated newspaper headlines through the coming months. Brougham used events on the Continent as a rhetorical trope against Wellington, and his denunciation of arbitrary despotism abroad led naturally to questions of colonial slavery, commercial monopolies, and the state of parliamentary representation at home.[138] Anti-slavery sentiment fuelled local enthusiasm behind Brougham's campaign, though the balance of parties at Westminster shaped his broader strategy. A pamphlet Brougham published anonymously soon before the election again likened Wellington to Polignac and accused the Duke of exceeding his abilities by monopolizing the power normally shared with colleagues in the cabinet. Only the forbearance of Whigs, Canningites, and ultras kept the present government in its place.[139] Along with Brougham's Yorkshire speeches, the pamphlet indicated his plan to lead the opposition challenge when Parliament met in the autumn.

The election began on Thursday, 5 August 1830, when candidates and supporters assembled at York. Although hoarse from canvassing, Brougham called again for parliamentary reform and abolition. The speech marked the height of his campaign, and Brougham used every issue to emphasize the need for respectable and prosperous men to have their interests fairly represented in Parliament. Stapylton demanded a poll after the customary show of hands in favour of the candidates, and the High Sheriff closed polling the next day with the other candidates' consent when it became clear that Stapylton had abandoned the contest. Morpeth led the poll, with Brougham second and the other two candidates taking the remaining seats.[140] The results having been announced, the newly-elected Knights of the Shire closed the proceedings with the local custom of riding on a charger around the castle yard and through city streets with sword, cocked hat, and spurs. Another lawyer reportedly told Brougham, 'whose ease and gracefulness upon horseback do not exactly square with Yorkshire standards... "you may do very well for a member for the county, but you will never do for a *Riding* member"'. Brougham declared it in his memoirs the proudest moment of his life.[141]

Observers reacted predictably. *The Times* and *Morning Chronicle* congratulated Yorkshire for returning Brougham and Morpeth. Local Tory papers expressed their disgust, with the *Leeds Intelligencer* calling the election a farce and warning that Brougham would use the county only as a path to office. According to the *Sheffield Iris* the election proved that the Whigs' political creed had won general acceptance.[142] The *Leeds Mercury* declared the proceedings 'a signal triumph for Purity of election' and the principles of freedom. Brougham's election 'discharged the debt due by England to this champion of right and liberty, this illustrious friend of knowledge and humanity'. The only possible cause for regret lay in the fact that four liberal candidates, rather than just two, might have been elected. Baines concluded that organizers had 'judged well on the present occasion', though it remained 'a fair matter for consideration whether the same conduct shall be pursued at future elections'.[143]

Brougham gave his own view of the political scene in an article hastily prepared as a Whig manifesto for the July *Edinburgh Review*. The piece reviewed Brougham's pamphlet and again compared Wellington with Polignac's ultra royalist ministry in words taken from his Yorkshire speeches.[144] Insisting the Duke must not presume that men can be manoeuvred in politics with the same ease as in battle, Brougham predicted that, like Polignac, Wellington would face a new Parliament more troublesome than its predecessor. The article closed by describing Brougham's 'nearly unanimous choice' as Yorkshire's representative as the most appalling 'of all the portentous signs of the times for the present ministry'. Its profession of support for Brougham's principles marked the most extraordinary event that had raised him 'to the pinnacle of popular influence'.[145]

Brougham capitalized on that influence during the round of congratulatory dinners and meetings that typically followed elections. Indeed, his tour as the newly elected MP for Yorkshire amounted to a second canvass that received as much, if not more, press coverage. Brougham drew criticism from *The Times*, which still supported Wellington, for accusing his ministry of wishing Polignac's government well 'almost in the very last stages of its madness' during a dinner at Leeds on 14 August 1830. The *Morning Chronicle* thought Brougham's remarks deserved public notice, and the paper noted that the ultra Tory Sir Richard Vyvyan had made the same claim during his election for Cornwall.[146] Many Tories, particularly ultras like Vyvyan who had opposed Catholic Emancipation to the bitter end, adopted liberal views on Europe and the Bourbon regime's overthrow from an almost paranoid concern over a perceived Catholic threat. Their position drew them even further from Wellington and encouraged cooperation with the Whigs.[147] Brougham joined Milton, Russell, and other Whig leaders at a dinner in London 'to celebrate the late triumph of freedom in France'. Milton told the assembly that the greatest number possible of society's higher ranks ought to lead in expressing their approval. Brougham praised the revolution's leaders for having done more over three days to prevent despotism in England and France 'than its vile abettors can now accomplish in as many ages'.[148] Foreign affairs were no longer the Whigs' Achilles heel or the government's best security against an opposition challenge.

Reform still remained the central issue, and Brougham raised the political stakes by pledging to introduce a measure when Parliament met. He outlined his plan at an election dinner in Sheffield on 27 September where he shared the stage with Morpeth and Milton. Besides extending representation to industrial towns like Sheffield, Leeds, and Manchester, Brougham demanded multiple polling places for county elections to reduce the freeholders' expense and inconvenience and a thorough reform of representation in Scotland, which amounted to a pocket borough under government control.[149] A few days earlier, he had told another gathering in Saddleworth that Liverpool and other boroughs ought to extend their franchise beyond freemen elected by the corporation to include many 'of the most wealthy, the most intelligent, and most influential inhabitants of Liverpool [who now] had no share whatever in electing its representatives'.[150] Brougham cited as an example the abolitionist William Roscoe's family that had no votes even though it included four or five adults. While pushing reform further than past Whig proposals, Brougham's programme excluded radical demands for universal suffrage or secret ballots and remained within the bounds of moderate opinion.

Another pamphlet Brougham wrote against Wellington's government entitled *Result of the General Election; or What Has the Duke of Wellington Gained by the Dissolution* drew more press attention. Brougham discussed it in the October *Edinburgh Review*, and a print depicted the bewigged lawyer flinging ink at an alarmed Wellington and Peel from behind copies of the journal and pamphlet.[151] By late September 1830, Whig leaders agreed that only errors on their part could prevent Wellington from being driven from power. Huskisson's death in a freak railway accident in September ended the possibility that Canningites might join the government, and Holland's conversation with Palmerston and Melbourne revealed that nothing precluded a union with the Whigs. Significantly, the two men's only doubts involved 'Althorp's judgement and Brougham's lack of it'. Brougham's behaviour had become a matter of renewed concern among Whigs, many of whom feared the Yorkshire election had turned his head.[152] Brougham clearly meant to seize the initiative on parliamentary reform and abolition regardless of his colleagues' wishes, and the *Morning Chronicle* noted that his advocacy of popular rights made him more feared than loved by the aristocracy.[153] The problem of keeping Brougham safely harnessed to avoid an outburst that might throw Whig hopes into confusion seemed unavoidable.

Illustration 6.4 Print depicting Brougham flinging ink at an alarmed Wellington and Peel, from behind the *Edinburgh Review* of October 1830 and his recent pamphlet. Reproduced with kind permission of the British Museum.

The opening of Parliament on 26 October 1830 forced the pace of events. On 2 November, Brougham declared in measured tones his intention to bring forward the question of parliamentary reform. Although his declaration in Yorkshire had taken the issue away from Lord John Russell, its longtime advocate, Sir James Graham supported the move and told Brougham that

> the public will be satisfied with less from you than from any other member of the House of Commons, when you declare that you bring forward all, which you can hope to carry with a due regard to the circumstances of the present time.[154]

Wellington, rather than Brougham, made the fatal error of the session by declaring against reform of any degree in absolute terms. Grey urged his fellow peers that parliamentary reform not be postponed as Catholic Emancipation had been, 'but considered in time, so that measures may be introduced by which gradual reform can be effected without danger to the country'.[155] After touching on various other issues, Wellington replied that the present system answered all good purposes and 'possessed the full and entire confidence of the country – deservedly possessed that confidence'. If called upon to form a legislature for another country, Wellington declared he would take Britain's present system as his model. Not only unwilling to propose a measure of his own, he closed the speech by insisting that 'as long as he held any station in the government of the country, he should always feel it his duty to resist such measures when proposed by others'.[156] As he sat down amidst stunned silence, Wellington asked his Foreign Secretary, the Earl of Aberdeen, 'I have not said too much, have I?' Aberdeen replied 'you'll hear of it', and when another peer later asked what Wellington had said the Earl responded, 'He said that we were going out'.[157]

On the same day, Althorp stepped forward as Whig leader in the Commons to declare that the present government lacked the skill and care to guide the country through its present troubles. He thus had no objections to any effort that might displace them.[158] Public opinion strongly backed some degree of parliamentary reform, and Wellington's flat refusal left his administration dangerously isolated. Observers saw Brougham's motion for parliamentary reform as the key test of government support, but the crisis came on 11 November 1830 when Sir Henry Parnell proposed referring the civil list to a select committee. Public demands for economy made it a dangerous issue for the government that drew independents and country members to an opposition now comprised of Whigs, ultras, and Canningites. The division went against the government by 204 to 233, and John Cam Hobhouse asked Peel whether the cabinet would retain their places and carry on the government after the Commons had expressed itself against them.[159] Peel made no reply, but Wellington answered the question by resigning the next day to avoid another defeat over Brougham's motion. No government had been forced from office by a Commons vote since 1804, and Wellington's resignation marked the end of the ascendancy Pitt and his heirs had exerted over British politics.

William IV called upon Grey to form a new government, and the challenge of handling Brougham now cast the Whigs' prospects in doubt. At Althorp's request Brougham grudgingly agreed to postpone his motion until 25 November. He would then, 'and at no more distant period bring forward the question of parliamentary reform, whatever may be the condition of circumstances, and whosoever may be His Majesty's ministers'.[160] Beyond the Whigs' desire to postpone a difficult and controversial question now that they had gained power, Brougham had to be brought into the cabinet lest he attack it. Grey could not appoint him Master of the Rolls, for the appointment would leave Brougham in the Commons and free to break with the government without fear of losing office or salary. Althorp, who had become Whig leader in the Commons only after Brougham persistently declined the post, refused to serve as leader if Brougham received the Mastership.[161] Brougham then spoke of repeating the part of disinterested supporter he had played during Canning's brief government and repeated his earlier view that no office could equal the prestige of representing Yorkshire except that of Lord Chancellor.[162]

Grey called a conference at Lansdowne's house of the prospective cabinet's leading members who agreed to the 'dangerous experiment' of giving Brougham the Chancellorship. Holland quietly said 'then we shall never have a comfortable moment in this room'.[163] Grey met Brougham the next morning to make the offer, insisting that a government could not be formed without him. Though he refused at first, Brougham agreed to speak with Althorp before a final decision. Althorp brought Duncannon, the party whip, Lord Sefton, and James Brougham to repeat the proposal. Brougham insisted that the Chancellorship would take him from the Commons and end a lucrative career at the bar that he could not afford to abandon. Althorp had no reply, but he privately told Brougham that refusal would make him responsible for keeping the Whigs out of power.[164]

174

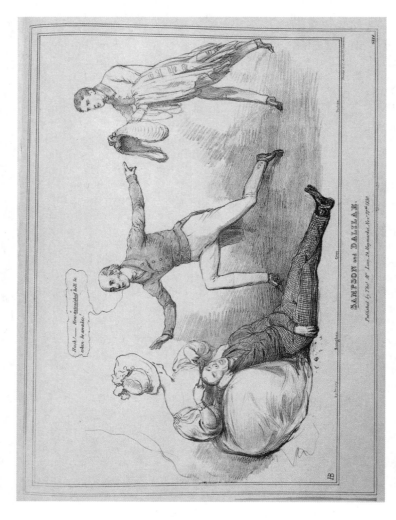

Illustration 6.5 Lady Holland and Grey replay the biblical story. By conferring on Brougham the wig and robes of the Lord Chancellorship, the Whigs neutralized the power their colleague had exercised through his oratory in the House of Commons and the country. Reproduced with kind permission of the British Museum.

Brougham could have dismissed Althorp's claim easily. With the collapse of Wellington's government, a Whig ministry of some kind provided the only alternative. Brougham might well have called Althorp's bluff in the knowledge that the Tories could not take his party's victory away by returning to office. Brougham's mother had warned him earlier not to give up the position he held as MP for Yorkshire by leaving the Commons. His election that summer, she insisted, had earned him a greater position than any king or minister could bestow.[165] No one was more conscious of the fact than Brougham himself, and the reasons why he finally acceded to Althorp's demand remain obscure. Refusal might have severed Brougham's Whig ties and forced him to the dangerous expedient of relying on outside support against his own party. The rejection of his claims to lead the Commons by rank-and-file Whigs who liked and trusted Althorp may have had an influence, though Althorp only had come forward after Brougham himself had refused the post many times. More importantly, the Lord Chancellorship was a glittering prize for an Edinburgh-bred lawyer who had spent years excluded from the rewards of his profession. The *Morning Chronicle* called him 'the only man who ever hesitated one second as to the acceptance of the Chancellorship' and remarked on the prestige and patronage connected with the position.[166] Along with the demands of party loyalty, the allure of so prestigious a legal post cannot be doubted for a man who had insisted that he was only qualified for appointments within his profession. Under great pressure, Brougham finally accepted the party's demands and took his place on the Woolsack as Lord Chancellor on 22 November. Years of opposition thus closed as Grey's ministry gained office to initiate its programme of reform.

Conclusion

Although the new reform ministry in 1830 included Canningites and a single ultra Tory, the Duke of Richmond, a relative of Lord Holland, Grey presided over a Whig-dominated coalition government. As a coalition, it invites comparison with the Talents ministry of 1806–7 while raising questions about factionalism among the Whigs themselves. Whig attitudes had shifted over the intervening years, however, toward a much broader view that drew support beyond the political world at Westminster and engaged a wider set of issues. The inclusion of five veterans of earlier Tory administrations did not dilute the government's Whig character, but rather it provided a welcome infusion of new talent committed to its agenda.[1] Pressed forward at times against their will by Brougham during the 1810s and 20s, the Whigs had overcome great difficulties to gain power, and the experience from those years helped sustain them in office. Decades in opposition had forged a consensus within a Whig party that reunited in mid-1830 just as its opponents collapsed into factional quarrels. Having broadened their appeal during the 1820s, the Whigs now stood pledged to a general programme of measured reform.

Reform had become the dominant theme in British political discourse by 1830. As *The Times* noted at Grey's accession to office, the new government 'must *redress our grievances*, or be forever ruined'.[2] Such pressures enhanced the government's cohesion and suited its plans. Far from ignoring public demands, Grey and his colleagues sought to calm tension by restoring the political order according to Whig principles adumbrated in the 1820s. The 1832 Reform Act and other measures that followed created a political realignment in the Whigs' favour that lasted remarkably well until the 1880s. So successfully had the Whigs positioned themselves within a broad centre-left alliance by 1840, that their precarious earlier years in opposition before 1830 became easy to forget. The Whig-Liberal ascendancy arguably provided a more effective centre-left coalition before 1880 than the Labour party from the 1920s.[3] Between 1830 and 1886 the broad Whig-Liberal coalition found itself out of office for barely a dozen years and lost only two of fourteen general elections. One of those election defeats in 1874 actually saw them draw more votes than the Tories.[4] Whig efforts to revitalize their party in opposition and gain power made a significant contribution to the establishment of Liberalism as the dominant political force in Victorian Britain.

By 1830, the Whigs had moved beyond eighteenth-century concerns about circumscribing the power of the Crown to engage a much broader spectrum of respectable opinion. Where the Rockingham Whigs backed such initiatives as Dunning's motion on the influence of the Crown in 1780, their successors after 1808 showed a greater concern with the liberties of other groups within the nation. The changed focus helped them successfully combine traditional social groups with newer, highly dynamic ones to create a formidable political force. Cooperation with provincial interests had enabled Whig leaders to take Francis Jeffrey's advice from 1810 and guide an unsettled public opinion as they rebuilt their own party into a body that could viably govern.[5] The struggle to move from opposition to office brought about deeper, structural changes in British politics that went beyond the Whigs themselves. No longer occasionally enlisting outside support to force their claims to office on the Crown, Whigs focused on constructing a sustainable working coalition of varied interests that reached beyond the metropolitan preoccupations of high politics. Despite subsequent changes in its composition, that coalition sustained Whig governments in power after 1830 and broadened the political nation to include greater participation by provincial interests and elites. The participatory ethos of the Whig–Liberal ascendancy that came to dominate Victorian politics supplanted both the administrative mindset that had defined the Pittite regime and the disciplinary ethos of militant loyalism.[6]

Coalition building and participation by respectable members of the public not only assisted the Whigs' move from opposition to office, it also shaped the party's broader transition from Whig to Liberal. During the 1820s and 30s, Whiggery developed into a broader tradition of aristocratic leadership of reform movements rather than an exclusive property of one group of families.[7] The word 'liberal' itself, an adjective that originally described openness or generosity, took on a political meaning in the late 1810s and 1820s as counterpoint to orthodoxy or authoritarianism that brought it into general usage as ·a noun. Liberalism then became reified into a concept that described the shared agenda of Whigs and reformers into the 1840s and beyond.[8] Tactics and strategies that had brought Whigs and provincial Liberals together in the struggle to gain power later influenced its use by Grey's administration. The participatory ethos behind the Whig revival involved a particular approach to governance that emphasized responsiveness to public opinion and reconciling competing interests with the framework of law. Liberals would later alter their perceptions and make overtures to new interests as the political nation expanded through the nineteenth century, but the essential approach that they developed in opposition over the 22 years before 1830 remained constant.[9]

The struggle for power that brought the Whig revival also promoted the development of the party system. Despite the electoral changes of 1832, much of what historians associate with Victorian politics operated within the very different framework of the unreformed electoral system.[10] Whigs already had an intellectual justification for party activity from Burke's writing in the 1770s, and a parliamentary party focused on the charismatic leadership of Fox gradually became a coalition of interests that connected politicians at Westminster with sympathetic groups in the country. Occasional splits aside, the party became more cohesive over time as its members gained experience working together. Cooperation and party ties became increasingly necessary to managing parliamentary business as the abolition of emoluments and patronage removed incentives that had bolstered executive influence over eighteenth-century politics. With a more evenly poised balance in the Commons created by the removal of 140 seats in 1832, ministers also required party support far more than in the unreformed system.[11] Building an effective opposition before 1830 had given the Whigs valuable experience and networks of support beyond Parliament that became all the more important after they took office.

Local interests became increasingly tied with the party conflict at Westminster as Whigs and the government alike bid for support at the constituency level. The opening of constituency politics and the organizational infrastructure of clubs and committees that facilitated it created a national arena for party politics. Local interests had developed sophisticated infrastructures for electioneering at the constituency level during the eighteenth century, especially where contested elections were common. Conflict at the constituency level, however, only engaged national politics on occasion before the early nineteenth century. The opening of county and borough politics to party rivalries extending from Westminster marked an important development that Brougham and other Whigs actively promoted. Changes in the allocation of seats brought by the 1832 Reform Act increased the importance of party in the Commons and meant that general elections came to determine a government's tenure. Whigs and Tories quickly responded to the new dynamic with more sophisticated means for coordinating electioneering. Permanent constituency associations recruited electors as well as handling the business of candidates and electioneering between contests. The formation of central registration committees helped coordinate local efforts, and political clubs like the Carlton Club founded in 1832 to promote Tory efforts in opposition marked an important step toward the emergence of centralized party organizations in the 1830s.[12] Earlier Whig initiatives during the 1810s and 1820s, however, had set the pattern that linked vibrant aspects of the old order with these developments in engaging public opinion and building permanent national political organizations.

What of Brougham's own career? Although a leading figure in the Whigs' revival, his role later became overshadowed by events in the 1830s. Campaigns against the Orders in Council, the income tax, and slavery, along with his widely publicized speeches at Westminster, had linked Brougham indelibly with reform in the broadest sense. He was the most famous Whig leader, and the Yorkshire election gave him credit among the public for the Tories' final defeat. Alexander Somerville, a Scottish labourer who wrote an autobiography in the 1840s, described the scene when a boy approached him and his fellow workmen at a quarry on the Lothian coast to bring word of the Tories having been driven from power. 'Those of us who knew least of politics knew enough to understand the importance of this announcement...and loud above the north wind, and the roaring sea, shouted 'Henry Brougham for ever!'"[13] Longtime readers of the *Leeds Mercury, Manchester Guardian*, and other liberal papers in the provinces might have drawn a similar conclusion.

Nonetheless, Brougham's election for Yorkshire and later accession to office as Lord Chancellor marked the peak of his career. Not only did the Chancellorship take Brougham from the Commons where he stood out as a leading debater, it also pushed him from politics into an essentially professional office. As he might have foreseen, a peerage ended Brougham's ability to portray himself as the people's tribune in Parliament. Charles Greville wrote that with Brougham's peerage, 'all men feel that he is emasculated and drops on the Woolsack as on his political deathbed; once in the H. of Lords, there is an end to him, and he may rant, storm, and thunder without hurting anybody'.[14] As Wellington had said in 1818 of Grey and Lansdowne, both also noted for their success in the Commons, 'they are lost by being in the House of Lords. Nobody cares a damn for the House of Lords; the House of Commons is everything in England and the House of Lords nothing'.[15]

Grey and Lansdowne, like Lord Liverpool among the Tories, made the transition to the peerage without losing their standing as party leaders. Brougham's acceptance of the Chancellorship set in stone his earlier dictum to Holland in 1827 that he would place his legal work above political office. No Lord Chancellor had proceeded to fill another leading office or act as a party leader. John Scott, Earl of Eldon, despite his ultra ties, held aloof from the Pittites and acted from a loyalist commitment to defend the interests of Church and State. An earlier Chancellor, Lord Thurlow, showed his independence by negotiating with the Prince of Wales to retain his office when the Regency crisis of 1788 threatened to drive Pitt from power, but the increasing sense of the cabinet's collective responsibility by the 1830s made it unthinkable that a Lord Chancellor could act independently in this way. After Brougham, no leading politician besides F.E. Smith accepted the Chancellorship, and, as Lord Birkenhead after 1919, even the redoubtable Smith saw his influence fade after leaving the Commons.

Brougham lived up to his reputation as a reformer during the early years of his tenure as Lord Chancellor. He immediately redeemed the commitment to judicial reform made in 1828 by introducing the measure for a cheap and easy administration of the law that he previously had carried through several stages in the Commons.[16] The two previous Chancellors, Eldon and Lyndhurst, had left a massive backlog of cases in the Court of Chancery that amounted to a grievance in itself. Brougham worked through almost all the arrears by the end of his first year in office through an unrivalled display of activity that combined his judicial duties with political responsibilities as leader of the House of Lords and party strategist. Sydney Smith praised his achievement at a public meeting in Taunton, Somerset, describing

the gigantic Brougham, sworn in at 12 o'clock, and before 6 has a bill on the table, abolishing the abuses of a Court which has been the curse of the people of England for a century...[and] in an instant the iron mace of Brougham shivered to atoms this house of fraud and of delay; and this is the man who will help to govern you; who bottoms his reputation on doing good to you; who knows, that to reform abuses is the safest basis of fame and the surest instrument of power....Look to Brougham, and turn you to that side where he waves his long and lean finger; and mark well that face which nature has marked so forcibly – which dissolves pensions – turns jobbers into honest men – scares away the plunderer of the public – and is a terror to him who doeth evil to the people.[17]

After passage of the 1832 Reform bill cleared the way for other measures, Brougham put forward additional legislation for legal reforms.

Smith's praise came at the height of the crisis over parliamentary reform and confirmed that Brougham's popular standing remained a strong electoral asset for the Whigs. Grey excluded Brougham from the cabinet committee formed to draft the Reform bill so that the Chancellor would not upset its deliberations or leak details of the measure to the press. Brougham retained control of the Whigs' press relations, however, and Lord John Russell claimed that he had coined the slogan 'the Bill, the whole Bill, and nothing but the Bill' during the 1831 general election.[18] Guiding the Reform bill through bitter resistance in the House of Lords further enhanced Brougham's reputation. Besides concerting strategy with Grey, he led the debate on 8 October 1831 with the longest speech ever given in the House of Lords.[19] Althorp reported the view of Holland and Grey that it was a superhuman effort uniting 'all the excellencies of the ancient with those of modern oratory, and that the action and delivery were as much applauded as the speech itself'.[20] After the peers rejected the measure by 46 votes, Brougham opposed the suggestions of a compromise urged by some of his colleagues and kept up the pressure that finally ensured the Reform Act's passage. Holland attributed the government's eventual narrow victory to the perseverance of Brougham, Grey, and William IV.[21]

Despite such triumphs, Brougham's political career was already in eclipse. The querulousness and propensity toward intrigue that had previously set Brougham's mixed reputation within political circles at odds with his fame in the provinces plagued the Whigs. His fiery temperament remained a disruptive influence that only grew worse over time. When *The Times* sharply criticized Grey in early 1831 for nepotism, Brougham's past differences with Grey and his relationship with its editor, Thomas Barnes, aroused suspicions of his involvement. Grey's conciliatory attitude and the pressure of other business averted a serious quarrel, but the incident exacerbated all the old doubts about Brougham's reliability. The government's mishandling of Irish affairs brought Grey's resignation in mid-1834, and many Whigs blamed the situation on Brougham, who indeed had interfered in matters outside his departmental responsibility. Differences over the new Poor Law between Brougham and Barnes sparked a dispute in the spring of 1834 that quickly became personal and turned the *Times* and other newspapers against the Lord Chancellor. Barnes used Brougham's eccentricities, particularly his slovenly attire, and muted criticism among fellow Whigs to lash him mercilessly in *The Times*. By opening a campaign against the paper and failing to win it, Brougham drew scorn from colleagues and observers alike. His political touch clearly had gone.

During the autumn of 1834, Brougham conducted what Holland called 'an indecorous exhibition of public oratory' on a speaking tour through Northern England and Scotland intended as a response to his critics.[22] At a dinner for Grey in Edinburgh, Brougham spoke in defence of his own achievements and disparaged those, like Durham, who urged a faster pace of reform. It fuelled a dispute between Brougham and the fiery-tempered Durham that involved both Brougham's disloyalty to Grey and his struggle with Durham for the Whig Mountain's allegiance. Brougham made a bad situation worse with a series of public indiscretions that included a drunken appearance at the Edinburgh races in his full regalia as Lord Chancellor. His behaviour offended William IV and embarrassed the government. Grey told Holland that Brougham seemed determined to undermine the government: 'You cannot conceive the degree to which he has injured both the administration generally and himself personally, by his conduct'.[23] Before the year closed, the King dismissed the Whig government now led by Lord Melbourne, who had succeeded Grey as Prime Minister. When Melbourne returned to office in early 1835, he deliberately excluded Brougham from the cabinet, and the former Chancellor never again held office. Far from a reprise of his Westmorland and Yorkshire campaigns, Brougham's speaking tour had marked what Benjamin Disraeli aptly called a 'vagrant and grotesque apocalypse' to his career.[24]

Brougham's temperament was the tragic flaw that ended his career and marred his reputation. Greville shrewdly described Brougham in 1828 as

> a living and very remarkable instance of the inefficacy of the most splendid talents unless they are accompanied with other qualities, which scarcely admit of definition, but which must serve the same purpose as ballast does for a ship...As a statesman he is not considered eligible for the highest offices, and however much he may be admired or feared as an orator or debater, he neither commands respect by his character nor inspires confidence by his genius, and in this contrast between his pretensions and his situations more humble abilities may find room for consolation and cease to contemplate with envy his immense superiority.[25]

Lord John Russell numbered among Brougham's faults recklessness of judgement, an omnivorous appetite for praise, a habitual interference in matters not of his concern, and a disregard for truth.[26] An excess of charisma, in the sense of effortlessly commanding attention, spoiled Brougham's talents by feeding his ambition and vanity. Creevey, Althorp, Durham, and Grey all quarrelled with Brougham or fell victim to his scheming. Consequently, like Canning among the Tories, Brougham aroused more respect, and occasionally fear, than affection.

Before the late 1820s, Brougham's fellow Whigs excused his often erratic behaviour as an unfortunate accompaniment to his abilities. But his part in the events surrounding the formation of Canning's short-lived government in 1827 and the tenor of his Yorkshire campaign in 1830 finally cost Brougham the Whigs' confidence. Unable to do without him, party leaders in the 1830s failed to solve the problem of what they could do with him. The Lord Chancellor's interference with policies outside his department and his petty quarrels with colleagues and the press led Melbourne to conclude by 1835 that nothing could be done about Brougham. Melbourne likened his character to that of Burke:

> as a man of violent, often intensely violent passions; that he was a man as unmeasured in his invectives as he was profuse in panegyric, that he disregarded the moral maxim *ne quid nimis* – that such was the extreme recklessness, such the unequalled eccentricity of his conduct, that he often proved a most pernicious and dangerous guide.[27]

Melbourne's words showed how far Brougham's reputation had fallen from earlier days in 1809 when Grey had compared him with Burke in terms of talent and eloquence.[28]

Despite the failure of his own career, Brougham had led the Whigs to power and transformed British politics. Indeed, the contrast between Brougham's ultimate failure as a politician and the tremendous achievements of his early career obscured his impact on the Whigs and politics generally between 1808 and 1830. While promoting an essentially moderate programme that marginalized popular radicals, he made the Whigs a more aggressive opposition party. Brougham's work with the press and his cultivation of middle class provincial opinion gave his party a formidable base of support that Grey's ministry confirmed through its measures. All Brougham's achievements depended upon seizing opportunities contingent on events, but his fundamental programme to broaden political representation and revive the Whigs remained consistent. Brougham's sustained criticism of government policies on a range of issues laid the basis for subsequent reforms that began with repeal of the Test and Corporation Acts in 1828 and continued through the Municipal Corporations Act in 1835. Simply by reinvigorating the Whig opposition and connecting high politics with provincial interests and public opinion, Brougham contributed substantially to the development of a two-party system that became the hallmark of British parliamentary liberalism.

In the years before 1830, Brougham showed a remarkable grasp of British politics that allowed him to bring the Whigs out of the margins and lay the basis of Victorian liberalism. His ideas on reform in politics, economic policy, law, and relations between church and state deeply influenced nineteenth-century Britain. Brougham's behaviour in office, however, eclipsed his earlier achievements as much as it destroyed his career. The events that led to his exclusion from power by Melbourne and his subsequent attacks on the Whigs who had rejected him, cast a pall over Brougham's entire career. Both contemporaries and later historians often failed to distinguish between the two periods of Brougham's public life, and his reputation suffered as a result.

Ironically, a similar fate has befallen the closing years of the unreformed political system marked by Brougham's greatest successes and the revival of the Whig party. Historians have tended to focus on either the late eighteenth century period characterized by rivalry between Pitt and Fox or the crisis over the 1832 Reform Act and its aftermath. Recent scholarship has not engaged early nineteenth century British politics on its own terms, presenting it instead as the conclusion or prologue to another era. By casting a shadow over the Whig revival and its broader impact, this perspective understates the importance for British politics of the revitalization of parliamentary opposition and its linkage with support in the provinces. What John Wilson Croker aptly described in September 1831 as 'a revolution gradually accomplished by due form of law' followed directly from Whig efforts to rebuild their party and gain advantage over Tory administrations led by Liverpool and his colleagues.[29] Whig tactics in the 1820s drove contingencies that led to the political crisis between 1827 and 1832, and those tactics emerged after 1808 in response to the party's exclusion from power. Close study of the Whig revival and political culture during the early nineteenth century thus engages important questions about the nature of party and relations between metropolitan and provincial interests with broader significance. It also relates a narrative interesting on its own terms as a study in party transformation and political realignment.

Notes

Introduction

1. Peter Mandler, *Aristocratic Government in the Age of Reform: Whigs and Liberals, 1830–1852* (Oxford: Clarendon Press, 1990), 14.
2. Roy Porter, *English Society in the Eighteenth Century* (Harmondsworth, England: Penguin Books, 1990), 112.
3. Byron, 'Don Juan', Canto 11; John Cannon, 'New Lamps for Old: the End of Hanoverian England' in *The Whig Ascendancy: Colloquies on Hanoverian England*, Cannon, ed. (London: Edward Arnold, 1988), 115.
4. Robert Stewart, *Henry Brougham, 1778–1868: His Public Career* (London: Bodley Head, 1985), 43–4, 120.
5. Donald Read, *The English Provinces c. 1760–1960: A Study in Influence* (London: Edward Arnold, 1964).
6. Brougham, 'Rights and Duties of the People', *Edinburgh Review* (November 1812):424, Dror Wahrman, *Imagining the Middle Class: The Political Representation of Class in Britain c. 1780–1840* (Cambridge: Cambridge University Press, 1995), 255.
7. J.C.D. Clark, *English Society, 1660–1832: Religion, Ideology and Politics During the Ancien Regime* (Cambridge: Cambridge University Press, 2000), 513.
8. T.A. Jenkins, *The Liberal Ascendancy, 1830–86* (New York: St Martin's Press, 1994), 19.
9. Jonathan Parry, *The Rise and Fall of Liberal Government in Victorian Britain* (New Haven: Yale University Press, 1993), 3–4.
10. Walter Bagehot, *The English Constitution* (Ithaca, NY: Cornell University Press, 1966), 152.
11. Ibid., 28.
12. Richard Brent, *Liberal Anglican Politics: Whiggery Religion and Reform, 1830–1* (Oxford: Clarendon Press, 1990), 28, 37, 39.
13. James Abercrombie to George Tierney, 1818, Tierney MSS.
14. Horner to Francis Jeffrey, 15 September 1806, *Horner Papers* 427.
15. Chester H. New, *The Life of Henry Brougham to 1830* (Oxford: Clarendon Press, 1961), 2–3; David Hackett Fisher, *Albion's Seed: Four British Folkways in America* (Oxford: Oxford University Press, 1989), 647–8.
16. Arthur Aspinall, *Lord Brougham and the Whig Party* (London: Longmans, Green & Co., 1927), 2–5.
17. Holland *Memoirs*, II: 228–9.
18. Aspinall, *Lord Brougham and the Whig Party* 15; Brougham to John Allen, January 1807, Add. MSS 52177.
19. New, 8, 16, 19.
20. William Thomas, *The Quarrel of Macaulay and Croker: Politics and History in the Age of Reform* (Oxford: Oxford University Press, 2000), 80.
21. Creevey Papers, I: 108.
22. Thomas, *Quarrel of Macaulay and Croker*, 81.

23. Frank O'Gorman, *Voters, Patrons, and Parties: The Unreformed Electoral System of Hanoverian England, 1734–1832* (Oxford: Clarendon Press, 1989), 1–2; H.T. Dickinson, *The Politics of the People in Eighteenth Century Britain* (New York: St Martin's Press, 1995), 15–17.

1   Party Structure and the Whigs in British Politics

1. James J. Sack, *From Jacobite to Conservative: Reaction and Orthodoxy in Britain, c. 1760–1832* (Cambridge: Cambridge University Press, 1993), 42–5; Philip Harling, *The Waning of 'Old Corruption:' The Politics of Economical Reform in Britain, 1777–1846* (Oxford: Clarendon Press, 1996), 47–9.
2. Mandler, 45, 52.
3. S.H. Romilly, *Letters to Ivy from the First Earl of Dudley* (London: Longmans, Green & Co., 1905), 58.
4. J. Parry, 'Constituencies, Elections, and Members of Parliament, 1790–1820', *Parliamentary History*, 7.1(1988),153.
5. Denis Gray, *Spencer Perceval: The Evangelical Prime Minister, 1762–1812* (Manchester: Manchester University Press, 1963), 102.
6. Croker Papers, I: 372.
7. Thorne, I: 73, 99.
8. Thorne, I: 192; Memorandum in Lord Liverpool's papers, Add. MSS 38363, f. 65.
9. Austin Mitchell, *The Whigs in Opposition, 1815–30* (Oxford: Clarendon Press, 1967), 60.
10. Thorne, I: 237.
11. Peter Fraser, 'Party Voting in the House of Commons, 1812–27', *English Historical Review* 98(October 1983): 763–4; Thorne, I: 263.
12. Robert Stewart, *The Foundations of the Conservative Party, 1830–67* (London: Longmans, 1978), 16–17.
13. Harling, 179–80.
14. Mitchell, 79–80.
15. Caroline Robbins, 'Discordant Parties: A Study of the Acceptance of Party by Englishmen', *Political Science Quarterly*, 73(1958):505; Robert Willman, 'The Origins of "Whig" and "Tory" in English Political Language', *Historical Journal*, 17:2(1974), 264.
16. Mitchell, 64.
17. Frederick A. Pottle, ed., *Boswell in Holland, 1763–64* (New York: McGraw Hill, 1952), 129–30.
18. *Parliamentary Debates*, 2nd ser., 17(4 May 1827): 558.
19. Frank O'Gorman, *The Emergence of the British Two Party System, 1760–1832* (London: Edward Arnold, 1982), 56.
20. Croker to Brougham, 14 March 1839, Brougham MSS. Croker proceeded to state that it was possible for a man to be in the wrong party, 'always hankering after the opposite doctrine'.
21. A.S. Foord, *His Majesty's Opposition, 1714–1830* (Oxford: Clarendon Press, 1964), 444; Josceline Bagot, *George Canning and His Friends*, 2 vols (New York: E.P. Dutton and Co., 1909), I,148; Hawkesbury's speech, *Parl. Deb.*, 1st ser., 4(May 10, 1804): 691; Sack, *Jacobite to Conservative*, 67–9, 73.

22. O'Gorman, *Emergence of the British Two Party System*, viii.
23. Jenkins, 38.
24. J.E. Cookson, *Lord Liverpool's Administration: The Crucial Years, 1815–22* (Edinburgh: Scottish Academic Press, 1975), 40; Mitchell, 2.
25. O'Gorman, *Emergence of the British Two-Party System*, viii.
26. J.C.D. Clark, 'The Decline of Party, 1740–60', *English Historical Review*, 93.368(July 1978):511.
27. Stewart, *Foundations of the Conservative Party*, 15.
28. Thorne, I:126, 149, 185, 192, 135, 263.
29. O'Gorman, *Voters, Patrons and Parties*, 300.
30. W. Thomas, 'Whigs and Radicals in Westminster: The Election of 1819', *Guildhall Miscellany* 3.3(October 1970):184; Jenkins, 14; Clark, *English Society*, 499.
31. A.D. Kriegel, *Holland House Diaries, 1831–40: The Diary of Richard Vassal Fox, 3rd Lord Holland with Extracts from the Diary of Dr. John Allen* (London: Routledge & Kegan Paul, 1977) xiv; Francis Place MSS, Add. MSS 36626, f. 21.
32. Castlereagh's speech, *Parl. Deb.* 1st ser., 35(7 February 1817):270–1; Western's speech, *Parl. Deb.* 2nd ser., 9(11 June 1823):834.
33. Creevey Papers, I:25.
34. Croker Papers, I:401; Croker to Liverpool, 13 October 1824. Add. MSS 38299.
35. Cannon, *The Fox–North Coalition: The Crisis of the Constitution* (Cambridge: Cambridge University Press, 1969), 235–6.
36. Thorne, I:348; William Banks Taylor, 'The Foxite Party and Foreign Politics, 1806–16', (Ph.D. diss., University of London, 1974), 18; F. O'Gorman, 'Pitt and the "Tory" Reaction', in *Britain and the French Revolution, 1789–1815*, H.T. Dickinson, ed., (London: Macmillan Education, 1989), 27, 36.
37. Taylor, 418–9.
38. J.J. Sack, *The Grenvillites, 1801–29: Party Politics and Faction in the Age of Pitt and Liverpool* (Urbana: University of Illinois Press, 1979), 70–5; Peter Jupp, *Lord Grenville, 1759–1834* (Oxford: Clarendon Press, 1985), 328–9.
39. Sack, *The Grenvillites*, 125; *Examiner*, 16 April 1809;
40. Grey to Tierney, 27 June 1809, Tierney MSS; Grey to Grenville, 17 November 1812, Dropmore Papers, X:311–13; Grey to Sir Arthur Piggott, 21 January 1809, Grey MSS.
41. Henry Brougham, *Historical Sketches of Statesmen Who Flourished in the Time of George III*, 2 vols (Philadephia: Parry & Macmillan, 1842), I:202; Sack, *Grenvillites*, 153.
42. Dean Rapp, 'The Left–Wing Whigs: Whitbread, The Mountain and Reform, 1809–15', *Journal of British Studies* 21:2(Spring 1982), 35–6, 59; 'The Anti-Royal Menagerie', *Satirist*, 1 December 1812, listed in *English Cartoons and Satirical Prints, 1320–1832 in the British Museum* (Cambridge: Chadwyck-Healey, 1978) as Print 11, 916.
43. Taylor, 290; E.A. Wasson, *Whig Renaissance: Lord Althorp and the Whig Party, 1782–45* (New York: Garland Publishing, 1987), 39.
44. Holland to Brougham, February 1811, in Creevey Papers, I:144; Holland, *Further Memoirs*, 216; Richard W. Davis, 'Whigs in the Age of Fox and Grey', *Parliamentary History*, 12:2(1993), 203.

45. Kriegel, xvi, xviii; Clark, *English Society*, 445.
46. Holland to Brougham, 2 January 1810, Brougham MSS. Holland wrote that the seat was offered 'free of all expense', and Bedford only required a clear statement of Brougham's position 'to prevent all possibility of misunderstanding'; Michael A. Rutz, 'The Politicizing of Evangelical Dissent, 1811–13', *Parliamentary History*, 20:2(2001),189.
47. John Clive, *Scotch Reviewers: The Edinburgh Review, 1802–15* (London: Faber & Faber 1957), 83.
48. Thomas, *The Philosophical Radicals: Nine Studies in Theory and Practice, 1817–41* (Oxford: Clarendon Press, 1979), 47; Jupp, 126; Mitchell, 21.
49. Earl of Ilchester, ed., *The Journal of Elizabeth, Lady Holland 1791–1811*, 2 vols (London: Longmans, Green & Co., 1908), II:325–6.
50. Tierney to Grey, 26 November and 7 December 1807, Tierney MSS; Thorne, IV:94–5, 854.
51. Creevey Papers, I:181, 327; Brougham to Grey, 2 August 1812, Brougham MSS; Thorne, IV:861.
52. Thorne, IV: 856.
53. Holland to Grey, 17 November 1811, Add. MSS 51545; Creevey to H.G. Bennet, 30 December 1818, Creevey Papers, I:290.
54. Roberts, 106–7
55. Taylor, 272.
56. For two examples, see speeches by Robert Milnes, *Parl. Deb.*, 1st ser., 10(3 February 1808), 295; and Sir Thomas Turton, Ibid., 10(8 April 1808), 1360. Milnes had become an adherent of Portland's government after the Talents' collapse and responded to Whitbread's 6 July 1807 motion on the state of the nation with a call for national unity. Turton was an independent who defeated Tierney at Southwark in 1806, Thorne, IV:598–9, V:420.
57. Grey to Sir Arthur Pigott, 21 January 1809, Grey MSS.
58. *Parl. Deb.*, 1st ser., 10(29 January 1808):182; Tierney's speech, Ibid., 179.
59. Ponsonby's speech, *Parl. Deb.*, 1st ser., 10(3 February 1808):253; Ibid., 310; *Parl. Deb.*, 1st ser., 10(21 March 1808):1235; Sharp's speech, Ibid., 1197–8.
60. Whitbread's speech, *Parl. Deb.*, 1st ser., 10(8 April 1808):1353–6, 1358; Turton's speech. Ibid., 1360.
61. Grey to Brougham, 29 September 1808, Henry Brougham, *The Life and Times of Henry, Lord Brougham*, 3 vols (London: William Blackwood & Sons, 1871), I:413–4; *Morning Chronicle*, 15 June 1808; Brougham to Allen, July 1808, Add. MSS 52178.
62. Brougham to Allen, July 1808, Add. MSS 52178.
63. Brougham and Francis Jeffrey, 'Don Pedro Cevallos on the French Usurpation of Spain', *Edinburgh Review* (October 1808), 223.
64. Ibid., 222.
65. Sydney Smith to Francis Jeffrey, October or November 1808, *Letters of Sydney Smith* Nowell C. Smith ed., 2 vols (Oxford: Clarendon Press, 1953), I:145–6; Rory Muir, *Britain and the Defeat of Napoleon, 1807–15* (New Haven: Yale University Press, 1996), 260.
66. Muir, 59, 77.
67. Taylor, 248.

68. Roberts, 153–5.
69. Polypus (Eaton Stannard Barrett), *The Talents Run Mad or 1816* (London: Henry Colburn, 1816), 27–8.
70. Creevey Papers, I:97.
71. Romilly's speech, *Parl. Deb.*, 1st ser., 15(26 January 1810):199; *Parl. Deb.*, 1st ser., 16(30 March 1810):421–2
72. Roberts, 147.
73. Horner Papers, 633.
74. Irving Brock, *The Patriots and the Whigs: The Most Dangerous Enemies of the State* (London: J.M. Richardson, 1810), 44–5, 4; 'Sketch for a Prime Minister or how to purchase a Peace', *English Cartoons and Satirical Prints in the British Museum*, Print 11,710.
75. Roberts, 168.
76. S.H. Romilly, ed., *Letters to Ivy*, 140–1.
77. *Liverpool Mercury*, 11 August 1812.
78. Nicholas C. Edsall, *Richard Cobden: Independent Radical* (Cambridge, MA: Harvard University Press, 1986), 71; Stewart, *Henry Brougham*, 74.
79. Eli F. Hecksher, *The Continental System* (Oxford: Clarendon Press, 1922), 90.
80. Cabinet Memorandum of 12 October 1807, Perceval MSS, Add. MSS 41977. The file also contains other ministers' responses to Perceval's proposal.
81. *Parl. Deb.*, 1st ser., 10(27 January 1808):150–1.
82. Brougham, 'Late Orders in Council', *Edinburgh Review* (January 1808): 484–98.
83. Petty's speech, *Parl. Deb.*, 1st ser., 10(5 February 1808):314–20; Perceval's speech, Ibid., 328–30.
84. *Parl. Deb.*, 1st ser., 10(1808):671–6.
85. *Parl. Deb.*, 1st ser., 10(24 February 1808):726; Ibid., 10(11 March 1808):1076.
86. Hecksher, 171; François Crouzet, 'Towards an Export Economy: British Exports During the Industrial Revolution', in *Britain Ascendant: Comparative Studies in Franco–British Economic History* (Cambridge: Cambridge University Press, 1990), 222–3.
87. Muir, 423–4; Donald R. Hickey, *The War of 1812, A Forgotten Conflict* (Urbana: University of Illinois Press, 1989), 22–3; B.H. Tolley, 'The Liverpool Campaign Against the Orders in Council and the War of 1812', in *Liverpool and Merseyside*, J.R. Harris ed. (London: Frank Cass & Co., 1969), 109.
88. Arthur Gayer, W.W. Rostow, and Anna Jacobson Schwartz, *The Growth and Fluctuation of the British Economy, 1790–1850: An Historical, Statistical, and Theoretical Study of Britain's Economic Development* (Hassocks: Harvester Press, 1975), 109.
89. Peter Fraser, 'Public Petitioning and Parliament Before 1832', *History*, 158(1961):208–9.
90. Brougham to Thomas Thornley, 14 and 22 November 1811, Brougham MSS.
91. Roscoe to Brougham, 11 March 1812, Roscoe MSS.
92. *Liverpool Mercury*, 11 December 1811.

93. D.J. Moss, 'Birmingham and the Campaign against the Orders in Council and the East India Company Charter 1812–13', *Canadian Journal of History*, 11.2(1976):176; J.E. Cookson, *The Friends of Peace: Anti-war Liberalism in England, 1793–1815* (Cambridge: Cambridge University Press, 1982), 226.
94. *Leeds Mercury*, 25 January and 29 February 1812; *Morning Chronicle*, 10 March 1812.
95. Brougham to Holland, 11 March 1812, Add. MSS 51561.
96. Whitbread's speech, *Parl. Deb.*, 1st ser., 21(13 February 1812):769–72.
97. Brougham's speech, *Parl. Deb.*, 1st ser., 21(3 March 1812):1092–8; Rose's speech, Ibid., 1121–3.
98. Baring's speech, *Parl. Deb.*, 1st ser., 21(3 March 1812):1126; Perceval's speech, Ibid., 1151; Vote, Ibid., 1163.
99. *Parl. Deb.*, 1st ser., 22(27 March 1812):1; Ibid., 22(27 April 1812):1057–8.
100. *Parl. Deb.*, 1st ser., 21(April, 1812):1064–8; Moss, 178; *English Cartoons and Satirical Prints in the British Museum*, Print 11,876.
101. Castlereagh's speech, *Parl. Deb.*, 1st ser., 22(29 April 1812):1092; Stephen's speech, Ibid., 1111.
102. *Leeds Mercury*, May 2, 1812.
103. Holland, *Further Memoirs*, 132.
104. 'Minutes of Evidence Taken in the House of Commons Against the Orders in Council', *Parliamentary Papers*, 3(1812):95–135.
105. *Parl. Deb.*, 1st ser., 23(16 June 1812):489.
106. Rose's speech, *Parl. Deb.*, 1st ser., 23(16 June 1812):529; Baring's speech, Ibid., 536.
107. *Parl. Deb.*, 1st ser., 23(16 June 1812):538–45.
108. Grey to Grenville, 24 June 1812, Dropmore Papers, X:289.
109. Grey to Brougham, 20 October 1812, Brougham MSS; Thanet to Holland, 9 June 1812, Add. MSS 51571; Thomas Grenville to Lady Grenville, 24 April 1812, Dropmore Papers, X:240–1; Taylor, 342.
110. Rutz, 197, 204.
111. Perceval to Melville, 19 January 1807, Add. MSS 49174.
112. Romilly, *Letters to Ivy*, 99.

2   Elections, the Press and Whig Tactics in Opposition

1. Francis Jeffrey, 'The State of the Nation', *Edinburgh Review*, (January 1810):505, 513.
2. Mandler, 14.
3. John W. Derry, *Charles, Earl Grey: Aristocratic Reformer* (Oxford: Blackwells, 1992), 89; Cookson, *The Friends of Peace*, 158–62.
4. Brougham to Lansdowne, [no date], 1817, Lansdowne MSS.
5. Brougham to Allen, 1 May 1810, Add. MSS 52178.
6. Brougham to Allen, 21 June 1811, Add. MSS 52178.
7. Dickinson, *Politics of the People*, 13.
8. Brougham to Leigh Hunt, [no date], late 1812, Leigh Hunt MSS, Add. MSS 38108.
9. Brougham to Grey, 6 September 1811, Brougham MSS.

10. Taylor, 346–7.
11. Brougham to Creevey, 7 February 1814, cited in D. Rapp, *Samuel Whitbread, A Social and Political Study* (New York: Garland Publishing (1987)), 46.
12. Brougham to Roscoe, 21 October 1812, Roscoe MSS.
13. Romilly, *Letters to Ivy*, 107.
14. *Leeds Mercury*, 20 June 1812.
15. *Liverpool Mercury*, 17 July 1812.
16. *Liverpool Mercury*, 3 July 1812.
17. Sefton to Roscoe, 6 July 1812; Roscoe to Sefton, 9 July 1812, Roscoe MSS.
18. Cookson, *Friends of Peace*, 221.
19. E.M. Menzies, 'The Freeman Voter in Liverpool, 1802–35', *Transactions of the Historic Society of Lancashire and Cheshire*, 124(1972):85–8.
20. Brougham to Hunt, Tuesday (1812), Add. MSS 38108.
21. Thorne, II:230–2; *Times*, 8 October 1812.
22. Sefton to Roscoe, 23 September 1812, Roscoe MSS.
23. Thorne, I:231.
24. *An Impartial Collection of Addresses, Songs, Squibs, & etc. Published During the Election of Members of Parliament for the Borough of Liverpool, October 1812* (Liverpool: Timothy Herring, 1812), 5, 12–13.
25. *Times*, 8 October 1812.
26. Creevey to Mrs. Creevey, October 1812. Cited in Thorne II:232.
27. Aspinall notes the omission to spare Victorian sensibilities, in 'Lord Brougham's Life and Times', *English Historical Review*, 59.233(January 1944):102.
28. Brougham to Grey, 16 October 1812, Brougham MSS.
29. *Collected Speeches*, I:485–6.
30. Creevey to Mrs. Creevey, 17 October 1812, Creevey Papers, I:172.
31. *An Impartial Collection*, 15.
32. 'An Impartial Review of the Candidates', *Liverpool Mercury*, 9 October 1812.
33. *An Impartial Collection*, 117, 42–3. The tune of 'Yankee Doodle' may have been chosen to highlight Brougham's support for conciliation with the United States.
34. Tarleton to Grey, 11 October 1812, Grey MSS.
35. Brougham to Grey, 16 and 18 September 1812, Brougham MSS; Grey to Brougham, 10 August and 1 October 1812, Grey MSS.
36. New, *The Life of Henry Brougham to 1830*, 76; *Times*, October 15, 1812.
37. *Times*, 20 October 1812; Brougham to Grey, 16 October 1812, Brougham MSS.
38. *Courier*, 20 October 1812.
39. Creevey to Mrs. Creevey, 17 October 1812, Creevey Papers, I:171.
40. Horner to J. Murray, 21 October 1812, Horner Papers, 742.
41. *Morning Chronicle*, 30 October 1812.
42. Brougham to Allen, 28 October 1812., Add. MSS 52178; Brougham to Grey, 16 October 1812, Brougham MSS.
43. Barbara Whittingham-Jones, 'Liverpool's Political Clubs, 1812–30', *Transactions of the Historic Society of Lancashire and Cheshire* 111(1959):117; Brougham likened Liverpool to Camelford, the close borough he represented earlier, and told Hunt the two boroughs were

exactly the same in their proportion of inhabitants to voters and access to the suffrage. Brougham to Hunt, [no date] (October 1812), Add. MSS 38108.

44. Lansdowne to Allen, 1 November 1812, Add. MSS 52194.
45. Brougham to Grey, November 1812, Brougham MSS.
46. *Courier*, 23 October 1812.
47. Liverpool to Egremont, 14 October 1812, Add. MSS 38249; Croker to Peel, 26 October 1812. Cited in Thorne, I:230.
48. *Courier*, 24 October 1812.
49. *Morning Chronicle*, 26 October 1812.
50. Tierney to Grey, 17 September 1812, Grey MSS; Horner to Mrs. Dugald Stewart, 21 October 1812, Horner Papers, 745.
51. Thorne, I:231.
52. Ibid., I:237. Treasury officials combined sure supporters with a proportion of those counted hopeful or doubtful to calculate expected support.
53. Mitchell, 81, 116.
54. *Courier*, 24 October 1812.
55. Mitchell, 45–7.
56. Horner Papers, 596–601.
57. Tierney to Grey, 17 September 1812, Grey MSS.
58. Lamb to Grey, 3 November 1812; Grey to Holland, 11 November 1812, Grey MSS.
59. Brougham to Leigh Hunt, 20 October 1812, Add. MSS 38108.
60. Brougham to Grey, November 1812, Brougham MSS.
61. Romilly, *Letters to Ivy*, 173.
62. Brougham to Roscoe, 25 September 1812, Roscoe MSS; *An Impartial Collection*, 132.
63. *Courier*, 29 October 1812.
64. Brougham, 'Rights and Duties of the People', *Edinburgh Review*, November 1812, 424.
65. Brougham to Hunt, [no date] (1812), Add. MSS 38108.
66. Ian R. Christie, 'British Newspapers in the Late Georgian Age', in *Myth and Reality in Late Eighteenth Century British Politics and Other Papers* (Berkeley: University of California Press, 1970), 237.
67. A.P. Wadsworth, 'Newspaper Circulations, 1800–1954', *Transactions of the Manchester Statistical Society* (1954–5), 3–5.
68. *Cobbett's Political Register*, 16 November 1816.
69. John Ranby, *An Inquiry Into the Supposed Increase of the Influence of the Crown* (London: Hatchard, 1811), 45.
70. Scott to Lockhart, 3 April 1829, *Letters of Sir Walter Scott*, Sir Herbert Grierson ed., 12 vols (London: Constable & Co., 1936), XI:162.
71. A. Aspinall, 'The Social Status of Journalists at the Beginning of the Nineteenth Century', *Review of English Studies*, 21(1945):216, 220–5.
72. John Penn Tinney, *The Rights of Sovereignty Vindicated: With Particular Reference to Political Doctrines of the Edinburgh Review and of Other Periodical Publications* (London: C. & R. Baldwin, 1809), 190.
73. *History of the Times: 'The Thunderer' in the Making, 1785–1841* (New York: Macmillan, 1935), viii.
74. Brougham to Allen, [no date]. Cited in A. Aspinall, *Politics and the Press* (London: Home & Van Thal Ltd, 1949): 292.

75. Ivon Asquith, 'Advertising and the Press in the Late Eighteenth and Early Nineteenth Centuries: James Perry and the Morning Chronicle', *Historical Journal*, 18.4(1975):721.

76. *Morning Chronicle*, 22 March 1812.

77. Asquith, 'Advertising and the Press', 720.

78. Rapp, 43.

79. Grey to Holland, 23 March 1818, Add. MSS 51553.

80. Aspinall, *Politics and the Press*, 299–302; Brougham to Grey, 7 December 1821, Brougham MSS. The Whig *Guardian* should not be confused with the famous Manchester paper founded in the 1820s or the Tory weekly that Croker established from 1819 to 1824.

81. Wadsworth, 7.

82. Brougham's ties with Barnes and *The Times*' criticism of Grey in 1831 sparked an embarrassing quarrel that hurt Brougham's standing among the Whigs, Stewart, *Henry Brougham*, 260–2.

83. Trowbridge H. Ford, 'Political Coverage in *The Times*, 1811–41: The Role of Barnes and Brougham', *Bulletin of the Institute of Historical Research*, 49.139(May 1986):95–106.

84. Aspinall, *Politics and the Press*, 350.

85. Christie, 'British Newspapers in the Late Georgian Age' in *Myth and Reality in Late Eighteenth Century British Politics and other Papers*, 326.

86. Aspinall, *Politics and the Press*, 352.

87. *Leeds Mercury*, 26 September 1812.

88. Donald Read, *Press and People, 1790–1850: Opinion in Three English Cities* (London: Edward Arnold, 1961), 201.

89. Edward Baines, Jr, *The Life of Edward Baines, Late MP for the Borough of Leeds* (London: Longmans, Brown, Green & Longmans, 1851), 75, 64; Wahrman, 41; *Leeds Mercury*, 18 April 1812.

90. David Nicholls, 'The English Middle Class and the Ideological Significance of Radicalism, 1760–1886', *Journal of British Studies*, 24(October 1985):425–6.

91. Grey to Holland, 17 January 1817, Grey MSS.

92. Jenkins, 18.

93. Joanne Shattock, *Politics and Reviewers: The Edinburgh and The Quarterly in the Early Victorian Age* (Leicester: Leicester University Press, 1989), 13, 132.

94. Holland, *Further Memoirs*, 386.

95. R. Wharton, *Remarks on the Jacobinical Tendency of the Edinburgh Review in a Letter to the Earl of Lonsdale* (London: Hatchard, 1809), 6.

96. Shattock, 4.

97. Smith to Lady Holland, 10 January 1809, Smith, *Letters of Sydney Smith* I:152; John Clive, 'The Earl of Buchan's Kick: A Footnote to the History of the Edinburgh Review', *Harvard Library Bulletin*, 5.3(1951):362–70.

98. Brougham to Grey, 20 August 1808. Brougham MSS; Smith accused Brougham of acting in an 'unwhiglike manner' in a undated letter to Lady Holland from late 1808 and complained that it was hard to 'keep him right', *Letters of Sydney Smith*, I:151.

99. Clive, *Scotch Reviewers*, 113.

100. Macro, *The Scotiad, or Wise Men of the North* (London: J.J. Stockdale, 1809), 49.

101. Polypus, *The Talents Run Mad: or 1816*, 55.

102. Tinney, 163, 41.
103. *Courier*, 2 December 1808; Wharton, 7.
104. Aspinall, 'Social Status of Journalists', 220.
105. Wharton, 6.
106. Taylor, 398.
107. W.W. Rostow, 'Trade Cycles, Harvests and Politics: 1790–1850', in *The British Economy of the Nineteenth Century* (Oxford: Clarendon Press, 1948), 123–5.
108. Ibid., 123–5.
109. Dror Wahrman examines this theme in *Imagining the Middle Class*.
110. Boyd Hilton, *Corn, Cash, and Commerce: The Economic Policies of the Tory Governments 1815–30* (Oxford: Oxford University Press, 1977), 153.
111. Taylor, 352–3.
112. Grenville to Grey, 14 November 1813, Grey MSS.
113. Thomas Grenville to Grenville, 4 March 1814, Dropmore Papers, X:384.
114. Grey to Holland, 14 January 1816, Grey MSS.
115. Taylor, 400; Sack, *Grenvillites*, 159–61.
116. Tierney to Grey, 1 November 1815, Grey MSS; Grey to Holland, February 1816., Add. MSS 51553.
117. Taylor, 381.
118. Brougham to Grey, 2 August 1812, Brougham MSS.
119. Brougham to Leigh Hunt, 20 October 1812, Add. MSS 38108; 'A New Song in Favor of Peace and Plenty', in *An Impartial Collection*, 62–3.
120. B.E.V. Sabine, *A Short History of Taxation* (London: Butterworths, 1980), 115–9; Patrick O'Brian, 'The Political Economy of British Taxation 1660–1815', *Economic History Review*, 2nd ser., 41:1(1988): 21–2.
121. W. Smart, *Economic Annals of the Nineteenth Century*, 2 vols (London: Macmillan & Co., 1910 and 1917.) I:67–8.
122. *Parl. Deb.*, 1st ser., 29(1815):885.
123. Brougham to Leigh Hunt, 29 February 1816, Add. MSS 38108.
124. Grey to Brougham, 13 November 1815, Grey MSS.
125. *Morning Chronicle*, 12 and 24 January 1816.
126. *Leeds Mercury*, 27 January 1816.
127. *Parl. Deb.*, 1st ser., 32(1 February 1816):36; Ibid., 39, 44.
128. *Parl. Deb.*, 1st ser., 32(2 February 1816):65.
129. *Times*, 6 February 1816.
130. *Parl. Deb.*, 1st ser., 32(7 February 1816):332–3.
131. *Parl. Deb.*, 1st ser., 32(13 February 1816):434.
132. Burrell's speech, *Parl. Deb.*, 1st ser., 32(23 February 1816):820; Althrop's speech, Ibid., 32(26 February 1816):833.
133. *Leeds Mercury*, 10 February 1816.
134. *Morning Chronicle*, 9 February 1816.
135. *Times*, 15 February 1816.
136. *Parl. Deb.*, 1st ser., 33(7 March 1816):26.
137. *Leeds Mercury*, 17 February 1816.
138. *Liverpool Mercury*, 9 and 23 February 1816.
139. *English Cartoons and Satirical Prints in the British Museum*, Print 12,786.
140. *Parl. Deb.*, 1st ser., 32(26 February 1816):833–4.
141. *Parl. Deb.*, 1st ser., 32(26 February 1816):837.

142. Tierney's speech, *Parl. Deb.*, 1st ser., 32(27 February 1816):887; Brougham's speech, Ibid., 889; Mackintosh's speech, Ibid., 908.
143. Brougham's speech, *Parl. Deb.*, 1st ser., 32(27 February 1816): 887.
144. *Parl. Deb.*, 1st ser., 32(5 March 1816): 1120–2.
145. Hilton, *Corn, Cash, and Commerce*, 32.
146. Ibid., 31–2.
147. Mitchell, 94–5; E.A. Smith, *Whig Principles and Party Politics: Earl Fitzwilliam and the Whig Party, 1748–1833* (Manchester: Manchester University Press, 1975), 333.
148. *Morning Chronicle*, 23 February 1816.
149. *Parl. Deb.*, 1st ser., 33(18 March 1816):450–1.
150. Stewart, *Henry Brougham*, 107; *English Cartoons and Satirical Prints in the British Museum*, Print 12,752.
151. *Morning Chronicle*, 20 March 1816; *Leeds Mercury*, 23 March 1816; *Times*, 19 March 1816.
152. Tierney to Grey, 20 January 1815, Grey MSS.
153. Mitchell, 94–5. Austin Mitchell rightly points out the difficulty of assessing 'the Whigs' share in the petitioning campaign' and he applies Tierney's verdict from 1815 to subsequent events. His conclusion that the Whigs' part has been overstated, however, neglects Brougham's management of debate in the Commons and his role in originating 'petition and debate' tactics earlier.
154. Polypus, *The Talents Run Mad, or 1816*, 54.
155. Francis Place's 'History of General and Westminster Politics, 1803–18', Add. MSS 27850; Stewart, *Henry Brougham*, 107.
156. Brougham's speech, *Parl. Deb.*, 1st ser., 33(20 March 1816):495–7.
157. Holland, *Further Memoirs* 233–4; Thomas Wishaw to Thomas Smith, Lady Seymour *Pope of Holland House*, (London: T.F. Unwin, 1906) 149; Brougham to Grey, 21 March 1816, Brougham MSS.
158. Stewart, *Henry Brougham*, 107–9.
159. Cookson, *Lord Liverpool's Administration*, 73–7.
160. Cookson, *Lord Liverpool's Administration*, 7; Boyd Hilton, 'The Political Arts of Lord Liverpool', *Transactions of the Royal Historical Society*, 5th ser., 38(1988):154.
161. Grey to Holland, 3 March 1816, Add. MSS 51553.
162. Grey to Lady Holland, 12 January 1817, Add. MSS 51553; Holland to Grey, [no date (January 1817)] Add. MSS 51553.
163. Robert Southey, 'Rise and Progress of Popular Disaffection', *Quarterly Review* (January 1817):512–3, 345.
164. Mitchell, 103.
165. Smart, I:548–50.
166. Mitchell, 107; Sack, *Grenvillites*, 163.
167. Clark, *English Society*, 516
168. Canning's speech, *Parl. Deb.*, 1st ser. (25 February 1817):654–94.
169. Cochrane's speech, *Parl. Deb.*, 1st ser., 35 (17 February 1817): 369–72; Place complained bitterly about Brougham response to the Seditious Meetings Act and, remarking on Cochrane's opposition to the bill, asked 'where were the shuffling Whigs?', Add. MSS 36672.
170. Stewart, *Henry Brougham*, 116.

171. *English Cartoons and Satirical Prints in the British Museum*, Print 12,867A.
172. *Times*, 24 February 1816; Brougham to Hunt, 29 February 1816, Add. MSS 38108.
173. Holland, *Further Memoirs*, 46.
174. Brougham to Lambton, [no date (1817)], Brougham MSS.

3 The Westmorland Election

1. Brougham to Creevey, 1814, Creevey Papers, I:192.
2. Ibid., 132.
3. Thorne, I:253–4.
4. Darlington to Brougham, 7 January 1818, Brougham MSS.
5. *Kendal Chronicle*, 6 December 1817.
6. O'Gorman, *Voters, Patrons, and Parties*, 336.
7. Lonsdale to James Law Lushington, 12 September 1825, Lowther MSS, Cumbria Record Office, Carlisle.
8. Stuart Reid, *Life and Letters of Lord Durham, 1792–1840*, 2 vols (London: Longmans, Green and Co., 1906): I:68.
9. Thorne, II:406; Smith to John Wishaw, 13 April 1818, Smith, *Letters of Sydney Smith*, I:289.
10. Hugh Owen, *The Lowther Family: Eight Hundred Years of 'A Family of Ancient Gentry and Worship'* (Chichester: Philimore, 1990), 284–8, 381–6.
11. Charles Long to Viscount Lowther, 14 October 1806; Lowther to Charles Long, 27 October 1806, *Papers of the Earl of Lonsdale. Historical Manuscripts Commission 13th Report, Part 7* (London: HMSO, 1893), 204, 217; Buckingham to Thomas Grenville, 10 April 1807, Dropmore Papers, XI:134–5.
12. Thorne, I:408–9. Information on Thanet's views and career largely derive from his letters in the Brougham and Holland MSS and comments from William Banks Taylor, to whom I am indebted.
13. Brougham to Grey, 20 February 1818, Brougham MSS.
14. Thanet to James Atkinson, 7 December 1817; Thanet to James Brougham, 11 January 1818, Brougham MSS.
15. William Wordsworth to Lord Lonsdale, 11 March 1818, Mary Moorman and Alan G. Hill, eds, *Letters of William and Dorothy Wordsworth*, 3 vols (Oxford: Clarendon Press, 1970) II:438.
16. Aspinall, *Politics and the Press* 354; Stuart Melvin Brown, 'The Growth of Middle Class Leadership in Kendal Society and its Influence on Politics, 1790–1850' (MA diss., University of Lancaster, 1971), 8.
17. Carol Anne Dyhouse, 'Social Institutions in Kendal, 1790–1850' (MA diss., University of Lancaster, 1971), 25–6, 28.
18. John Burgess, 'A Religious History of Cumbria, 1780–1920' (Ph.D. diss., University of Sheffield, 1984), 418,339, 323.
19. Francis Nicholson and Ernest Axon, *The Older Nonconformity in Kendal* (Kendal: Titus Wilson, 1915), 347.
20. Alice Palmer, 'Local Government and Social Problems in Kendal and Westmorland, c. 1760–1860' (MA diss., University of Lancaster, 1972), 6–7.
21. J.D. Marshall and Carol Anne Dyhouse, 'Social Transition in Kendal and Westmorland, c. 1760–1860', *Northern History* 12(1976):129; Cornelius

Nicholson, *The Annals of Kendal: Being an Historical and Descriptive Account of Kendal and the Neighbourhood*, 2nd edn (London: Whitaker & Co., 1861), 240–2.

22. J.D. Marshall and John K. Walton, *The Lake Counties from 1830 to the mid-Twentieth Century: A Study in Regional Change* (Manchester: Manchester University Press, 1981), 1, 15.

23. David Stoker, 'Elections and Voting Behaviour: A Study of Elections in Northumberland, Durham, Cumberland and Westmorland, 1760–1832' (Ph.D. diss., University of Manchester, 1980), 3.

24. John Bateman, *Great Landowners of Great Britain and Ireland* 4th edn (Leicester: Leicester University Press, 1971), 60, 279.

25. Thanet to Atkinson, 7 December 1817, Brougham MSS.

26. *Liverpool Mercury*, 26 December 1817; *Kendal Chronicle*, 3 January 1818.

27. Lonsdale to Lowther, 11 January 1818, Lowther MSS.

28. *Kendal Chronicle*, 17 January 1818.

29. Lowther to Lonsdale, 15 January 1818, Lowther MSS.

30. Lord Darlington to Brougham, 7 January 1818, Brougham MSS. Darlington's mother was the sister of James Lowther, the 1st Earl from whom Lonsdale had inherited his political interest.

31. Thanet to Brougham, 23 January 1818, Brougham MSS.

32. *Kendal Chronicle*, 24 January 1818. The January 17 issue of *Carlisle Patriot*, a newspaper the Lowthers influenced, also mentioned Brougham as the London Committee's candidate.

33. J.R. McQuiston, 'The Lonsdale Connection and its Defender, William Viscount Lowther, 1818–1830', *Northern History*, 11(1976):146–7; *Kendal Chronicle*, 31 January 1818.

34. *Morning Chronicle*, 3 February 1818.

35. Brougham to James Brougham, January 1818, Brougham MSS.

36. *Kendal Chronicle*, 21 January 1818.

37. Thanet to James Brougham, 1 February and 5 February 1818; Thanet to Henry Brougham, 1 February 1818, Brougham MSS.

38. *Kendal Chronicle*, 7 February 1818.

39. Stoker, 24, 33, 114–5.

40. Wordsworth to Lonsdale, 29 January and 10 February 1818, Moorman and Hill, *Wordsworth Letters*, II:418, 125.

41. *Kendal Chronicle*, 7 February 1818; *Times*, 8 April 1818. Report copied from the *Carlisle Journal*.

42. Lowther to John Wilson Croker, 22 February 1818, Croker MSS, William L. Clements Library, University of Michigan.

43. Brown, 12.

44. O'Gorman, 'Campaign Rituals and Ceremonies: The Social Meaning of Elections in England, 1780–1860', *Past and Present*, 135(1992):79–115.

45. Stoker, 98, 87–8.

46. *Times*, 23 February 1818.

47. *Kendal Chronicle*, 3 January 1818.

48. Brougham to James Brougham, undated packet of circular letters from 1818, Brougham MSS.

49. *Kendal Chronicle*, 7 February 1818.

50. *Times*, 23 February 1818.

51. *Kendal Chronicle*, 17 January 1818, letter signed Old Noll.

52. *Kendal Chronicle*, 14 February 1818. Presenting a total calculated for seven years represented the income derived over the maximum life of a Parliament under the Septennial Act.
53. *New Times*, 26 February and 2 April 1818.
54. *Courier*, 4 July 1818.
55. *Kendal Chronicle*, 10 January 1818.
56. *Courier*, 23 February 1818.
57. Ibid.
58. Election Poster, D/LONS/L13/11, Box 4, Westmorland Election 1818, Lowther MSS.
59. *British Monitor*, 21 June 1818.
60. Ibid.
61. Enclosed in Wordsworth to Lonsdale, 24 March 1818, Moorman and Hill, *Wordsworth Letters*, 443.
62. *Courier*, 9 April 1818.
63. *New Times*, 1 April 1818.
64. *Courier*, 3 February 1818; *New Times*, 4 February 1818.
65. Thomas Harrison, *An Impartial Narrative of the Riotous Proceedings Which Took Place in Kendal on Wednesday, 11 February 1818* (Kendal: Airey & Bellingham, 1818), *passim*.
66. 1818 Election handbills, WD/CU/32, Cumbria Record Office, Kendal.
67. Colonel Henry Lowther to Lonsdale, 13 February 1818; Lord Lowther to Lonsdale, 11 February 1818, Lowther MSS.
68. *New Times*, 3 April 1818, letter signed 'An Old Englishman'.
69. *Morning Chronicle*, 16 February 1818.
70. *Leeds Mercury*, 21 February 1818.
71. O'Gorman, 'Campaign Rituals and Ceremonies', 84–6. Cultivating support through dinners and other entertainments became a common practice, albeit one disliked by the patrons and candidates forced to subsidize it. Before Brougham's challenge, however, Lonsdale organized few such overtly political entertainments.
72. James Losh to Brougham, 3 March 1818, Brougham MSS.
73. Thanet to Brougham, 15 February 1818, Brougham MSS.
74. McQuiston, 148.
75. Thanet to James Brougham, 5 February 1818, Brougham MSS; Owen, 290.
76. Stoker, 61.
77. Thanet to James Brougham, 18 February 1818, Brougham MSS.
78. Stoker, 67; *Kendal Chronicle*, 9 May 1818; O'Gorman, *Voters, Patrons, and Parties*, 238.
79. Lowther to Lonsdale, 27 February 1818, Lowther MSS.
80. *Carlisle Patriot*, 11 April 1818.
81. Lowther to Lonsdale, 21 March 1818, Lowther MSS.
82. Stoker, 59, 124.
83. Stewart, *Henry Brougham*, 130.
84. McQuiston, 152; Brougham to Atkinson, 8 March 1818, Brougham MSS.
85. *Carlisle Patriot*, 28 March 1818; *Kendal Chronicle*, 28 March 1818. Accounts of the event and Brougham's speech differed slightly between the two papers.

86. John Edwin Wells, 'Wordsworth and DeQuincey in Westmorland Politics, 1818', *Publications of the Modern Language Association of America*, 55.4(1940):1099.
87. *Carlisle Patriot*, 28 March 1818.
88. *Kendal Chronicle*, 28 March 1818.
89. *Kendal Chronicle*, 23 March 1818.
90. Dorothy Wordsworth to Sara Hutchinson, 24 March 1818 and Wordsworth to Lowther, 6 May 1818, Moorman and Hill, *Wordsworth Letters*, II:470, 448–9; *Carlisle Patriot*, 2 May 1818.
91. Brougham to Lady Holland, 28 March 1818, Add. MSS 51564.
92. Brougham to Lady Holland, 24 and 28 March 1818, Add. MSS 51564.
93. *Liverpool Mercury*, 10 April 1818.
94. R.J. Mackintosh, ed., *Memoirs of the Life of the Right Honourable Sir James Mackintosh*, 2 vols (London: Edward Moxon, 1836), II:353.
95. Lowther to Lonsdale, 28 and 30 March 1818, Lowther MSS.
96. Wordsworth to Lonsdale, 6 April 1818, Moorman and Hill, *Wordsworth Letters*, II:462.
97. *Carlisle Patriot*, 4 April 1818.
98. F.S. Janzow, 'DeQuincey Enters Journalism: His Contributions to the Westmorland Gazette 1818–19' (Ph.D. diss., University of Chicago, 1968), 2–3.
99. Thomas DeQuincey, *Close Comments on a Straggling Speech* (Kendal: Airey & Bellingham, 1818). Reprinted in Wells, 'Wordsworth and DeQuincey in Westmorland Politics', 1100–10.
100. Owen, 383.
101. Iain Robertson Scott, 'From Radicalism to Conservatism: The Politics of Wordsworth and Coleridge, 1797–1818' (Ph.D. diss., University of Edinburgh, 1987), 231–2, 241, 161–2.
102. William Wordsworth, *Two Addresses to the Freeholders of Westmorland* (Kendal: Airey & Bellingham, 1818). Reprinted in *The Prose Works of William Wordsworth*, W.J.B. Owen and Jane Worthington Smyser, eds. 3 vols (Oxford: Clarendon Press, 1974), III:155.
103. Ibid., 161, 162–3.
104. Ibid, 171 and *passim*.
105. Stoker, 241–3; DeQuincey, *Close Comments*, 1102.
106. Brougham to Creevey [1818] Creevey Papers, I:120. The letter is misdated and printed with another from 1810.
107. Aspinall, *Politics and the Press*, 304.
108. McQuiston, 150.
109. Thanet to Brougham, 12 and 15 February 1818, Brougham MSS.
110. Thorne, II:90–1.
111. Brougham to Lady Holland, 23 June 1818, Add. MSS 51564.
112. Lady Morpeth to Devonshire, 1 June 1818, cited in Thorne, II:91.
113. Brougham's Speech, *Parl. Deb.*, 1st ser. (27 May 1818):988–90.
114. Thorne, I:4.
115. *Kendal Chronicle*, 4 April 1818. The announcement appeared over several weeks.
116. *Parl. Deb.*, 1st ser. (27 May 1818):990–2.
117. Brougham's speech, *Parl. Deb.*, 1st ser. (31 May 1818):1053–4.

118. Lowther's speech, *Parl. Deb.*, 1st ser. (31 May 1818):1054.
119. *Carlisle Patriot*, 6 June 1818; *Westmorland Gazette*, 6 June 1818; *Parl. Deb.*, 1st ser. (4 May 1818):499–501.
120. Thorne, I:254; *The Late Elections; An Impartial Statement of All Proceedings Connected with the Progress and Result of the Late Elections* (London: Bensley & Sons, 1818), iv–vi; *Courier*, 11 June 1818.
121. Lambton to Grey, 30 June 1818, Grey MSS.
122. Ibid., 20, 24, 33; Poll Book, Westmorland Election, 1818, Box 3, D/LONS/L13/11, Lowther MSS.
123. Croker to Lowther, 4 July 1818; Poll Book, Westmorland Election, 1818, Lowther MSS.
124. *Westmorland Election 1818* (Kendal: Richard Lough, 1818), 20–2, 25; Lambton to Grey, 31 June 1818, Grey MSS; *Liverpool Mercury*, 3 and 10 July; G. Butt, *Suggestions as to the Conduct and Management of a County Contested Election* (London: James Duncan, 1826), 119–21.
125. Lambton to Grey, 6 July 1818, Grey MSS; Brougham to Lady Holland, 3 July 1818, Add. MSS 51564.
126. *Westmorland Election, 1818*, 34–5.
127. *Leeds Mercury*, 10 July 1818.
128. *Courier*, 6 and 7 July 1818.
129. *Westmorland Gazette*, 18 July 1818.
130. Thomas Grenville to Lord Grenville, 3 July 1818, Dropmore Papers, X:440.
131. Brougham to Grey [late summer] 1818, Brougham MSS. Emphasis in original.
132. Smith to Grey, 12 August 1818, Smith, *Letters of Sydney Smith*, I:298.
133. Thorne, II:260–1; Mitchell, 116.
134. *Leeds Mercury*, 10 July 1818; Thorne, I:235, 263.
135. Cookson, *Lord Liverpool's Administration*, 142–3.
136. Brougham to Holland, 28 May 1818, Add. MSS 51561.
137. Thorne, IV:865
138. Holland to Grey, 18 March 1818, Add. MSS 51545.
139. Mitchell, 33–4.
140. Requisition to Tierney, 1818, Tierney MSS.
141. Creevey to Henry Grey Bennet. December 30, 1818, Creevey Papers, I:290–1.
142. Lambton to Wilson, 19 July 1818, Add. MSS 30108.
143. Stewart, *Henry Brougham*, 119.
144. Tierney to Grey, 22 August 1818, Grey MSS.
145. Brougham, 'State of Parties', *Edinburgh Review* (June 1818), 203, 205.

4   Social Tension and Party Politics

1. Ibid., 194.
2. Ibid., 197–8.
3. Tierney to Holland, 6 September 1818, Add. MSS 51584.
4. Wilson to Grey, 4 January 1819, Add. MSS 30123.
5. Lambton to Grey, 13 January 1819; Ibid., 15 January 1819, Grey MSS.
6. *Morning Chronicle*, 6 January 1819.
7. Grey to Wilson, 8 February 1819, Grey MSS.

8. *Leeds Mercury*, 30 January 1819.
9. Holland to Grey, 8 December 1818, Add. MSS 51545.
10. Cookson, *Lord Liverpool's Administration*, 158n; Vansittart's speech, *Parl. Deb.*, 1st ser., 39(2 February 1819):229–30.
11. *Parl. Deb.*, 1st ser., 39(2 February 1819):175.
12. Lambton to Grey, 3 February 1818, Grey MSS.
13. Thorne, I:268.
14. Castlereagh's speech, *Parl. Deb.*, 1st ser., 39(8 February 1819):350–1; Canning's speech, Ibid., 355–6; Calcraft's speech, Ibid., 350; William Wynn's speech, Ibid., 356.
15. Tierney's speech, *Parl. Deb.*, 1st ser., 39(8 February 1819):351; Morpeth's speech, Ibid., 358
16. *Parl. Deb.*, 1st ser., 39(8 February 1819):358.
17. Cited in Cookson, *Lord Liverpool's Administration*, 161.
18. Gerrit P. Judd, *Members of Parliament, 1734–1832* (New Haven: Yale University Press, 1955), 28.
19. Tierney to Grey, 18 February 1819, Grey MSS.
20. *Parl. Deb.*, 1st ser., 39(2 March 1819):845.
21. Thomas, 'Whigs and Radicals in Westminster', 174.
22. Thorne, II:267, 279–81.
23. *Parl. Deb.*, 1st ser., 39(1 April 1819):1351–2.
24. Thorne, I:78–9; Cookson, *Lord Liverpool's Administration*, 166–7.
25. Hamilton's speech, *Parl. Deb.*, 1st ser., 40(6 May 1819):178–80.
26. Canning's speech, *Parl. Deb.*, 1st ser., 40(6 May 1819):195–6.
27. *Parl. Deb.*, 1st ser., 40(6 May 1819):197–8; Cookson, *Lord Liverpool's Administration*, 168.
28. Tierney's speech, *Parl. Deb.*, 1st ser., 40(18 May 1819):474–9.
29. Ibid., 490–1, 495.
30. Castlereagh's speech, *Parl. Deb.*, 1st ser., 40(18 May 1819):348, 501–3.
31. Canning's speech, *Parl. Deb.*, 1st ser., 40(18 May 1819):527–8, 546.
32. Mitchell, 124.
33. Holland, *Further Memoirs*, 268.
34. *Parl. Deb.*, 1st ser., 40(18 May 1819):527–8.
35. *Courier*, 20 May 1819.
36. Smart, 683–6; Cookson, *Lord Liverpool's Administration*, I:169–71.
37. *New Times*, 14 July 1819.
38. *Courier*, 14 June 1819.
39. Ibid.
40. Lambton to Grey, 5 February 1818, Grey MSS.
41. Fulford, Roger and Lytton Strachey, eds, *The Greville Memoirs*, 7 vols (London: Macmillan & Co., 1936), I:74.
42. *Courier*, 25 January 1819.
43. Mackintosh to Holland, 6 January 1819, Add. MSS 51653.
44. Smart, I:689–91.
45. Donald Read, *Peterloo: The 'Massacre' and its Background* (Manchester: Manchester University Press, 1958), 16–17.
46. *Leeds Mercury*, 19 June 1819.
47. *Times*, 22 June 1819.
48. *Leeds Mercury*, 26 June 1819.

49. Letter published in the *Morning Chronicle* on 2 August.
50. *Morning Chronicle*, 4 August 1819.
51. *Times*, 12 August 1819.
52. Smart, I:720; *Times*, 15 July 1819; Read, *The English Provinces*, 74.
53. Smart, I:720–1.
54. Cookson, *Lord Liverpool's Administration*, 180–2.
55. Mitchell, 126; Wahrman, 201–2.
56. Grey to Brougham, 25 August 1819, Grey MSS.
57. Grey to Wilson, 24 October 1819, Add. MSS 30109.
58. Holland to Grey, 6 September 1819, Add. MSS 51546.
59. Tierney to Grey, 6 September 1819, Grey MSS.
60. *Leeds Mercury*, 28 August 1819.
61. *Times*, 23 September 1819.
62. Fitzwilliam to Holland, 11 September 1819, Add. MSS 51593; E.A. Smith, *Whig Principles and Party Politics*, 349–50.
63. *Leeds Mercury*, 2 October 1819.
64. *Leeds Mercury*, 16 October 1819.
65. *Courier*, 20 October 1819; *New Times*, 18 October 1819.
66. Grey to Holland, 21 September 1819, Grey MSS.
67. Mitchell, 128–9.
68. Tierney to Grey, 25 September 1819, Grey MSS.
69. Brougham to Lady Holland, 11 September 1819, Add. MSS 51561.
70. Brougham to Holland, 19 September 1819, Add. MSS 51561.
71. *Kendal Chronicle*, 2 October 1819; *Times*, 2 October 5 1819.
72. Brougham to Grey [no date (September 1819)], Brougham MSS.
73. *Carlisle Patriot*, 16 October 1819.
74. *Carlisle Patriot*, 30 October 1819.
75. *Leeds Mercury*, 6 November.
76. Mitchell, 131.
77. *Times*, 23 and 25 October 1819.
78. *Leeds Mercury*, 20 November 1819.
79. *Morning Chronicle*, 1 October 1819.
80. Horace Twiss, *The Public and Private Life of Lord Chancellor Eldon*, 3 vols (London: John Murray, 1844), II:346; Liverpool to Canning, 10 October 1819, Add. MSS 38568.
81. Read, *Peterloo*, 185–6.
82. Grey's speech, *Parl. Deb.*, 1st ser., 41(23 November 1819):4–10.
83. Liverpool to Canning, 10 October 1819. Add. MSS 38568.
84. Althrop's Speech, *Parl. Deb.*, 1st ser., 41(30 November 1819):518–9.
85. Bathurst's Speech, *Parl. Deb.*, 1st ser., 41(30 November 1819):526–7.
86. Lascelles' Speech, *Parl. Deb.*, 1st ser., 41(30 November 1819):341.
87. Milton's speech, *Parl. Deb.*, 1st ser., 41(30 November 1819):544–7.
88. Castlereagh's speech, *Parl. Deb.*, 1st ser., 41(30 November 1819):557–60.
89. Tierney's speech, *Parl. Deb.*, 1st ser., 41(30 November 1819):560–9.
90. Brougham's speech, *Parl. Deb.*, 1st ser., 41(24 November 1819):218–28.
91. Read, *Peterloo*, 196–7.
92. Brougham's speech, *Parl. Deb.*, 1st ser., 41(6 December 1819):705–6.
93. Read, *Peterloo*, 197–8, 200.
94. Parry, 14.
95. Wilson to Grey, 24 December 1819, Add. MSS 30123.

5 Public Opinion and the Limits of Opposition

1. *Parl. Deb.*, 1st ser., 35(4 March 1817):881.
2. Castlereagh's speech, *Parl. Deb.*, 1st ser., 41(18 February 1820):1604–6.
3. *Morning Chronicle*, 31 January 1820.
4. *Westmorland Gazette*, 5 January 1820.
5. Stoker, 186.
6. *Kendal Chronicle*, 26 February 1820.
7. *Westmorland Gazette*, 18 March 1820; *Times*, 20 March 2920.
8. *Kendal Chronicle*, 18 March 1820; *Carlisle Journal*, 18 March 1820.
9. *Westmorland Gazette*, 18 March 1820.
10. Lowther to Lonsdale, Monday morning [March 20, 1820] Lowther MSS.
11. *Kendal Chronicle*, 25 March 1820; *Carlisle Journal*, 25 March 1820. The Kendal paper gave a more detailed account.
12. Thanet to Lady Holland, 18 March 1820, Add. MSS 51571; Thanet to Lord Holland, 21 March 1820, Add. MSS 51571.
13. *Westmorland Gazette*, 25 March 1820.
14. Thanet to Holland, 22 March 1820; 24 March 1818, Add. MSS 51571.
15. Lowther to Lonsdale, Sunday morning [March 1820], Lowther MSS.
16. Thanet to Holland, 24 March 1820, Add. MSS 51571.
17. Brougham to Holland, 21 March 1820, Add. MSS 51562.
18. Grey to Brougham, 18 April 1820, Grey MSS.
19. Mitchell, 66.
20. *Morning Chronicle*, 14 April 1820; Mitchell, 140–1.
21. *Parl. Deb.*, 2nd ser., 1(5 May 1820):163.
22. Cookson, *Lord Liverpool's Administration*, 215–6.
23. Grey to Brougham, 19 January 1815, Grey MSS.
24. New, 102–18.
25. *Morning Chronicle*, 31 January 1820.
26. Cookson, *Lord Liverpool's Administration*, 206–12; Liverpool to Eldon, 3 April 1820, Add. MSS 38284.
27. Grey to Holland, 18 and 20 February 1820, Add. MSS 51553.
28. Grey to Holland, 18 February 1820, Add. MSS. 51553.
29. E.A. Smith, *A Queen on Trial: The Affair of Queen Caroline* (Stroud: Alan Sutton, 1993), 20–2; Caroline to Brougham (copy), 4 June 1820, 5 o'clock, Add. MSS. 38565.
30. Croker Papers, Croker's Diary, 12 April 1820, I:172; Croker to Lord Yarmouth, 6 June 1820, I:172.
31. Canning to Liverpool, 2 April 1820, Add. MSS 38193; Liverpool to Eldon, 3 April 1820, Add. MSS 38284; Liverpool to Hutchinson, 12 June 1820, Add. MSS 38565; Hutchinson to Liverpool, 16 June 1820, Add. MSS 38565.
32. Grey to Lady Grey, 20 May and 7 June 1820, Grey MSS.
33. *Parl. Deb.*, 2nd ser., 1(7 June 1820):905–6.
34. Castlereagh's speech, *Parl. Deb.*, 2nd ser., 1(7 June 1820):908; Brougham's speech, Ibid., 949.
35. Tierney's speech, *Parl. Deb.*, 2nd ser., 39(7 June 1820):978; Tierney to Grey, 8 June 1820; Lambton to Grey, 8 June 1820, Grey MSS.
36. Wilberforce's speech, *Parl. Deb.*, 2nd ser., 39(7 June 1820):281–2; Ibid., 983–5.

37. Lansdowne to Grey, 12 June 1820, Grey MSS.
38. Tierney to Grey, 12 June 1820, Grey MSS.
39. Cookson, *Lord Liverpool's Government*, 238–9, 241–2.
40. Brougham's speech, *Parl. Deb.*, 2nd ser., 2(17 August 1820):638–51.
41. *Parl. Deb.*, 2nd ser., 2(23 August 1820):871–4.
42. *Parl. Deb.*, 2nd ser., 3(14 October 1820):641–2.
43. Grey's speech, *Parl. Deb.*, 2nd ser., 3(3 November 1820):1573–4.
44. Mitchell, 151–3.
45. Sack, *Jacobite to Conservative*, 142.
46. Thomas Babbington Macaulay, 'The Present Administration', *Edinburgh Review* (June 1827):262–3.
47. Grey to Holland, 21 November 1820, Grey MSS; Parry, 74.
48. *Times*, 3 August, 17 August, 4 September, and 20 September 1820.
49. Thomas W. Laqueur, 'The Queen Caroline Affair: Politics as Art in the Reign of George IV', *Journal of Modern History*, 54.3(September 1982):439, 454–3.
50. William Hazlitt, 'Commonplaces', no. LXXIII, in *The Round Table. Northcote's Conversations. Characteristics*, W. Carew Hazlitt ed. (London: Bell & Daldy, 1871), 549–52; Laqueur, 454–63.
51. Croker Papers, I:180.
52. Sack, *Grenvillites*, 185.
53. Grey to Holland, 21 November 1820, Add. MSS 51553; Aspinall, *Lord Brougham and the Whig Party* (Manchester: Manchester University Press, 1927), 120; Lady Seymour, *Pope of Holland House*, Wishaw to Smith, 20 November 1820, 209–10.
54. Smith, *Letters of Sydney Smith*, Smith to Lady Grey, 9 February 1921, I:347.
55. Liverpool to Charles Bathurst, 29 December 1820, Add. MSS 38288.
56. Sack, *The Grenvillites*, 190–3.
57. Cookson, *Lord Liverpool's Administration*, 366–92.
58. Canning's speech, *Parl. Deb.*, 2nd ser., 12(3 February 1825):72; Mitchell, 186–7.
59. Hilton, *Corn, Cash, Commerce*, 153.
60. Norman Gash, 'The State of the Nation (1822)', in *Pillars of Government and Other Essays on State and Society c. 1770–1880* (London: Edward Arnold, 1986), 26–42.
61. *Morning Chronicle*, 8 February 1821.
62. Peel to Croker, 23 March 1820, Croker Papers, I:170; E.A. Wasson, 'The Great Whigs and Parliamentary Reform, 1809–30', *Journal of British Studies*, 24(October 1985):460.
63. Lord John Russell's speech, *Parl. Deb.*, 1st ser., 41(14 December 1819):1091–1107; Castlereagh's speech, Ibid., 1110–6.
64. Cookson, *Lord Liverpool's Administration*, 305–6.
65. *Parl. Deb.*, 2nd ser., 5(17 April 1821):453.
66. *Parl. Deb.*, 2nd ser., 5(9 May 1821):621–2, 624.
67. Russell's speech, *Parl. Deb.*, 2nd ser., 7(25 April 1822):60.
68. Canning's speech, *Parl. Deb.*, 2nd ser., 7(25 April 1822):123; Ibid., 139.
69. Lambton to Grey, 13 May 1820, Grey MSS.
70. Wishaw to Smith, 6 March 1817, Lady Seymour, *Pope of Holland House*, 174.
71. Grey to Lady Grey, 23 June 1820, Grey MSS.

72. Edward Hughes, ed., *The Diaries and Correspondence of James Losh*, 2 vols (Durham: Andrews & Co., 1962), I:178–9.
73. Grey to Brougham, 30 August 1822, Grey MSS.
74. Brougham to Grey, 2 September 1822, Brougham MSS.
75. Grey to Brougham, 5 September 1822, Grey MSS.
76. Harling, 125.
77. Grey to Holland, 17 January 1817, Grey MSS.
78. Parry, 15.
79. Clark, *English Society*, 521; Brent, 23
80. Smith, 'Dissenters' Marriages', *Edinburgh Review*, 35(March 1821):62–72.
81. Nicholson and Axon, 380.
82. *Liverpool Mercury*, 21 September 1821.
83. *Durham Chronicle*, 10 August 1821.
84. *Morning Chronicle*, 15 November 1821.
85. *Times*, 15 November 1821.
86. Brougham to Creevey, 16 August 1822, John Gore, ed., *Creevey's Life and Times*, 154–6.
87. Clark, *English Society*, 487.
88. *A Letter to Henry Brougham, Esq. MP upon his Durham Speech and the Three Articles in the Last Edinburgh Review* (London: C. & J. Rivington, 1823), 3.
89. *The Speech of Henry Brougham, Esq. in the Case of the King v. Williams for a Libel on the Clergy* (London: J. Limbird, 1822), 1–18.
90. *Morning Chronicle*, 10 August 1822; *Times*, 10 August 1822.
91. 'The Bishop of Peterborough and His Clergy', *Edinburgh Review*, 36(November 1822):436.
92. Brougham, 'Durham Case, Clerical Abuses', *Edinburgh Review*, 36(November 1822):350–79.
93. *A Letter to Henry Brougham*, 1.
94. *The Age*, 28 May 1826.
95. See P.F. Dixon, 'The Politics of Emancipation: the Movement for the Abolition of Slavery in the British West Indies 1807–1833', (D.Phil. diss: Oxford, 1971), *passim*.
96. *Parl. Deb.*, 2nd ser., 11(13 April 1824):400–1.
97. *Morning Chronicle*, 17 April 1824; *Times*, 17 April 1824.
98. Brougham's speech, *Parl. Deb.*, 2nd ser., 11(1 June 1824):123; Ibid., 139.
99. Canning's speech, *Parl. Deb.*, 2nd ser., 11(11 June 1824):1277–8, 1288.
100. Brougham's speech, Ibid., 1309–12.
101. Brougham's speech, Ibid., 1295.
102. *Times*, 14 June 1824; *Leeds Mercury*, 19 June 1824.
103. *Morning Chronicle*, 3 July 1826.
104. New, 273; Brougham's speech, *Parl. Deb.*, 2nd ser., 9(31 May 1825):954.
105. Brougham's speech, *Parl. Deb.*, 2nd ser., 12(3 February 1825):58–66.
106. Althorp to Brougham, [no date (early 1824)], Althorp MSS.
107. Parry, 14.
108. Brougham's speech, *Parl. Deb.*, 2nd ser., 12(15 February 1825): 498–9, 505–6, 513–4.
109. Brougham to Holland, August 1826., Add. MSS 51562.
110. *Kendal Chronicle*, 5 February 1825; Lowther to Lonsdale, 27 January and 4 February 1825, Lowther MSS.

111. Holland to Lansdowne, 27 July 1825, Lansdowne MSS.
112. Lowther to Lonsdale, 14 September 1825, Lowther MSS.
113. Tierney to Lady Holland, 2 December 1825, Add. MSS 51586; Grey to Holland, 15 May 1826., Add. MSS 51554.
114. G.I.T. Machin, *The Catholic Question in English Politics, 1820 to 1830* (Oxford: Clarendon Press, 1964), 58–9.
115. Linda Colley, *Britons: Forging the Nation 1707–1837* (New Haven: Yale University Press, 1992), 329–32; Sack, *Jacobite to Conservative*, 231–8.
116. *Kendal Chronicle*, 6 May 1826; *Times*, 9 May 1826; Brougham's letters to his election agent, James Atkinson, contain a draft copy of the requisition and reply dated May 1826, Brougham MSS.
117. *Courier*, 2 May 1826; *New Times*, 20 June 1826; *Kendal Chronicle*, 13 May 1826.
118. *Kendal Chronicle*, 27 May and 3 June 1826.
119. Wordsworth to Lonsdale, 15 May 1826, Moorman and Hill, *Wordsworth Letters*, III:445–7.
120. Draft declaration in Lowther to Lonsdale, 5 June 1826; Lowther to Lonsdale, 8 June 1826, Lowther MSS; *Courier*, 16 June 1826.
121. *Times*, 19 June 1826.
122. *Morning Chronicle*, 27 June 1826; *Times*, 27 June 1826.
123. Colonel Lowther to Lonsdale, 26 May 1826, Lowther MSS.
124. *Morning Chronicle*, 3 July 1820; *Times*, 1 July 1820.
125. John Becket to Lonsdale, 30 June 1826, Lowther MSS.
126. Brougham to Grey, 6 July 1826, Brougham MSS.
127. *Times*, 4 July 1826; 'Westmorland Election, 1826', Lowther MSS.
128. *Kendal Chronicle*, 8 July 1826; *Manchester Guardian*, 8 July 1826.
129. William Vizard to James Brougham, 15 September 1826, Brougham MSS.
130. McQuiston, 166; 'Expenses of the Election for Westmorland, 1818', Westmorland Election, 1818, Box 4, Lowther MSS; Lowther to Lonsdale, 14 January, 29 July and 17 August 1826, Lowther MSS.
131. Stoker, 206, 195.
132. Mitchell, 185–6.

6 A Revolution in Parties

1. *Times*, 19 February 1827.
2. *Morning Chronicle*, 19 February 1827.
3. Holland to Grey, 2 September 1825, Add. MSS 51547.
4. Francis Bamford and Duke of Wellington, eds., *The Journal of Mrs. Arbuthnot, 1820–32*, 2 vols (London: MacMillan & Co. Ltd., 1950), I:275–6.
5. N. Gash, '1812–30', in *How Tory Governments Fall: The Tory Party in Power Since 1783*, Anthony Seldon, ed. (London: Fontana, 1996), 84–5; Hilton, 'Political Arts of Lord Liverpool', 165.
6. Croker to Sir Benjamin Bloomfield, 10 May 1824, Croker Papers I:265.
7. Holland to Grey, 2 September 1825, Add. MSS 51547.
8. Grey to Holland, 10 February 1826, Grey MSS.
9. New, *Life of Brougham*, 305.
10. *Times*, 20 February 1827.

11. Brougham to Allen, 25 February 1827, Add. MSS 52179.
12. Peel to Wellington, 18 February 1827; Canning to Huskisson, 21 February 1827, *Formation of Canning's Ministry*, 1,7; Norman Gash, *Lord Liverpool: The Life and Political Career of Robert Banks Jenkinson, Second Earl of Liverpool 1770–1828* (London: Weidenfeld & Nicholson, 1984), 248–9.
13. Tierney's speech, *Parl. Deb.*, 2nd ser., 17(30 March 1827):157–64
14. Canning to George IV, 30 March 1827, A. Aspinall, *Letters of George IV*, III:212–3; *Times*, 31 March 1827.
15. Lushington to Sir William Knighton, 26 March 1827, Aspinall, *Letters of George IV*, III:207–10.
16. A. Aspinall, *Formation of Canning's Ministry*, xxxiii–vii.
17. Brougham to Wilson, March 1827, Add. MSS 30111.
18. Wilson, *Narrative*, 3–6.
19. Brougham to Wilson. March 26, 1827. Copy in Canning MSS; West Yorkshire Archive Service, Leeds.
20. Wilson, *Narrative*, 6–7.
21. Fulford and Strachey, *Greville Memoirs*, 23 September 1834, III:88.
22. Before succeeding his father in 1825 the Earl of Carlisle had been styled Viscount Morpeth, and had been MP for Cumberland as Lord Morpeth prior to his defeat in 1820.
23. Darlington to Lansdowne, 16 April 1827, Aspinall, *Formation of Canning's Ministry*, 94–5.
24. Brougham to Lansdowne, 16 April 1827, Lansdowne MSS.
25. Croker to Lowther, 17 April 1827, Aspinall, *Formation of Canning's Ministry*, 106–7.
26. Holland to Lansdowne, 18 April 1827, Lansdowne MSS.
27. Grey to Lansdowne, 16 April 1827; Grey to Lansdowne, 17 April 1827, Lansdowne MSS.
28. Lansdowne Memorandum, 19 April 1827, Aspinall, *Formation of Canning's Ministry*, 118–23.
29. Brougham to Althorp, 20 April 1827, Althorp MSS.
30. New, 311–4; Dudley to Canning, 20 April 1827, Aspinall, *Formation of Canning's Ministry*, 134.
31. Essex to Wilson, 22 April 1827, Add. MSS 30111.
32. Wilson, *Narrative*, 23–5; Lansdowne to Holland. Saturday Morning, 21 April 1827, *Formation of Canning's Ministry*, 144–5.
33. Aspinall, *Formation of Canning's Ministry*, xlvii–iii.
34. *Times*, 19 April and 21 April 1827.
35. *Morning Chronicle*, 11 and 25 April 1827.
36. Mitchell, 200.
37. Brougham to Creevey, 21 April 1827, Creevey Papers, II:114.
38. Tavistock to Althorp, 25 April 1827, Aspinall, *Formation of Canning's Ministry*, 222–3.
39. Althorp to Brougham, 18 April 1827, Althorp MSS.
40. Althorp's speech, *Parl. Deb.*, 2nd ser. (7 May)583.
41. E.A. Wasson, 'The Coalitions of 1827 and the Crisis of Whig Leadership', *Historical Journal*, 20.3(1977):603.
42. Grey to Lansdowne, 27 April 1827; Brougham to Lansdowne, [early 1827], Lansdowne MSS.

43. Wilson, *Narrative*, 17; Abercrombie to Althorp [April, 1827]; Aspinall, *Formation of Canning's Ministry*, 104–6.
44. Grey to Holland, 7 March 1827, Add. MSS 51554.
45. Grey's speech, *Parl. Deb.*, 2nd ser. 17(10 May 1827), 720–33.
46. E.A. Smith, *Lord Grey, 1761–1830* (Oxford: Clarendon Press, 1990) 247; Mitchell, 201.
47. *Leeds Mercury*, 26 May 1827; *Morning Chronicle*, 11 May 1827.
48. Holland's speech, *Parl. Deb.*, 2nd ser. 17(17 May 1827):857–66.
49. Brougham to Allen, 26 August 1827, Add. MSS 52179.
50. Brougham to Holland, 15 August 1827, Add. MSS 51562.
51. *English Cartoons and Satirical Prints in the British Museum*, Print 15378; *Times*, 30 April 1827; *Morning Chronicle*, 24 April 1827.
52. Aspinall, *Formation of Canning's Ministry*, liii.
53. *Times*, 5 July 1827; New, *Life of Brougham*, 316. The patent of precedence that Brougham received granted the same rank as a King's Counsel of the same date. It restored his rank as the former Queen's Counsel, allowing him once more the privilege of appearing before the bar in a silk gown.
54. *English Cartoons and Satirical Prints in the British Museum*, Prints 15406, 15416, and 15385.
55. *Leeds Mercury*, 23 June 1827.
56. *Manchester Guardian*, 23 June 1827; *Liverpool Mercury*, 22 June 1827.
57. Croker to Lord Hertford, 8 August 1827, Croker Papers, I:382–3.
58. King's Memorandum, 8 August 1827, Aspinall, *Letters of George IV*, III:275–6; Cabinet to the King, 9 August 1827, Ibid., III:276–8.
59. George IV to Goderich, 10 and 12 August 1827, Aspinall, *Letters of George IV*, III:275–6, 284.
60. Abercrombie to Huskisson, cited in A. Aspinall, 'The Coalition Ministries of 1827: Goderich', *English Historical Review* 42(October 1827):533–59.
61. Holland to Lansdowne, 22 and 27 August 1827, Lansdowne MSS.
62. Tierney to Lady Holland, 31 August 1827, Add. MSS 51586.
63. Brougham to Lansdowne [August 1827.] Lansdowne MSS; Brougham to Abercrombie [August 1827] in Mitchell, 204.
64. Aspinall, 'The Coalition Ministries of 1827: Goderich', 541–3.
65. Althorp to Earl Spencer, 9 September 1827, in Sir Denis Le Marchant, *Memoir of John Charles, Viscount Althorp, 3rd Earl Spencer* (London: Richard Bently & Son, 1876), 225–6.
66. Grey to Creevey, 21 August 1827, *Creevey's Life and Times* 245; Grey to Holland, 16 September 1827, Add. MSS 51554.
67. Rosslyn to Brougham, 20 October 1827, *Brougham's Life and Times*, II:492.
68. Brougham, 'State of Parties', *Edinburgh Review* (October 1827): 415–32.
69. *The Age*, 20 September 1827.
70. Mitchell, 209; Althorp to Russell, 13 January 1828, *Early Correspondence of Lord John Russell*, I:271–2.
71. Brougham to Lansdowne, 22 October 1827, in Aspinall, *Brougham and the Whig Party*, 285.
72. Stewart, *Henry Brougham*, 226–8; Grey to Creevey, 13 December 1827, *Creevey Papers*, I:140; Creevey to Miss Ord, 3 March 1828, Gore, *Creevey's Life and Times*, 260.
73. *Courier*, 18 January 1828.
74. *Morning Chronicle*, 28 January 1828; *Times*, January 28, 1828.

75. Brougham's speech, *Parl. Deb.*, 2nd ser. 18(29 January 1828):55.
76. Mitchell, 210.
77. Machin, 'Resistance to Repeal of the Test and Corporation Acts, 1828', *Historical Journal*, 22.1(1979)117–8: John Smith's speech, *Parl. Deb.*, 2nd ser., 18(4 February 1828):596–7; William Smith's speech, Ibid., (6 February 1828):124–5.
78. Russell's speech, *Parl. Deb.*, 2nd ser., 18(26 February 1828): 678–93; Huskisson's speech, Ibid., 734; Peel's speech, Ibid., 750–1.
79. Clark, *English Society*, 438, 435; *New Times*, 2 February 1828.
80. Brougham's speech, *Parl. Deb.*, 2nd ser., 18(26 February 1828):769.
81. Ibid., 779–81.
82. *Parl. Deb.*, 2nd ser., 18(26 February 1828):781–4.
83. *Times* February 28, 1828; *Leeds Mercury* March 1, 1828.
84. Machin, 'Resistance to Repeal of the Test and Corporation Acts', 125–6.
85. *Leeds Mercury*, 1 March 1828.
86. *Morning Chronicle*, 27 February 1828.
87. *Courier*, 27 February 1828.
88. *John Bull*, 10 March 1828; *The Age*, 6 April 1828.
89. Abercrombie to Brougham, 13 July 1828, Brougham MSS.
90. *Times*, 19 June 1828.
91. Wendy Hinde, *Catholic Emancipation: A Shake to Men's Minds* (Oxford: Blackwell, 1992), 64–9.
92. Althorp to Brougham, 30 September 1828, Althorp MSS.
93. *Manchester Guardian*, 11 October 1828.
94. Brougham to Althorp, 30 December 1828, Althorp MSS.
95. Grey to Holland, 10 January 1829, Add. MSS 51555.
96. King's speech, *Parl. Deb.*, 2nd ser., 20(5 February 1829):4–5; Wellington's speech, Ibid., 13; Eldon's speech, Ibid., 15–23.
97. Inglis's speech, *Parl. Deb.*, 2nd ser., 20(5 February 1829):62–3.
98. Brougham's speech, *Parl. Deb.*, 2nd ser., 20(5 February 1829):88–94.
99. Grattan's speech, *Parl. Deb.*, 2nd ser., 20(5 February 1829):97.
100. Althorp to Brougham, 14 February 1829, Althorp MSS.
101. Grey to Holland, 10 January 1829, Grey MSS.
102. Sack, *Jacobite to Conservative*, 236–7.
103. J.J. Sack, 'Wellington and the Tory Press', in *Wellington: Studies of the Political and Military Career of the First Duke of Wellington*, Norman Gash, ed. (Manchester: Manchester University Press, 1990), 159–68.
104. *Leeds Mercury*, 7 January 1829.
105. *Manchester Guardian*, 6 June 1829.
106. Althorp to Brougham, 17 June 1829, Althorp MSS.
107. Neville Thompson, *Wellington After Waterloo* (London: Routledge & Keegan Paul, 1986), 97–8, 89; Bamford and Duke of Wellington, *Journal of Mrs. Arbuthnot*, II:251.
108. Mitchell, 219–20.
109. Smart, II:454, 466–7.
110. *Manchester Guardian*, 5, 19, and 26 September 1829.
111. Smart, II:511–6; Grey to Holland, 5 March 1830, Grey MSS.
112. *The Age*, 6 June 1830.
113. *Parl. Deb.*, 2nd ser., 22(23 February 1830):915–8; *Times*, 24 February 1830.

114. Russell's speech, *Parl. Deb.*, 2nd ser., 22(23 February 1830):860.
115. *Sheffield Iris*, 15 June 1830.
116. Stewart, *Henry Brougham*, 239–40.
117. Brougham's speech, *Parl. Deb.*, 2nd ser., 25(13 July 1830):1191; Ibid., 1214; *Sheffield Iris*, 20 July 1830.
118. Grey's speech, *Parl. Deb.*, 2nd ser., 25(30 June):765; Brougham's speech, Ibid., (30 June 1830):824–5.
119. N. Gash, 'Brougham and the Yorkshire Election of 1830', *Proceedings of the Leeds Philosophical and Literary Society*, 8(May 1956):20–1.
120. F.M.L. Thompson, 'Whigs and Liberals in the West Riding, 1820–1832', *English Historical Review*, 74.291(April 1959):215.
121. Robert Worthington Smith, 'Political Organization and Canvassing: Yorkshire Elections Before the First Reform Bill', *American Historical Review*, 74(1969):1541–3, 1547–8.
122. A.S. Turberville and Frank Beckwith, 'Leeds and Parliamentary Reform, 1820–1832', *Publications of the Thoresby Society: Miscellany*, 41.1(1943):18; Thompson, 218; Gash, 'Brougham and the Yorkshire Election', 20.
123. *Leeds Mercury*, 26 September 1812.
124. *Leeds Mercury*, 17 July 1830.
125. Gash, 'Brougham and the Yorkshire Election', 26–7; *Leeds Mercury*, 24 July 1830 and *Leeds Intelligencer*, 29 July 1830 gave reports of the meeting.
126. *Sheffield Iris*, 27 July 1830.
127. *Sheffield Iris*, 3 August 1830.
128. *Yorkshire Gazette*, 24 July 1830.
129. *Yorkshire Gazette*, 7 August 1830.
130. *Leeds Mercury*, 17 July; Fulford and Strachey, *Greville Memoirs*, 30 July 1830, II:18–9.
131. Aspinall, *Lord Brougham and the Whig Party*, 176.
132. *Leeds Mercury*, 27 July 1830.
133. *Leeds Mercury*, 27 and 31 July 1830.
134. Gash, 'Brougham and the Yorkshire Election', 31.
135. *Leeds Mercury*, 27 and 31 July 1830.
136. Brougham, *Brougham's Life and Times*, III:40.
137. *Sheffield Iris*, 3 August 1830.
138. For two views on the impact of events in France, see Gash, 'English Reform and the French Revolution in the General Election of 1830', in *Essays Presented to Sir Lewis Namier*, Richard Pares and A.J.P. Taylor, eds. (London: Macmillan, 1956), 258–88 and R. Quinault, 'The French Revolution of 1830 and Parliamentary Reform', *History* 79(1994):377–93.
139. Henry Brougham, *The Country Without a Government; or Plain Questions upon the Unhappy State of the Present Administration* (London: James Ridgeway, 1830), 4–5, 9–10.
140. *Leeds Mercury*, 7 August 1830. The *Morning Chronicle* reprinted its reports of the Yorkshire canvass and election.
141. *Manchester Guardian*, 21 August 1830; Brougham, *Brougham's Life and Times*, III:42.
142. *Times*, 9 August 1830; *Morning Chronicle*, 9 August 1830; *Leeds Intelligencer*, 12 August 1830; *Sheffield Iris*, 24 August 1830.
143. *Leeds Mercury*, 7 August 1830.

144. *Yorkshire Gazette*, 4 September 1830.
145. Brougham, 'The Ministry and the State of Parties', *Edinburgh Review* (July 1830): 579,582.
146. *Leeds Mercury*, 14 August 1830; *Times*, 17 August 1830; *Morning Chronicle*, 16 August 1830.
147. Sack, *Jacobite to Conservative*, 246–8.
148. *Morning Chronicle*, 19 August 1830.
149. *Sheffield Iris*, 28 September 1830.
150. *Manchester Guardian*, 2 October 1830.
151. *English Cartoons and Satirical Prints in the British Museum*, Print 16281. Henry Brougham, *The Result of the General Election, or, What has the Duke of Wellington gained by the Dissolution?* (London: J. Ridgway, 1830).
152. Mitchell, 236–8, 240; Grey to Holland, 8 October 1830, Grey MSS.
153. *Morning Chronicle*, 26 October 1830.
154. *Parl. Deb.*, 3rd ser., 1(2 November 1830):54–5; Graham to Brougham., 1 November 1830, Brougham MSS.
155. Grey's speech, *Parl. Deb.*, 3rd ser., 1(2 November 1830):37.
156. Wellington's speech, *Parl. Deb.*, 3rd ser., 1(2 November 1830):52–3.
157. Muriel Chamberlain, *Lord Aberdeen, A Political Biography* (London: Longman, 1983), 252.
158. Althorp's speech, *Parl. Deb.*, 3rd ser., 1(2 November 1830):63–4.
159. *Parl. Deb.*, 3rd ser., 1(2 November 1830):548.
160. Brougham's speech, *Parl. Deb.*, 3rd ser., 1(16 November 1830):562–3.
161. Le Marchant, *Memoir of Althorp*, 261.
162. Aspinall, *Brougham and the Whig Party*, 187.
163. Grey to Lansdowne, 18 November 1830, Lansdowne MSS; Lord Broughton, *Recollections of a Long Life*, Lady Dorchester ed., 6 vols (London: John Murray, 1909–11), IV:256.
164. Brougham, *Brougham's Life and Times*, III:79.
165. Brougham, *Brougham's Life and Times*, III:80.
166. *Morning Chronicle*, 22 November 1830.

Conclusion

1. Brent, 21; Jenkins, 2–3.
2. *Times*, 22 November 1830.
3. Clark, *English Society*, 515; Jenkins, x.
4. Parry, 1.
5. Jenkins, ix, 19; Francis Jeffrey, 'The State of the Nation', *Edinburgh Review* (January 1810):505.
6. Philip Harling defines the Tory 'disciplinary ethos' in 'Robert Southey and the Language of Social Discipline', *Albion*, 30.4 (winter 1998).
7. Jenkins, 4.
8. Clark, *English Society*, 6–8.
9. Jenkins, 44–5; H.J. Hanham, *The Reformed Electoral System in Great Britain, 1832–1914* (London: Historical Association, 1968), 12, 28–30; Parry, 3, 5. An example of the redefinition can be seen in the way Lord John Russell equated the people with the middle classes in 1832, but then by 1861 came to include the working classes in his definition.

10. O'Gorman, *Voters, Patrons, and Parties*, 392–3.
11. Clark, *English Society*, 550–1.
12. N. Gash, *Politics in the Age of Peel: A Study in The Technique of Parliamentary Representation*, 2nd edn (Hassocks: Harvester, 1977), xiii, 393–6, Hanham, 18–22.
13. [Alexander Somerville], *Autobiography of a Working Man* (London: Turnstile Press, 1848), 143.
14. Fulford and Strachey, *Greville Memoirs*, 20 November 1830, II:64–5.
15. Creevey Papers, I:287
16. *Manchester Guardian*, 11 December 1830.
17. *Times*, 12 October 1831.
18. Russell, *Recollections and Suggestions, 1813–1873* (London: Longmans, Green & Co., 1875), 74. Durham's biographer, however, noted that others attributed the phrase to Edward Ellice, Grey's brother-in-law and government whip in the Commons. Reid, *Life and Letters of Durham*, I:259.
19. Brougham thus holds credit for the longest speeches given to date in both Houses of Parliament for this speech and his 1828 address to the Commons on legal reform.
20. Le Marchant, *Memoir of Althorp*, 352
21. Kriegel, *Holland House Diaries, 1831–40* 106.
22. Kriegel *Holland House Diaries*, 264.
23. Grey to Holland, 25 October 1824, Grey MSS.
24. Donald Southgate, *The Passing of the Whigs, 1832–86* (London: Macmillan, 1962), 55n.
25. Fulford and Strachey, *Greville Memoirs*, January 1828, I:196.
26. Russell, *Recollections and Suggestions*, 140.
27. Melbourne's speech, *Parl. Deb.* 3rd ser., 44(3 August 1838):976.
28. Grey made the comment to Creevey in late September or early October 1809, Creevey Papers, I:107–8.
29. Croker Papers, II:125.

Bibliography

Unpublished manuscripts sources

British Library, Department of Manuscripts, London

Additional Manuscripts:

Holland Papers
John Allen Papers
Sir James Mackintosh Papers
Lansdowne Papers
Althorp (Spencer) Papers
Sir Robert Wilson Papers
Liverpool Papers
Sir Robert Peel Papers
Francis Place Papers
Leigh Hunt Papers
Spencer Perceval Papers

British Library, Newspaper Archive, Colindale
University College, London
Brougham Papers

Cumbria Record Office, Carlisle
Lowther Papers

Hampshire Record Office, Winchester
George Tierney Papers

Durham University Library
Earl Grey Papers

Liverpool Record Office
William Roscoe Papers

West Yorkshire Archive Service, Leeds
George Canning Papers

William L. Clements Library
University of Michigan, Ann Arbor

John Wilson Croker Papers

Newspapers and periodicals

The Age
Anti-Jacobin and True Churchman Magazine
Blackwoods Edinburgh Magazine

British Monitor
Carlisle Journal
Carlisle Patriot
Cobbett's Political Register
Courier
Durham Chronicle
Edinburgh Review
Examiner
Guardian
John Bull
Kendal Chronicle
Leeds Intelligencer
Leeds Mercury
Liverpool Mercury
Manchester Guardian
Morning Chronicle
New Times
Quarterly Review
Satirist
Sheffield Iris
Times
Westminster Review
Westmorland Gazette
Yorkshire Gazette

Printed primary sources

An Account of Mr. Brougham's Visits to the the Freeholders of the East and West Wards of Westmorland (Kendal: Gough, 1818).

An Address to the Yeomanry of the Counties of Westmorland and Cumberland on the Present State of their Representation in Parliament (Carlisle: Jollie, 1818).

Aspinall, Arthur, ed., *The Correspondence of Charles Arbuthnot* (London: Royal Historical Society, 1941 (Camden Society 3rd. ser., vol 59)).

Aspinall, Arthur, ed., *The Letters of George IV, 1812–30*, 3 vols (Cambridge: Cambridge University Press, 1938).

Aspinall, Arthur, ed., *The Formation of Canning's Ministry, February to August 1827* (London: Royal Historical Society, 1927).

Bagehot, Walter, *The English Constitution* (Ithica, NY: Cornell University Press, 1966).

Bagot, Josceline, ed., *George Canning and His Friends*, 2 vols (New York: E.P. Dutton & Co., 1909).

Baines, Edward Jr, *The Life of Edward Baines, Late MP for the Borough of Leeds* (London: Longmans, Brown, Green & Longmans, 1851).

Bamford, Francis and the Duke of Wellington, eds, *The Journal of Mrs Arbuthnot, 1820–32*, 2 vols (London: Macmillan, 1954).

Bourne, Kenneth and William Banks Taylor, eds, *The Horner Papers: Selections from the Letters and Miscellaneous Papers of Francis Horner MP, 1795–1817* (Edinburgh: Edinburgh University Press, 1994).

Brock, Irving, *The Patriots and the Whigs: The Most Dangerous Enemies of the State* (London: J.M. Richardson, 1810).

Brougham, Henry, *Speeches of Henry, Lord Brougham upon Questions relating to Public Rights, Duties, and Interests; with Historial Introductions, and a Critical Dissertation upon the Eloquence of the Ancients*, 4 vols (Edinburgh: A. & C. Black, 1838).

Brougham, Henry, *Henry, Life and Times of Henry, Lord Brougham*, 3 vols (London: William Blackwood & Sons, 1871).

Brougham, Henry, *Historical Sketches of Statesmen Who Flourished in the Time of George III*, 2 vols (Philadelphia: Parry & Macmillan, 1842).

Brougham, Henry, *The Country Without a Government; or Plain Questions upon the Unhappy State of the Present Administration* (London: James Ridgeway, 1830).

Brougham, Henry, *The Speech of Henry Brougham, Esq. in the Case of the King v. Williams for a Libel on the Clergy* (London: J. Limbird, 1822).

Brougham, Henry, *The Result of the General Election, or, What has the Duke of Wellington gained by the Dissolution?* (London: J. Ridgway 1830)

Brougham, Henry, *A Letter to Sir Samuel Romilly, MP from Henry Brougham, Esq. MP., F.R.S. Upon the Abuse of Charities* (London: J. Ridgeway, 1818).

Broughton, Lord, *Recollections of a Long Life*, Lady Dorchester, ed., 6 vols (London: John Murray, 1909–11).

Butt, G., *Suggestions as to the Conduct and Management of a County Contested Election* (London: James Duncan, 1826).

DeQuincey, Thomas, *Close Comments on a Straggling Speech* (Kendal: Airey & Bellingham, 1818).

English Cartoons and Satirical Prints, 1320–1832 in the British Museum (Cambridge: Chadwyck-Healey, 1978).

Fulford, Roger and Lytton Strachey, eds, *The Greville Memoirs*, 7 vols (London: Macmillan & Co., 1938).

Gore, John, ed., *Creevey's Life and Times: A Further Selection from the Correspondence of Thomas Creevey* (London: Murray, 1837).

Grierson, Sir Herbert, ed., *Letters of Sir Walter Scott*, 12 vols (London: Constable & Co., 1936).

Harrison, Thomas, *An Impartial Narrative of the Riotous Proceedings Which Took Place in Kendal on Wednesday, 11 February 1818* (Kendal: Airey & Bellingham, 1818).

Hazlitt, William, 'Commonplaces', no. LXXII, in *The Round Table. Northcote's Conversations. Characteristics*, W. Carew Hazlitt, ed., (London: Bell & Daldy, 1871).

Holland, Henry Richard Vassal Fox, 3rd Baron, *Further Memoirs of the Whig Party, 1807–21 with Miscellaneous Recollections*. Lord Stavordale, ed. (New York: Dutton and Co., 1905).

Holland, Henry Richard Vassal Fox, 3rd Baron, *Memoirs of the Whig Party*, 2 vols (London: Longmans, Brown, Green & Longmans, 1852–4).

Hughes, Edward, ed., *The Diaries and Correspondence of James Losh*, 2 vols (Durham: Andrews & Co., 1962).

Ilchester, Earl of, ed., *The Journal of Elizabeth, Lady Holland, 1791–1811*, 2 vols (London: Longmans, Green & Co., 1908).

An Impartial Collection of Addresses, Songs, Squibs & etc. Published During the Election of Members of Parliament for the Borough of Liverpool, October 1812 (Liverpool: Timothy Herring, 1812).

Jennings, Louis J., ed., *The Croker Papers: The Correspondence and Diaries of John Wilson Croker*, 3 vols (London: John Murray, 1885).

Kriegel, A.D., ed., *Holland House Diaries, 1831–40: The Diary of Richard Vassall Fox, 3rd Lord Holland with Extracts from the Diary of Dr. John Allen* (London: Routledge & Keegan Paul, 1977).

The Late Elections An Impartial Statement of All Proceedings Connected with the Progress and Result of the Late Elections (London: Bensley & Sons, 1818).

Le Marchant, Sir Denis, *Memoir of John Charles, Viscount Althorp, 3rd Earl Spencer* (London: Richard Bently & Son, 1876).

A Letter to Henry Brougham, Esq. MP Upon His Durham Speech and the Three Articles in the Last Edinburgh Review (London: C. & J. Rivington, 1823).

A Letter to the Right Honorable Sir William Scott, MP for the University of Oxford in Answer to Mr Brougham's Letter to Sir Samuel Romilly on the Abuse of Charities, 4th edn, (London: J. Hatchard, 1818).

Mackintosh, R.J., ed., *Memoirs of the Life of the Right Honourable Sir James Mackintosh*, 2 vols (London: Edward Moxon, 1836).

Macro, *The Scotiad, or Wise Men of the North* (London: J.J. Stockdale, 1809).

Maxwell, Sir Herbert, ed., *The Creevey Papers: A Selection of the Correspondence and Diaries of the Late Thomas Creevey MP*, 2 vols (London: John Murray, 1903).

Moorman, Mary and Alan G. Hill, eds, *Letters of William and Dorothy Wordsworth*, 3 vols (Oxford: Clarendon Press, 1970).

Owen, W.J.B and Jane Worthington Smyser, eds, *The Prose Works of William Wordsworth*, 3 vols (Oxford: Clarendon Press, 1974).

Papers of the Earl of Lonsdale. Historical Manuscripts Commission 13th Report, Part 7 (London: HMSO, 1893).

Polypus, [Eaton Stannard Barrett], *The Talents Run Mad or 1816* (London: Henry Colburn, 1816).

Pottle, Frederick A., ed., *Boswell in Holland, 1763–64* (New York: McGraw Hill, 1952).

Ranby, John, *An Inquiry into the Supposed Increase of the Influence of the Crown* (London: Hatchard, 1811).

Reid, Stuart, *Life and Letters of Lord Durham, 1792–1840*, 2 vols (London: Longmans, Green & Co., 1906).

Report on the Manuscripts of J.B. Fortescue Esq. Preserved at Dropmore, 10 vols (London: HMSO, 1892).

Romilly, S.H., ed., *Letters to Ivy from the First Earl of Dudley* (London: Longmans, Green & Co., 1905).

Russell, Rollo, ed., *Early Correspondence of Lord John Russell, 1805–40*, 2 vols, (London: T. Fisher Unwin, 1913).

Russell, Lord John, *Recollections and Suggestions, 1813–73* (London: Longmans, Green & Co., 1875).

Septuagenarius, *An Address to the Freeholders of Westmorland Containing Observations on A Sermon Preached at Appleby on the 12th August, 1825* (Kendal: Tyrus Redhead, 1825).

Seymour, Lady, ed., *The 'Pope' of Holland House: Selections from the Correspondence of John Wishaw and His Friends, 1813–14* (London: T.F. Unwin, 1906).

Smith, Nowell C., ed., *The Letters of Sydney Smith*, 2 vols (Oxford: Clarendon Press, 1953).

[Somerville, Alexander], *Autobiography of a Working Man* (London: Turnstile Press, 1848).

Tinney, John Penn, *The Rights of Sovereignty Vindicated: With Particular Reference to Political Doctrines of the Edinburgh Review and of Other Periodical Publications* (London: C. & R. Baldwin, 1809).

Twiss, Horace, *The Public and Private Life of Lord Chancellor Eldon*, 3 vols (London: John Murray, 1844).

Westmorland Election 1818: An Account of the Proceedings at Appleby From Saturday the 27th of June to the Final Close of the Poll (Kendal: Richard Lough, 1818).

Wharton, R., *Remarks on the Jacobinical Tendency of the Edinburgh Review in a Letter to the Earl of Lonsdale* (London: Hatchard, 1809).

Wilson, Sir Robert, *Narrative of the Formation of Canning's Administration, 1827*, Herbert Randolph, ed., (London: Rivingtons, 1872).

Young, Charles Duke, *Life and Administration of Robert Banks, 2nd Earl of Liverpool*, 3 vols (London: Macmillan & Co., 1868).

Printed secondary works

Aspinall, Arthur, *Lord Brougham and the Whig Party* (Manchester: Manchester University Press, 1927).

Aspinall, Arthur, 'The Coalition Ministries of 1827: Goderich', *English Historical Review*, 2 parts (April and October 1827):201–26, 533–59.

Aspinall, Arthur, 'Lord Brougham's Life and Times', *English Historical Review* 59.233(January 1944): 87–112.

Aspinall, Arthur, 'The Social Status of Journalists at the Beginning of the Nineteenth Century', *Review of English Studies*, 21(1945):216–32.

Aspinall, Arthur, *Politics and the Press* (London: Home & Van Thal Ltd., 1949).

Aspinall, Arthur, 'English Party Organization in the Early Nineteenth Century'. *English Historical Review* (1926):389–411.

Asquith, Ivon, 'The Whig Party and the Press in the Early Nineteenth Century', *Bulletin of the Institute of Historical Research* (November 1976):264–83.

Asquith, Ivon, 'Advertising and the Press in the Late Eighteenth and Early Nineteenth Centuries: James Perry and the Morning Chronicle', *Historical Journal*, 18.4(1975):703–24.

Barnes, F. and J.L. Hobbs, *Handlist of Newspapers Published in Cumberland, Westmorland, and Lancashire* (Kendal: Wilson, 1951).

Bateman, John, *Great Landowners of Great Britain and Ireland*, 4th edn (Leicester: Leicester University Press, 1971).

Best, G.F.A., 'The Protestant Constitution and Its Supporters, 1800–29'. *Transactions of the Royal Historical Society*, 5th ser., 8(1959):105–27.

Belchem, J.C., 'Henry Hunt and the Evolution of the Mass Platform', *English Historical Review*, 93.369(October 1978):739–73.

Bouch, G.M. and G.P. Jones, *A Short Economic History of the the Lake Counties, 1500–1830* (Manchester: Manchester University Press, 1961).

Bouch, G.M. and G.P. Jones, *Prelates and People of the Lake Counties* (Kendal: Titus Wilson and Son, 1948).

Brent, Richard, *Liberal Anglican Politics: Whiggery Religion and Reform, 1830–1* (Oxford: Clarendon Press).

Cannon, John, *The Whig Ascendancy: Colloquies on Hanoverian England* (London: Edward Arnold, 1988).

Cannon, John, *The Fox–North Coalition: The Crisis of the Constitution* (Cambridge: Cambridge University Press, 1969).

Chamberlain, Muriel, *Lord Aberdeen, A Political Biography* (London: Longman, 1983).

Christie, Ian R., *Myth and Reality in Late Eighteenth Century British Politics and Other Papers* (Berkeley: University of California Press, 1970).

Clark, J.C.D., *English Society, 1660–1832: Religion, Ideology, and Politics During the Ancien Regime* (Cambridge: Cambridge University Press, 2000).

Clark, J.C.D., 'A General Theory of Party, Opposition, and Government, 1688–1832', *Historical Journal*, 23.3(1980):323–4.

Clark, J.C.D., 'The Decline of Party, 1740–60', *English Historical Review*, 93.368(July 1978):499–527.

Clive, John, *Scotch Reviewers: The Edinburgh Review, 1802–15* (London: Faber & Faber, 1957).

Clive, John, 'The Earl of Buchan's Kick: A Footnote to the History of the Edinburgh Review', *Harvard Library Bulletin*, 5.3.(1951):262–70.

Colley, Linda J., *Britons: Forging the Nation, 1707–1837* (New Haven: Yale University Press, 1992).

Colley, Linda J., 'The Principles and Practice of Eighteenth Century Party', *Historical Journal*, 22(1979):239–46.

Cookson, J.E., *The Friends of Peace: Anti-War Liberalism in England, 1793–1815* (Cambridge: Cambridge University Press, 1982).

Cookson, J.E., *Lord Liverpool's Administration: The Crucial Years, 1815–22* (Edinburgh: Scottish Academic Press, 1975).

Crouzet, François, *Britain Ascendant: Comparative Studies in Franco–British Economic History* (Cambridge: Cambridge University Press, 1990).

Crouzet, François, *L'économie britannique et le blocus continental, 1806–13* (Paris: Presses Universitaires de France, 1958).

Davis, Richard W., 'Whigs in the Age of Fox and Grey', *Parliamentary History*, 12:2(1993), 201–8.

Davis, Richard W., 'The Tories, the Whigs, and Catholic Emancipation, 1827–29', *English Historical Review*, 87(1982):89–98.

Davis, Richard W., 'The Whigs and the Idea of Electoral Deference: Some Further Thoughts on the Great Reform Act', *Durham University Journal*, 67.1(December 1978):79–91.

Davis, Richard W., 'The Strategy of "Dissent" in the Repeal Campaign, 1820–8', *Journal of Modern History*, 38.4(1966):374–93.

Derry, John W., *Charles, Earl Grey: Aristocratic Reformer* (Oxford: Blackwells, 1992).

Derry, John W., *Politics in the Age of Fox, Pitt, and Liverpool: Continuity and Transformation* (London: Macmillan, 1990).

Dickinson, H.T., *The Politics of the People in Eighteenth Century Britain* (New York: St Martin's Press, 1995).

Dickinson, H.T., ed., *Britain and the French Revolution, 1789–1815* (Basingstoke: Macmillan Education, 1989).

Douglas, Wallace W., 'Wordsworth in Politics: The Election of 1818', *Modern Language Notes*, 43.7(November 1948):437–49.

Eastwood, David, 'Amplifying the Province of the Legislature: The Flow of Information and the English State in the Early Nineteenth Century', *Historical Research*, 62(1989):419–43.

Edsall, Nicholas C., *Richard Cobden: Independent Radical* (Cambridge, MA: Harvard University Press, 1986).

Emsley, Clive, *British Society and the French Wars, 1793–1815* (London: Macmillan, 1979).

Ferguson, Richard Saul, *Cumberland and Westmorland MPs from the Restoration to the Reform Bill* (Carlisle: C. Thurnman & Son, 1871).

Fisher, David Hackett, *Albion's Seed: Four British Folkways in America* (Oxford: Oxford University Press, 1989).

Fontana, Biancamaria, *Rethinking the Politics of Commercial Society* (Cambridge: Cambridge University Press, 1985).

Foord, Archibald S., *His Majesty's Opposition, 1714–1830* (Oxford: Clarendon Press, 1964).

Ford, Trowbridge H., *Henry Brougham and His World: A Biography* (Chichester: B. Rose, 1995).

Ford, Trowbridge H., 'Political Coverage in the Times, 1811–41: The Role of Barnes and Brougham', *Bulletin of the Institute of Historical Research*, 49.139(May 1986):91–107.

Fraser, Peter, 'Party Voting in the House of Commons, 1812–27.' *English Historical Review*, 98(October 1983):736–84.

Fraser, Peter, 'Public Petitioning and Parliament Before 1832', *History*, 158(1961):195–211.

Gash, Norman, *Pillars of Government and Other Essays on State and Society c. 1770–1880* (London: Edward Arnold, 1986).

Gash, Norman, *Lord Liverpool: The Life and Political Career of Robert Banks Jenkinson, Second Earl of Liverpool 1770–1828* (London: Weidenfeld & Nicholson, 1984).

Gash, Norman, 'After Waterloo: British Society and the Legacy of the Napoleonic Wars', *Transactions of the Royal Historical Society*, 5th ser., 28:(1978):145–57.

Gash, Norman, *Politics in the Age of Peel: A Study in The Technique of Parliamentary Representation*, 2nd edn (Hassocks: Harvester, 1977).

Gash, Norman, 'Brougham and the Yorkshire Election of 1830', *Proceedings of the Leeds Philosophical and Literary Society*, Literary and Historical Section, 8(May 1956):19–35.

Gash, Norman, 'English Reform and French Revolution in the General Election of 1830', in *Essays Presented to Sir Lewis Namier*, Richard Pares and A.J.P. Taylor, eds., (London: Macmillan, 1956).

Gayer, Arthur, W.W. Rostow, and Anna Jacobson Schwartz, *The Growth and Fluctuation of the British Economy, 1790–1850: An Historical, Statistical, and Theoretical Study of Britain's Economic Development* (Hassocks: Harvester Press, 1975).

Gibson, Thomas, *Legends and Historical Notes on Places in East and West Westmorland* (Manchester: Heywood, 1877).

Gray, Denis, *Spencer Perceval: The Evangelical Prime Minister, 1762–1812* (Manchester: Manchester University Press, 1963).

Gunn, J.A., 'Influence, Parties, and the Constitution', *Historical Journal*, 17(1974):301–28.

Hanham, H.J., *The Reformed Electoral System in Great Britain, 1832–1914* (London: Historical Association, 1968).

Harling, Philip, 'Robert Southey and the Language of Social Discipline', *Albion*, 30.4(winter 1998):630–55.

Harling, Philip, *The Waning of 'Old Corruption': The Politics of Economical Reform in Britain, 1777–1846* (Oxford: Clarendon Press, 1996).

Heckscher, Eli F., *The Continental System* (Oxford: Clarendon Press, 1922).

Hickey, Donald R., *The War of 1812, A Forgotten Conflict* (Urbana: University of Illinois Press, 1989).

Hilton, Boyd, 'The Political Arts of Lord Liverpool', *Transactions of the Royal Historical Society*, 5th ser., 38(1988):147–70.

Hilton, Boyd, *Corn, Cash, and Commerce: The Economic Policies of the Tory Governments, 1815–30* (Oxford: Oxford University Press, 1977).

Hinde, Wendy, *Catholic Emancipation: A Shake to Men's Minds* (Oxford: Blackwell, 1992).

History of the Times: 'The Thunderer' in the Making, 1785–1841 (New York: Macmillan, 1935).

Holdgate, Martin W., *A History of Appleby; County Town of Westmorland* (Appleby: Whitehead, 1956).

Hudson, Derek, *Thomas Barnes of the Times* (Cambridge: Cambridge University Press, 1943).

Hughes, Edward, *North Country Life in the Eighteenth Century*, vol. II, *Cumberland and Westmorland, 1700–1830* (Oxford: Oxford University Press, 1965).

Jenkins, T.A., *The Liberal Ascendancy, 1830–86* (New York: St Martin's Press, 1994).

Judd, Gerrit P., *Members of Parliament, 1734–1832* (New Haven: Yale University Press, 1955).

Jupp, Peter, *Lord Grenville, 1759–1834* (Oxford: Clarendon Press, 1985).

Kriegel, A.D., 'Liberty and Whiggery in Early Nineteenth Century England', *Journal of Modern History*, 52(1980):253–78.

Laqueur, Thomas W., 'The Queen Caroline Affair: Politics as Art in the Reign of George IV', *Journal of Modern History*, 54.3(September 1982):417–66.

Large, David, 'The Decline in the Party of the Crown and the Rise of Parties in the House of Lords, 1738–1837', *English Historical Review*, 78(October 1963):669–95.

Machin, G.I.T., 'Resistance to Repeal of the Test and Corporation Acts, 1828', *Historical Journal*, 22.1(1979):115–39.

Machin, G.I.T., *The Catholic Question in English Politics, 1820 to 1830* (Oxford: Clarendon Press, 1964).

Main, J.M., 'Radical Westminster, 1807–20', *Historical Studies (Australia and New Zealand)*, 12.46(April 1966):186–204.

Mandler, Peter, *Aristocratic Government in the Age of Reform: Whigs and Liberals, 1830–52* (Oxford: Clarendon Press, 1990).

Marshall, J.D. and John K. Walton, *The Lake Counties from 1830 to the mid-Twentieth Century: A Study in Regional Change* (Manchester: Manchester University Press, 1981).

Marshall, J.D. and Carol Anne Dyhouse, 'Social Transition in Kendal and Westmorland, c. 1760–1860', *Northern History*, 12(1976):127–57.

McAdams, Donald R., 'Electioneering Techniques in Populous Constituencies, 1784–96', *Studies in Burke and His Times*, 14(1972):23–53.

McQuiston, Julian R., 'The Lonsdale Connection and its Defender, William Viscount Lowther, 1818–30', *Northern History*, 11(1976):143–79.

Menzies, E.M., 'The Freeman Voter in Liverpool, 1802–35', *Transactions of the Historical Society of Lancashire and Cheshire*, 124(1972):85–107.

Mitchell, Austin, *The Whigs in Opposition, 1815–30* (Oxford: Clarendon Press, 1967).

Morris, R.J., *Class, Sect, and Party: The Making of the British Middle Class, Leeds, 1820–50* (Manchester: Manchester University Press, 1990).

Moss, D.J., 'Birmingham and the Campaign against the Orders in Council and the East India Company Charter 1812–13', *Canadian Journal of History*, 11.2(1976):173–88.

Muir, Rory, *Britain and the Defeat of Napoleon, 1807–15* (New Haven: Yale University Press, 1996).

New, Chester H., *The Life of Henry Brougham to 1830* (Oxford: Clarendon Press, 1961).

Newbold, Ian, 'The Emergence of a Two Party System in England from 1830 to 1841', *Parliaments, Estates, and Representation*, 5(1985):25–32.

Nicholls, David, 'The English Middle Class and the Ideological Significance of Radicalism, 1760–1886', *Journal of British Studies*, 24(October 1985):415–33.

Nichols, Robert L., 'Surrogate for Democracy: Nineteenth Century British Petitioning', *Maryland Historian*, 5(1974):43–52.

Nicholson, Cornelius, *The Annals of Kendal: Being an Historical and Descriptive Account of Kendal and the Neighbourhood*, 2nd ed. (London: Whitaker & Co., 1861).

Nicholson, Francis and Ernest Axon, *The Older Nonconformity in Kendal* (Kendal: Titus Wilson, 1915).

O'Brian, Patrick, 'The Political Economy of British Taxation, 1660–1815', *Economic History Review*, 2nd ser., 41:1(1988):1–32.

O'Gorman, Frank, 'Campaign Rituals and Ceremonies: The Social Meaning of Elections in England, 1780–1860', *Past and Present*, 135(1992):79–115.

O'Gorman, Frank, 'Pitt and the "Tory" Reaction', in *Britain and the French Revolution, 1789–1815*, H.T. Dickinson ed., (London: Macmillan Education, 1989).

O'Gorman, Frank, *Voters, Patrons and Parties: The Unreformed Electoral System of Hanoverian England, 1734–1832* (Oxford: Clarendon Press, 1989).

O'Gorman, Frank, 'Party Politics in the Early Nineteenth Century', *English Historical Review*, 102(1987):63–84.

O'Gorman, Frank, 'The Unreformed Electorate of Hanovarian England: The mid-Eighteenth Century to 1832', *Social History*, 2.1(1986):33–52.

O'Gorman, Frank, 'Electoral Deference in Unreformed England, 1760–1832', *Journal of Modern History*, 56(1984):391–429.

O'Gorman, Frank, *The Emergence of the British Two Party System, 1760–1832* (London: Edward Arnold, 1982).

Olphin, H.K., *George Tierney, 1761–1830* (London: George Allen & Unwin Ltd., 1934).

Owen, Hugh, *The Lowther Family: Eight Hundred Years of 'A Family of Ancient Gentry and Worship'* (Chichester: Phillimore, 1990).

Parry, Jonathan, *The Rise and Fall of Liberal Government in Victorian Britain* (New Haven: Yale University Press, 1993).

Parry, Jonathan, 'Constituencies, Elections, and Members of Parliament, 1790–1820', *Parliamentary History*, 7.1(1988):147–60.

Pollitt, Charles, *DeQuincey's Editorship of the Westmorland Gazette* (Kendal: Atkinson & Pollitt, 1890).

Porter, Roy, *English Society in the Eighteenth Century* (Harmondsworth, England: Penguin Books, 1990).

Quinault, R., 'The French Revolution of 1830 and Parliamentary Reform', *History*, 79(1994):377–93.

Rapp, Dean, 'The Left-Wing Whigs: Whitbread, the Mountain, and Reform 1809–15', *Journal of British Studies*, 21:2(spring 1982), 35–66.

Rapp, Dean, *Samuel Whitbread, A Social and Political Study* (New York: Garland Publishing, 1987).

Read, Donald, *The English Provinces c. 1760–1960: A Study in Influence* (London: Edward Arnold, 1964).

Read, Donald, *Press and People, 1790–1850: Opinion in Three English Cities* (London: Edward Arnold, 1961).

Read, Donald, *Peterloo: The 'Massacre' and Its Background* (Manchester: Manchester University Press, 1958).

Rickworth, Edgell, *Radical Squibs and Loyal Ripostes: Satirical Pamphlets of the Regency Period* (Bath: Adams & Dart, 1971).

Roberts, Michael, *The Whig Party, 1807–15* (London: Macmillan, 1939).

Roberts, Michael, 'The Ministerial Crisis of May-June 1812', *English Historical Review*, 51(1936):466–87.

Robbins, Caroline, 'Discordant Parties: A Study of the Acceptance of Party by Englishmen', *Political Science Quarterly*, 73(1958):505–29.

Rostow, W.W., *The British Economy of the Nineteenth Century* (Oxford: Clarendon Press, 1948).

Rutz, Michael A., 'The Politicizing of Evangelical Dissent, 1811–13', *Parliamentary History*, 20:2(2001), 187–207.

Sabine, B.E.V., *A Short History of Taxation* (London; Butterworths, 1980).

Sack, James J., *From Jacobite to Conservative: Reaction and Orthodoxy in Britain, c. 1760–1832* (Cambridge: Cambridge University Press, 1993).

Sack, James J., *The Grenvillites, 1801–29: Party Politics and Faction in the Age of Pitt and Liverpool* (Urbana: University of Illinois Press, 1979).

Sack, James J., 'Decline of the Grenvillite Faction under the First Duke of Buckingham and Chandos, 1817–29', *Journal of British Studies*, 15.1(1975):112–34.

Shattock, Joanne, *Politics and Reviewers: The Edinburgh and The Quarterly in the Early Victorian Age* (Leicester: Leicester University Press, 1989).

Seldon, Anthony, ed., *How Tory Governments Fall: The Tory Party in Power Since 1783* (London: Fontana, 1996).

Smart, William, *Economic Annals of the Nineteenth Century*, 2 vols (London: Macmillan & Co., 1910 and 1917).

Smith, E.A., *A Queen on Trial: The Affair of Queen Caroline* (Stroud: Alan Sutton, 1993).

Smith, E.A., *Lord Grey, 1761–1830* (Oxford: Clarendon Press, 1990).

Smith, E.A., *Whig Principles and Party Politics: Earl; Fitzwilliam and the Whig Party, 1748–1833* (Manchester: Manchester University Press, 1975).

Smith, E.A., 'The Election Agent in English Politics, 1734–1832', *English Historical Review*, 84(January 1969):12–35.

Smith, M.J., 'The Mushroom Elections in Carlisle', *Transactions of the Cumberland and Westmorland Antiquarian and Archeological Society*, 80(1981):114–21.

Smith, Robert Worthington, 'Political Organization and Canvassing: Yorkshire Elections Before the First Reform Bill', *American Historical Review*, 74(1969):1538–60.

Southgate, Donald, *The Passing of the Whigs, 1832–86* (London: Macmillan, 1962.)

Stewart, Robert, *Henry Brougham, 1778–1868: His Public Career* (London: Bodley Head, 1985).

Stewart, Robert, *The Foundations of the Conservative Party, 1830–67* (London: Longmans, 1978).

Thomas, William, *The Quarrel of Macaulay and Croker: Politics and History in the Age of Reform* (Oxford: Oxford University Press, 2000).

Thomas, William, *The Philosophical Radicals: Nine Studies in Theory and Practice, 1817–41* (Oxford: Clarendon Press, 1979).

Thomas, William, 'Whigs and Radicals in Westminster: The Election of 1819', *Guildhall Miscellany*, 3.3(October 1970):174–215.

Thompson, F.M.L., 'Whigs and Liberals in the West Riding, 1820–32', *English Historical Review*, 74.291(April 1959):214–39.

Thompson, Neville, *Wellington After Waterloo* (London: Routledge & Keegan Paul, 1986).

Thorne, R.G., ed., *The House of Commons, 1720–1820*, 5 vols (London: Secker & Warburg, 1986).

Tolley, B.H., 'The Liverpool Campaign Against the Orders in Council and the War of 1812', in *Liverpool and Merseyside*, J.R. Harris, ed., (London: Frank Cass & Co., 1969).

Turberville A.S. and F. Beckwith, 'Leeds and Parliamentary Reform, 1820–32', *Publications of the Thoresby Society, Miscellany*, 41.1(1943):1–88.

Wahrman, Dror, *Imagining the Middle Class: The Political Representation of Class in Britain c. 1780–1840* (Cambridge: Cambridge University Press, 1995).

Wadsworth, A.P., 'Newspaper Circulations, 1800–1954', *Transactions of the Manchester Statistical Society*, (1954–5), 1–40.

Wasson, E.A., *Whig Renaissance: Lord Althorp and the Whig Party, 1782–1845* (New York: Garland Publishing, 1987).

Wasson, E.A., 'The Great Whigs and Parliamentary Reform, 1809–30', *Journal of British Studies*, 24(October 1985):434–64.

Wasson, E.A., 'The Coalition of 1827 and the Crisis of Whig Leadership', *Historical Journal*, 20.3(1977):587–606.

Wells, John Edwin, 'Wordsworth and DeQuincey in Westmorland Politics, 1818', *Publications of the Modern Language Association of America*, 55.4(1940):1080–128.

Whittingham-Jones, Barbara, 'Liverpool's Political Clubs, 1812–30', *Transactions of the Historic Society of Lancashire and Cheshire*, 11.1(1959):117–38.

Willman, Robert, 'The Origins of "Whig" and "Tory" in English Political Language', *Historical Journal*, 17:2(1974):247–64.

Wood, Marcus, *Radical Satire and Print Culture, 1790–1822* (Oxford: Clarendon Press, 1994).

Unpublished dissertations

Brown, Stuart Melvin, 'The Growth of Middle Class Leadership in Kendal Society and its Influence on Politics, 1790–1850', (MA thesis., University of Lancaster, 1971).

Burgess, John, 'A Religious History of Cumbria, 1780–1920' (Ph.D. diss., University of Sheffield, 1984).

Dixon, P.F., 'The Politics of Emancipation: the Movement for the Abolition of Slavery in the British West Indies 1807–33' (D.Phil. diss., Oxford University, 1971).

Dyhouse, Carol Anne, 'Social Institutions in Kendal, 1790–1850' (MA diss., University of Lancaster, 1971).

Janzow, F.S., 'DeQuincey Enters Journalism: His Contributions to the Westmorland Gazette 1818–19' (Ph.D. diss., University of Chicago, 1968).

Palmer, Alice, 'Local Government and Social Problems in Kendal and Westmorland c. 1760–1860' (MA diss., University of Lancaster, 1972).

Scott, Iain Robertson, 'From Radicalism to Conservativism: The Politics of Wordsworth and Coleridge, 1797–1818' (Ph.D. diss., University of Edinburgh, 1987).

Stoker, David, 'Elections and Voting Behaviour: A Study of Elections in Northumberland, Durham, Cumberland and Westmorland, 1760–1832' (Ph.D. diss., University of Manchester: 1980).

Sumner, L.V., 'The General Election of 1818' (Ph.D. diss., University of Manchester, 1969).

Taylor, William Banks, 'The Foxite Party and Foreign Politics, 1806–16' (Ph.D. diss., University of London, 1974).

Index

Abercrombie, James, 145, 152, 157
Aberdeen, 95–6
Aberdeen, George Gordon 4th Earl, 172
Abolitionism, 80, 129–30, 162, 165, 168, 170
Adamthwaite, Rev. John, 134
Age, The, 157
Allen, John, 6, 7, 139, 147
Althrop, John Charles Spencer Viscount, 5, 55, 84, 106–9, 124, 141, 143, 145, 152–3, 158–61, 172–3, 175, 181, 183
America, 27–9, 31–2
Appleby, 68, 71–2, 80, 86, 88, 112, 132
Anti-Corn Law League, 2, 25
Anti-Slavery Society, 129, 164
Arbuthnot, Charles, 115
Arbuthnot, Harriet, 161
Atkinson, James, 68, 206n
Attwood, Thomas, 29, 37
Auckland, William Eden, 1st Baron, 27
Austria, 23–4

Baines, Edward, 48, 77, 129
  reacts to Peterloo, 100, 103
  promotes Brougham's election for Yorkshire, 163–7, 168
Bagehot, Walter, 4
Baring, Alexander, 29, 32, 54
Barnes, Thomas, 47, 77, 181–2, 193n
Bathurst, Charles Bragge, 108
Bedford, John Russell, 6th Duke, 18, 36, 146
Bentham, Jeremy, 5
Birmingham, 29–30, 32, 37, 48, 101, 162
Blacow, Rev. Richard, 126, 128
Bonaparte, Napoleon, 21, 23–4, 26–8, 31, 50, 53, 55, 82–3, 98
boroughs, 38, 41–2, 67, 74, 89, 123, 136, 162, 178
Boswell, James, 13

Bristol, 41
Brougham, Eleanor (née Sime), 5, 175
Brougham, Henry, 12, 122
  political strategy, 2–4, 8, 35, 52, 66, 89–92, 106, 109–10, 111, 121, 125, 137, 160
  family and education, 5–6
  enters politics, 6–7
  temperament and reputation, 7, 59–61, 63, 98–9, 124, 138, 147, 153–4, 166, 170, 179–84, 193n
  enters Parliament, 18, 188n
  on Spain, 22
  defeats Orders in Council, 25–33, 36, 54
  Liverpool election (1812), 36–41, 191–2n
  attacks slavery, 38, 129–30, 162, 166, 168
  out of Parliament, 42–3
  relations with the press, 43–8, 181–2
  Yorkshire, 48
  Edinburgh Review, 49–51
  attacks income tax, 54–7
  defeats income tax, 58–61, 195n
  attacks Prince Regent, 59, 99
  attacks radicals, 63–4
  stands for Westmorland, 67–74, 85–7, 112–14, 132–6
  attacked as adventurer, 75–6, 83
  canvasses Westmorland, 79
  Cumberland politics, 84–5
  pledges to oppose Lowthers, 87–8
  parliamentary session in 1819, 94, 97–9
  reacts to Peterloo, 101, 104–8
  opposes Six Acts, 109
  defends Caroline of Brunswick, 116–20
  proposed as Whig leader in Commons, 124–5
  criticizes Established Church, 125–8

Brougham, Henry *continued*
on Catholic question, 131–2, 159
supports coalition with Canning,
    139–48
desire for office, 147, 149–50, 208n
supports coalition with Goderich,
    151–2
repeal of Test and Corporation Acts,
    155–8
elected for Yorkshire, 163–8
canvasses following election,
    169–70
leads opposition to Wellington,
    170–2
becomes Lord Chancellor, 173–9
career fails, 179–82
achievement, 183–4, 212n
Brougham, James
Westmorland interest, 67
prompts brother's candidacy, 71–2
visits Kendal, 76
distributes newspapers in
    Westmorland, 79
1826 Westmorland election, 133
presses brother to accept Lord
    Chancellorship, 173
Brougham, William, 133
Buckingham and Chandos, Richard
    Temple Nugent Bridges Chandos
    Grenville, 1st Marquess, 68, 121
Burdett, Sir Francis, 33, 36, 75, 95, 101
Burke, Edmund, 1, 2, 35, 106, 147,
    178
likened to Brougham, 7, 37, 183
critique of French Revolution, 75
Burrard, Sir Harry, 23
Burrell, Sir Charles, 55
business cycle, 52
Byron, George Gordon, Lord, 2

Calcraft, John, 94
Canning, George, 12, 42, 67, 84, 107,
    130–1, 153, 156, 173, 183
on Toryism, 14
duel with Castlereagh, 24
Liverpool election (1812), 38–41
attacks reform, 63, 124
parliamentary session in 1819, 94,
    96–7

on Brougham, 117
joins government in 1822, 121–3
relations with Tory party, 133,
    138–9
forms government, 137, 141–6,
    148–50, 154
death in 1827, 151
Canningites, 15, 42, 138, 145, 147,
    149, 153, 155, 157, 160–2, 170,
    173, 176
canvassing, 39, 72, 76–81, 86, 89,
    114, 133–5, 166, 169
Carlisle, 86
Carlisle, Earl of, *see* Morpeth,
    Viscount
Carlisle Patriot, 76, 79–81, 86, 122
Caroline, of Brunswick, 47, 110,
    127–8, 139, 149
marriage with George IV, 115
divorce negotiations, 116–17
trial of, 118–20, 124, 134
Cartwright, John, 62
Cartwright, William, 57
Castlereagh, Robert Stewart Viscount
    (later 2nd Marquess of
    Londonderry), 12, 59, 63–4, 94,
    111
defines Toryism, 14
on party, 14, 16
duel with Canning, 24
defends Orders in Council, 25, 30,
    32
defends income tax, 57, 60
parliamentary session in 1819,
    94–7
introduces Six Acts, 107–8
suicide in 1822, 121
Catholic Association, 131, 158
Catholic Emancipation, 2, 14, 38, 42,
    116, 125, 131, 133–4, 136, 138–41,
    143–6, 151, 155–62, 166, 169, 172
Cavendish family, 70, 83–4
Cavendish, Lord George, 84, 146
Cheshire, 100
Clapham, Samuel, 164
Clarkson, Thomas, 80
clergy, 73, 75, 77–8, 83, 125–8, 135
coalition, 16, 20, 35, 138, 141, 145–7,
    149, 160, 176–7

Cobbett, William, 44, 50, 62–4, 92
Cobden, Richard, 2, 44
Cochrane, Lord Thomas, 63–4, 195n
Cockermouth, 71, 113
Copenhagen, 21
Copley, John Singleton (later 1st
    Baron Lyndhurst), 141, 149, 180
constituencies, 36, 66, 178
Continental System, 27
Convention of Cintra (1808), 23
Corn Laws, 133, 138–9, 151, 166
Cornwall, 123
corruption, 40, 52–3, 74
Courier, 40–1, 43, 47, 51, 62, 63, 74–6,
    88, 97–9, 101, 105, 154, 157, 160
Crackenthorp, William, 105, 114, 133
Creevey, Thomas, 20
    on party, 16, 90
    depicted as a badger, 18
    Liverpool election (1812), 36–41
    and Brougham, 127, 154, 183
    opposes Canning, 146
Croker, John Wilson, 11, 41, 193n
    defines party, 14, 186n
    defends government, 61
    comments on Brougham, 87, 117
    conflict among Tories, 138, 141,
        151
Cruikshank, George, 57–59, 63–4
Cumberland, 70
    politics, 84–5, 88, 104–6, 113–4
Curtis, Sir William, 55
Curwen, John Christian, 70, 85, 105,
    113
Curwen's Act (1809), 12

Dalrymple, Sir Hew, 23
Darlington, William Harry Vane,
    2nd Earl (later 1st Marquess of
    Cleveland), 43, 66, 71, 132
    urges support for Canning, 141
    quarrel with Grey, 153–4
    joins Wellington, 162
Demerara, 129–30
DeQuincey, Thomas, 84
    *Close Comments on a Straggling
        Speech*, 81–2
    friendship with Wordsworth, 82
    edits *Westmorland Gazette*, 88

Derby, Lord, 84
Devonshire, William George Spencer
    Cavendish, 6th Duke, 84, 101,
    141, 143–4, 162, 166
Dewsbury, 167
Dissenters, 15, 33, 37, 49, 52, 69–70,
    73, 125–9, 134, 154–6, 163–4
Disraeli, Benjamin, 182
Duncannon, John William Ponsonby,
    Viscount, 89, 115, 173
Duncombe, Henry, 163
Dundas, Henry, 1st Viscount Melville,
    5, 11–12
Dundas, Lawrence, 102
Durham, 55, 67, 70, 77, 87, 104, 124
    clergy in, 126–8, 155
Durham Chronicle, 126

East India Company, 33, 48, 167
Edinburgh, 5–6, 68
Edinburgh Review, 5, 22–3, 25, 27,
    35, 43, 49–51, 57, 79, 90–1,
    97–8, 126, 128–9, 153, 155,
    169, 171
Eldon, John Scott, 1st Earl, 107, 111,
    115, 117, 142, 144, 148, 180
    and Catholic question, 131, 159
    excluded from Wellington's
        government, 154
Elections, 3, 36, 73, 76, 78, 177–9
    in 1807, 12, 14, 38
    in 1812, 12, 38, 42
    Liverpool (1812), 36–41
    in 1818, 66, 89, 92
    Westmorland (1818), 67, 71–87
    Westminster (1819), 95
    Westmorland (1820), 112–13
    Cumberland (1820), 113
    in 1826, 132
    Westmorland (1826), 132–6
    Yorkshire (1830, 165–9
Erskine, Thomas, 1st Baron, 107
Established Church, 14–5, 37, 73,
    125–8, 155
Examiner, 17, 46

faction, 8, 14, 16, 19, 25, 114, 137,
    145, 161
Fitzgerald, William Vesey, 158

Fitzwilliam, William Wentworth
   Fitzwilliam, 2nd Earl, 17, 48, 58,
   108, 119, 123–4, 163
   responds to Peterloo, 99–104,
   105–7
Fox, Charles James, 2, 14, 35, 52–3,
   67, 94, 184
   memory of, 16, 18, 46, 68, 90, 92,
   153, 178
   alliance with Grenville, 17
   on party, 20, 144, 147
Fox–North Coalition (1783), 16, 147,
   149
Foxites, *see* Whigs
France, 11, 17, 21, 24, 53, 55, 83, 132,
   146, 163, 169, 210n
franchise, 38, 41, 85–6, 170
freeholders, 67, 71, 78, 85–8, 112–4,
   120, 133–6, 160, 163–4, 166
French Revolution, 11, 17, 53, 75, 83,
   210n

Gascoigne, Issac, 37, 39–41
George III
   relations with ministers, 12
   appoints Pitt, 16
   unable to rule, 20
   Walcheren Expedition, 24
   dies in 1820, 111, 115
George IV, 10, 29, 34, 59, 62, 93,
   101–2, 105
   relations with ministers, 58, 121,
   139, 140–3, 151–3
   attacked by Brougham, 59, 61, 63,
   81, 118–19
   dissolves Parliament, 86
   and Caroline of Brunswick, 115–20
   refuses to accept Brougham, 147,
   149
   accepts Catholic Emancipation,
   159–60
   dies in 1830, 163
Gladstone, John, 38, 40
Gladstone, William, 1, 3, 79
Glasgow, 70
Goodwin, John, 42
Graham, Sir James, 86, 172
Grampound, 123
Grattan, Henry, 159

Grenville, Thomas, 19, 32, 53, 88, 141
Grenville, William Wyndham,
   1st Baron, 88, 102, 117, 120–1,
   145
   and Fox, 17
   economic views, 19
   rejects coalition, 20
   foreign policy, 21–3, 53–4, 62
   resists aggressive opposition, 24
   withdraws from active politics, 62
Grenvillites, 12, 15, 17, 19, 32–3, 42,
   53–4, 62, 89, 91, 121, 152, 154
Greville, Charles, 98, 166, 179, 182
Grey, Charles, 2nd Earl, 2, 10, 131,
   133, 179–80
   and Brougham, 7, 36–7, 39, 61, 88,
   98, 114, 117, 124–5, 146–7,
   153–4, 174–5, 180–3, 193n
   and Grenville, 17, 53–4
   economic policy, 19, 27, 52, 55
   rejects coalition, 20, 137–8, 141,
   144–5, 147, 149, 152
   foreign policy, 21–2
   repeal of Orders in Council, 32
   1812 elections, 42–3
   relations with press, 46
   principles, 49, 147, 153
   Whig party, 61, 110, 121, 139, 149
   political programme, 92–3, 116
   reacts to Peterloo, 102, 104–5, 107
   Caroline of Brunswick's trial,
   119–20
   attacks Canning, 145–6
   supports Wellington, 160–1
   revives opposition, 162
   urges parliamentary reform, 172
   forms government in 1830, 173,
   175–8
   passes 1832 Reform Act, 181

Hamilton, Lord Archibald, 95
Hampshire, 104
Harrison, John, 69
Hazlitt, William, 50, 120
Heckmond, 167
Henry, Patrick, 5
Herries, John Charles, 97, 151–2
Hertfordshire, 104
Hobhouse, John Cam, 95, 173

Holland, Lady Elizabeth Vassall, 25, 61, 80, 85, 104, 174
Holland, Henry Richard Vassal Fox, 3rd Baron, 25, 49, 75, 126, 139, 176, 181
 and Brougham, 6, 30, 36, 61, 63, 124, 132, 147, 182, 188n
 Whig party, 18, 20, 43, 53, 89, 92, 99, 116, 118, 120, 137–8, 141, 146, 151–2, 161–2, 170
 economic policy, 27, 52
 relations with press, 45
 and Thanet, 68, 114
 reacts to Peterloo, 102–4
 describes 'revolution in parties', 137, 160–1
Holland House, 35, 51
Hone, William, 75
Hook, Theodore, 119
Horner, Francis, 2, 25, 41
 and Whigs, 18, 42
 and *Edinburgh Review*, 49, 51
 attacks income tax, 57
House of Commons, 2, 10, 28, 43, 61, 89, 91–2, 105, 111, 126, 140, 149, 151, 154, 158–9, 163, 172–3, 175
 balance of seats, 11–12, 36, 93–4, 97, 114–15, 138, 178–9
 debates, 21, 24–5
 discusses Orders in Council, 27, 29–30, 32
 debates income tax, 55–7
 rejects income tax, 58–60, 195n
 aristocratic influence, 84
 debates Westmorland's land tax returns, 85–6
 1819 session, 93–7, 99
 debates Six Acts, 107–9
 and Caroline of Brunswick, 117–19
 debates parliamentary reform, 123–4
 debates Smith case and slavery, 129–31
 supports Catholic Emancipation, 133
House of Lords, 62, 151, 154, 179
 Caroline of Brunswick's trial, 118–19
 Catholic Emancipation, 133

 debates Canning's government, 146
 debates parliamentary reform, 172
Howard family, 70, 83
Howick, Henry Grey, Viscount, 161
Huddersfield, 163, 167
Hull, 56
Hunt, Henry, 62–4, 75, 89, 100–2, 106
Hunt, Leigh, 17, 38, 44, 46, 61, 191–2n
Huskisson, William, 89, 93, 115, 121, 138, 152, 155–8, 160, 170
Hutchinson, John Hely-Hutchinson, 1st Baron, 116–7

Income tax (property or land and funds tax) 2, 10, 54, 72, 97, 120, 122, 125, 179
 campaign against, 55–7
 defeated in Commons, 58–61
independents, 15, 25, 97, 123, 173
India, 33, 125
Inglis, Sir Robert, 155, 159
Ireland, 17, 115, 131, 158–9, 167, 181

Jacobins, 33, 43, 50–1, 79, 81–2
Jeffrey, Francis
 on Spain, 22–3
 political strategy, 35–6, 177
 editor of *Edinburgh Review*, 51
 reacts to Peterloo, 101
Jennings, William, 69
Jews, 126
John Bull, 119, 157, 160
journalists, 45, 48

Kendal, 71–2, 81, 86, 105–6, 126, 133, 135
 society, 69–70
 riot in, 76–7
 Brougham's visit, 79
Kendal Chronicle, 67, 69, 71, 77, 79, 86, 112, 135
Kinnaird, Douglas, 95
Kirkby Lonsdale, 71
Knatchbull, Sir Edward, 117

Labour Party, 177
Lamb, George, 95

Lamb, William (later 2nd Viscount Melbourne), 2, 42–3, 144, 170, 182–4
Lambton, John George (later 1st Earl of Durham) 55, 65, 67, 92–3, 95, 104, 174
  helps Brougham in Westmorland, 77, 84, 86–7
  Whig leadership, 90, 124
  on Brougham, 98
  urges parliamentary reform, 123–4
  Durham politics, 126
  quarrels with Brougham, 182–3
Lambton, Ralph, 67
Lancashire, 101, 133
Lancaster, 78
Lansdowne, Henry Petty-Fitzmaurice, 3rd Marquess, 19, 27, 41, 67, 117–8, 124, 132, 173, 179–80
  cooperation with Canning, 138, 141, 143–6, 148
  Whig leadership, 139
  cooperation with Goderich, 151–24
Lascelles family, 163
Lascelles, Henry, Viscount, 106, 108
Leach, Sir John, 117
Leeds, 29, 37, 48, 123, 162–3, 165–70
Leeds Intelligencer, 165, 168
Leeds Mercury, 29, 37, 48, 55–6, 59, 77, 89, 100, 102–3, 130, 144, 146, 149, 156–7, 164–6, 168
Lethbridge, Sir Thomas, 13
liberal, 4, 7, 19, 48–9, 91–2, 96, 125, 129, 131, 134, 136, 137, 139–40, 144–7, 152–4, 156–61, 163–5, 170, 176, 184
  defined in political terms, 177–8
Liverpool, 28–9, 33, 67, 70, 105, 149, 170, 191–2n
  Liverpool Election (1812), 36–41, 43, 54, 84, 87, 125, 153
  conflicting interests, 37–8
Liverpool Mercury, 39, 47, 56, 149
Liverpool, Robert Banks Jenkinson, 2nd Earl, 1–2, 25, 41, 58, 59, 66, 68, 94, 107, 116, 119, 133, 136, 138, 151, 157, 180, 184
  government of, 10–13, 20, 35, 53, 59–61, 68, 91, 96–7, 111, 115, 131–3, 140–1, 152

on Tory Party, 14
political strategy, 61, 122
suffers stroke, 137
local corporations, 37–8, 49
London, 3, 55, 70, 119, 143, 169
Lonsdale, William Lowther, 1st Earl, 3, 83–4, 113
  Westmorland interest, 67, 78–9, 88, 135–6
  party ties, 68
  social role, 69, 198n
  predicts challenge, 71
  attacked by Brougham, 80–1
  friendship with Wordsworth, 82
Losh, James
  assists Brougham in Westmorland, 77
  on Brougham, 124
Lowther, Colonel Henry, 67, 106
  canvasses Kendal, 76–7,
  urged to hear freeholders complaints, 78
  Westmorland election (1818), 86–7
  Westmorland election (1820), 112–13
  Westmorland election (1816), 134–6
Lowther interest, 67–9, 72, 87–8, 132–6, 164
  supported by clergy, 73, 75, 78, 125
  attacks Brougham, 75
  treating freeholders, 77
  canvassing system, 77–8
  threatened in Cumberland, 84–5
  challenged in 1820, 112–4
Lowther, Sir James, 68, 82
Lowther, Sir John, 85, 113–14
Lowther, William, Viscount, 67, 74, 86, 106, 132
  doubts Brougham's intentions, 71
  analyzes local opposition, 73
  canvasses Kendal, 76–8
  Westmorland election (1818), 86–7
  Westmorland election (1820), 112–14
  Westmorland election (1826), 134–6
loyalism, 53, 75, 110, 122, 177, 180
Lushington, Stephen, 85

Macaulay, Thomas Babbington, 119
Mackintosh, Sir James, 95–6, 99
  attacks income tax, 57
  Brougham's Westmorland canvass, 80
  attacks slavery, 129
Macon Act (1811), 28
Madison, James, 28
Majocci, Theodoro, 118
Manchester, 48, 100–6, 161–2, 170
Manchester Guardian, 135, 144, 149, 159, 161, 179, 193n
manufacturing interest, 25, 28, 58
Marshall, John, 163–4
mechanics institutes, 44, 132
Methodists, 33, 134
middle classes, 3–5, 48–9, 52–3, 56, 58, 101, 123, 164, 183, 194n, 211n
Middlesex, 83, 102, 104, 158, 163
Milton, Charles William Wentworth Fitzwilliam, Viscount, 4–5, 48, 124, 163–4, 167, 169–70
  reacts to Peterloo, 103, 108
  view of Canning's government, 145
Milton, John, 118–19
Ministry of all the Talents, 2, 6, 8, 10–11, 21, 24, 27, 38, 67–8, 84, 116, 176, 188n
Mitchell, James, 103
Morpeth, George Howard Viscount, (after 1825 6th Earl of Carlisle), 207n
  politics in Cumberland, 84–5
  defends Brougham, 94
  defeated in 1820 election, 113–14
  supports coalition with Canning, 141, 143–4
  son stands with Brougham for Yorkshire, 164
Morpeth, George William Frederick Howard, Viscount, 170
  nominated for Yorkshire, 164–5
  canvasses with Brougham, 166–7
monopoly, 48, 168
Monroe, James, 29
Moore, Sir John, 23
Morning Chronicle, 22, 41, 44–5, 55–6, 58–9, 77, 84, 95, 100, 106, 114–15, 122, 127–9, 137, 144, 146–7, 168–71, 175
Musgrave, Sir Philip, 84

Napoleonic Wars, 22, 47, 69–70, 163
New Times, 74, 76, 97, 103, 133, 155, 158
Newcastle, 77, 92
newspapers, 3, 44–8, 77, 79, 111–12, 136
  duty on, 44, 107, 109
  provincial, 44, 47–8, 127
North, Frederick, Viscount, 1, 13, 147
Northamptonshire, 5, 58
Northern Circuit, 6, 140, 164
Northumberland, 70, 104, 120

O'Connell, Daniel, 131–2, 158, 167
Orders in Council, 2, 7, 25–6, 36–7, 45, 48, 52, 58, 72, 84, 120, 149, 153, 179
  issued, 27
  repeal campaign, 28–33
  defeated, 32

Paine, Thomas, 51
Palmerston, Viscount, 152, 170
Parnell, Sir Henry, 172
party, 1, 13, 42, 72, 95, 97–8, 123, 133, 136, 140, 144, 147, 153, 154, 157–8, 168, 175
  definition, 14
  different from faction, 15
  system 16, 137–8, 177–9, 184
paternalism, 82
patrons, 42, 198n
patronage, 13, 72, 125, 136, 147, 149, 151, 175
Peel, Sir Robert, 122, 136, 138, 170–1, 173
  confronts Brougham, 99
  joins Liverpool's cabinet, 121
  relations with Canning, 140
  defends Test and Corporation Acts, 155–6
  accused of 'ratting', 157–60
Peninsular War (1808–14), 23
Perceval, Spencer, 12, 27–8, 30, 32–3, 57, 68, 146, 157

Perry, James, 45–6, 84, 95
Peterborough, 128
Peterloo (1819), 91, 101–4, 107, 109,
    115, 161
petitions, 28, 30, 37, 55–6, 58–60, 106,
    119, 125, 129, 131, 162–3, 195n
'petition and debate' tactics 2, 28, 33,
    58–60, 195n
Petty, Lord Henry, *see* Lansdowne, 3rd
    Marquess
philosophes, 50
Pitt, William, 1, 10, 16, 53–4, 68, 147,
    177, 180, 184
    memory of, 37, 39, 154
Place, Francis, 16, 60, 61, 63, 95, 195n
plumper votes, 87, 135
Poland, 51
Polignac, Jules-Auguste-Armand-
    Marie, Prince de, 163, 167–9
political clubs, 39
poll
    Liverpool 1812, 40
    Westmorland (1818), 86–7
    Westmorland (1820), 112–13
    Cumberland (1820), 113
    Westmorland (1826), 134–5
    Clare (1828), 158
    Yorkshire (1830), 165, 168
Ponsonby, George, 21
    Whig leader in Commons, 19–20, 89
    dies, 65
Portland, William Henry Cavendish-
    Bentinck, 3rd Duke, 11, 25, 78,
    146, 188n
press, 3, 36, 43–51, 55, 100, 109, 153
    provincial, 44, 47–8, 112
    periodical, 45–51
Prince Regent, *see* George IV
propaganda, 73
provinces, 3, 8, 32, 48, 92, 109–10,
    112, 129, 144, 151, 153, 158, 162,
    177–8, 183–4
Prussia, 23
public opinion, 3–4, 6–7, 11, 35, 32,
    43–6, 48–9, 57, 66, 79, 91–101,
    109, 119–20, 138, 147, 155, 160,
    163, 177–8, 183–4

Quakers, 126

Quarterly Review, 49–51, 62, 99

radicals, 3, 33, 35–6, 37, 49, 62–4, 75,
    89–90, 92, 95, 109, 118–20,
    123–4, 131, 139, 151, 158, 160,
    183
    view of party, 15–16
    agitation leading to Peterloo,
        99–101
    react to Peterloo, 102–3, 105–7
Raincock, Fletcher, 87
Ramsden, J.C., 164
reform, 3, 39, 48–9, 62, 93–6, 99, 123,
    129, 136, 143, 149, 160, 162,
    166–70, 172, 176–7, 181
Reform Act (1832), 2, 179, 176, 181,
    184
religion, 18, 49, 69, 125–31
representation, 49, 123–4
retrenchment, 53, 55–6, 72, 92, 94,
    116
rhetoric, 73, 120, 136, 167
Richmond, Charles Gordon Lennox,
    5th Duke, 176
Robertson, William, 5
Robespierre, Maxilimien, 18, 75
Robinson, Frederick (later 1st
    Viscount Goderich and 1st Earl of
    Ripon), 121, 137–8, 140
    forms government in 1827, 151–3
Rockingham Whigs, 1, 14, 16, 35,
    147, 177
Romilly, Sir Samuel, 18, 24, 40, 61,
    75, 89, 94–5
Roscoe, William, 28, 37–41, 47, 170
Rose, George, 28–32
Rosslyn, James Erskine, 2nd Earl, 152,
    161
Rostow, Walt Whitman, 52
rotten boroughs, 41, 73, 123
Russell family, 83
Russell, Lord John, 123, 139, 155–6,
    161, 166, 169, 181, 211n
Russia, 23, 98
Ryder, Richard, 27

Sacheverall, Henry, 126
Salkeld, Thomas, 105
Scales, Thomas, 165

scandal, 23, 52
Scarlett, James, 127, 144, 147, 161
scissors effect, 52
Scotland, 70, 93, 95–6, 115, 170, 182
Scott, Sir Walter, 45, 50
Sefton, William Philip Molyneux, 2nd
    Earl, 37–8, 40, 173
Sharp, Richard, 21
Sheffield, 29, 163, 165, 167, 170
Sheffield Iris, 165, 168
Shelburne, William Petty, 2nd Earl
    (later 1st Marquess of
    Lansdowne), 147
Sheridan, Richard Brinsley, 19, 117,
    147
Sidmouth, Henry Addington, 1st
    Viscount, 12, 17, 33, 54, 109,
    125, 147
Sidney, Algernon, 19
Six Acts, 107, 109, 112, 115–16
slave trade, 38, 129, 158, 162–3, 179
slavery, 5, 128–130, 158, 162–4, 166,
    168
Smith, Adam, 19
Smith case, 130
Smith, Frederick Edwin (later 1st Earl
    of Birkenhead), 180
Smith, Rev. John, 129–30, 155
Smith, Rev. Sidney, 121
    on anti-Catholicism, 18
    on Brougham, 23, 68, 88, 180–1
    Edinburgh Review, 49
    defends Dissenters' rights, 126
    criticizes Bishops, 128
Smith, William, 129, 155
social tension, 52, 91, 99, 132–3,
    161–2
Society for the Diffusion of Useful
    Knowledge, 7
Somerset, 180
Somerville, Alexander, 179
Southey, Robert, 49, 62, 119
Southwark, 119
Spain, 21–3, 50, 55, 146
Spa Fields Riot (1816), 62, 102
Spencer, George John, 2nd Earl, 17,
    84, 108
Spooner, Richard, 29
St Omer, 116

Staffordshire, 29–30
Stewart, Dugald, 5
Strickland, George, 164, 167
Stuart Wortley, James Archibald, 103,
    117

Tarleton, Banastre, 37, 40
Taunton, 180
Tavistock, Viscount, 141, 145
Test and Corporation Acts, 69, 143,
    145, 166, 184
    repealed, 154–9, 160–1
Thanet, Charles, 10th Earl, 132
Thanet, Sackville Tufton, 9th Earl, 32,
    62, 196n
    Westmorland interest, 68–9, 75,
        77–8, 82, 88
    supports Brougham in
        Westmorland, 71–2, 113
    appeals for Whig support in
        Westmorland, 84
    death, 132
Thornley, Thomas, 28
Thurlow, Edward, 1st Baron, 180
Tierney, George, 21, 38, 42, 121, 140,
    188n
    leadership in Commons, 19, 90,
        118, 124
    personality and reputation, 19–20
    on Grenville, 53–4
    attacks income tax, 57
    deprecates income tax repeal, 59,
        195n
    challenges Navy estimates, 61
    elected Whig leader in Commons,
        89–90
    parliamentary session in 1819,
        92–4, 96–7, 99
    reacts to Peterloo, 102, 104, 108–9
    defends Caroline of Brunswick,
        117–18
    supports coalition with Canning,
        144–5, 152
    dies in January 1830, 162
Times, The, 44, 47, 55, 59, 77, 100,
    106, 127–8, 130, 134, 139–40,
    144, 147, 156, 168–9, 176, 181–2,
    193n
toleration, 49, 125–6, 131, 155

Tooke, Horne, 48
Tory, 83, 106, 108, 127–8, 145
  party, 4, 10–11, 13, 35, 42, 49, 60,
    63, 89–90, 93, 97, 100, 102–3,
    120, 126, 131, 137–41, 146,
    151–5, 160–2, 164–5, 175, 179
  press, 10, 40, 49–51, 61–2, 68, 75–6,
    101, 107, 119, 129, 138, 157,
    160, 168, 193n
  ultras, 133–4, 140, 142, 144–5,
    154–5, 157, 159, 168–9, 173
  trade cycles, 52, 100, 122

Unitarians, 18, 126

Vansittart, Nicholas, 55–8, 93, 121
Vizard, William, 135
Vyvyan, Sir Richard, 169

Wakefield, James, 71
Wakefield, John, 133
Walcheren Expedition (1809), 24–5
Walpole, Sir Robert, 13, 74
Ward, John William (later 1st Earl of
    Dudley)
  on Whigs, 11, 34, 37
  on Brougham, 43
  in Canning's government, 143
Waterloo, 55, 93
Wedgwood, Josiah, 29–30
Wellesley, Richard Colley, 1st
    Marquess, 12, 42
Wellington, Arthur, 1st Duke of, 101,
    142, 148
  Peninsular War, 23–4
  and Canning, 138, 140, 151
  forms government, 153–4
  loses party support, 157–61, 169, 173
  recruits Whigs into government,
    161
  faces revived opposition, 163,
    166–72
  resigns, 173
  remarks on House of Lords, 179–80
Western, Charles, 16
Westminster, 3, 33, 36, 43–4, 86, 89,
    91, 110, 119, 153, 178–9
  radical interest, 15, 59, 63
  election (1819), 95

Westminster Review, 49
Westmorland, 3, 5, 8, 89, 164, 182
  politics, 67–8, 85, 125, 132–3
  society and economy, 69–70
  landed interest, 74–5
  Westmorland election (1818), 86–7
  county meetings in 1819, 104–6
  Westmorland election (1820), 112
  Westmorland election (1826), 132–6
Westmorland Gazette, 81, 86, 88, 112
Whig
  principles 4, 5, 17, 18, 49, 96, 125,
    144–5, 147
  metropolitan orientation, 4, 11, 83,
    177
  factionalism, 8, 36, 114, 137, 145,
    151–4
  public opinion of, 10–11, 98
  aristocracy, 11, 35, 114
  and French Revolution, 14
  synonymous with Foxite, 17
  Burkean or conservative Whigs, 17,
    62
  combination with Grenville, 17
  leadership, 17, 19–20, 62, 65,
    89–90, 124–5, 139, 143, 154,
    172–3, 175
  Mountain, 18–19, 21, 33, 37, 124,
    145, 154–5, 182
  and radicals, 18
  foreign policy, 22–4, 53–4, 169
  views on Brougham's Westmorland
    campaigns, 84–5
  reaction to Peterloo, 101–6
  Caroline of Brunswick, 118–20
  view of church reform, 128–9
  reunited in 1828, 158
  government formed in 1830, 173
Whitbread, Samuel, 17–9, 21, 29, 32,
    36–7, 48, 51, 53, 61, 117, 145,
    154–5, 188n
Wilberforce, William, 48, 67, 118,
    163–5
Wilkes, John, 83, 158
William IV, 173, 181–2
Williams, John Ambrose, 126–8
Wilson, Sir Robert, 23, 92, 95, 102, 110
  negotiations with Canning, 140–1,
    143

Winchelsea, 43, 66, 71, 114
Windemere, 80
Wishaw, Thomas, 61, 121, 124
Wolsey, Sir Charles, 101
Wolverhampton, 30
Wooler, Thomas, 103
Worcester, 36
Wordsworth, Dorothy, 75, 80
Wordsworth, John, 82
Wordsworth, William
    Westmorland politics, 69, 73–4, 106
    attacked by Brougham, 79
    advises Lonsdale, 81
    political views, 82
    Two Addresses to the Freeholders of
        Westmorland, 82–3

Wybergh, Thomas, 105
Wynn, Charles William Watkin, 86,
    94, 121, 152
Wyvill, Rev. Christopher, 3, 48, 163

York, 102, 165, 168
York, Frederick Augustus, Duke of, 93,
    133
Yorkshire, 3, 8, 29, 48, 55, 58, 70,
    100, 102–6, 119, 123, 129, 162,
    173, 175, 179, 182–3
    politics, 163–4
    West Riding of, 163–5
    Yorkshire Election (1830), 165–8
Yorkshire Association, 3, 163
Yorkshire Gazette, 165